Malta,
Mediterranean Bridge

Malta, Mediterranean Bridge

STEFAN GOODWIN

BERGIN & GARVEY
Westport, Connecticut • London

Library of Congress Cataloging-in-Publication Data

Goodwin, Stefan, 1941–
    Malta, Mediterranean bridge / Stefan Goodwin.
        p.   cm.
    Includes bibliographical references and index.
    ISBN 0–89789–820–6 (alk. paper)
    1. Malta—Civilization.   I. Title.
  DG989.7.G66   2002
  945.8'5—dc21   2001058317

British Library Cataloguing in Publication Data is available.

Library of Congress Catalog Card Number: 2001058317
ISBN: 0–89789–820–6

First published in 2002

Bergin & Garvey, 88 Post Road West, Westport, CT 06881
An imprint of Greenwood Publishing Group, Inc.
www.greenwood.com

Printed in the United States of America

The paper used in this book complies with the
Permanent Paper Standard issued by the National
Information Standards Organization (Z39.48–1984).

10 9 8 7 6 5 4 3 2 1

Contents

Preface

As a unique crossroads in the cultural development of humankind, the Mediterranean Basin has been of great interest to me for a long time, and my anthropological fascination with the Maltese Islands—located at its center—goes back at least 30 years. After writing the entry on Malta in the recently published encyclopedia titled *Countries and Their Cultures* and being allowed only a few thousand words to describe such a culturally rich and intriguing place, I realized that this book had to be written.

Although the presence of hominids close to the eastern Mediterranean goes back at least as far as certain australopithecines who lived a few million years ago, parts of the region remain scarcely documented in the scholarly literature, as epitomized even in the case of the Maltese Islands, which are centrally located. Malta is a missing link for understanding many regional interrelationships that remain hidden or poorly understood. Pejorative language and chauvinistic outlooks have often obfuscated an understanding both of Maltese experience and of Mediterranean life in general. Because Malta has a small population and much of the scholarly social science literature about it is very specialized or particularistic, much of it never comes to the attention of large audiences through major international publishing houses.

Malta annually attracts tourists in numbers far in excess of its population and is changing very rapidly. One consequence of this change is that popular literature intended to appeal to vacationers is being published much faster than that which is scholarly. Against this background the need for this rather holistic work is urgent. In addition to extensive primary research, it relies heavily on the findings of many other scholars to whom I am much indebted. Overall, however, it is an original treatment and I bear full responsibility for its interpretations and its conclusions.

Also, it would not have been possible for me to write *Malta, Mediterranean Bridge* without the assistance of numerous people who were willing to share their hospitality, wisdom, and insights with me. During the years when my research on Malta was beginning, it was extremely important that Professor Salvino Busuttil, Professor J. Aquilina, Mr. Guze Cardona, and Mr. Edward Zammit used their good offices to welcome me at the Royal University of Malta. I shall always be extremely grateful to them.

Over the years, so many wonderful and warm people have shared their perspectives with me on Maltese history, culture, and society that a mention of most of them would be impossible. Included among these are numerous families that agreed to be studied over extended periods of time provided only that I write honestly about them and protect their confidences.

While I feel much gratitude to all these people, I am compelled to acknowledge by name Edward Caruana, Joseph Abela, Donald Orr, Joseph Busuttil, Chevelier E. S. Tonna, Joseph Cassar Pullicino, Charles Iskander Yousif, Joseph Buttigieg, and Emidio and Carmen Galea for special favors. As this book uses Malta as a prism to sometimes focus on the larger Mediterranean Basin, I am similarly indebted to people in numerous places outside of Malta among whom I traveled and lived and who helped me gain insight into regional interrelationships.

As my mother, Dr. Helen Goodwin, promised me no peace until this book was written, she was a constant inspiration. Among those who gave generously of their time in reading and reacting to various parts of the manuscript were Father Stephen Jeselnick, Professor Dean R. Wagner, Dr. Delores G. Kelley, and Dr. William J. Megginson. However, this story is not exactly as any of these people would have told it. In the final analysis I therefore take credit where it elucidates and assume full responsibility if occasionally I have faltered.

AN INTRODUCTORY NOTE ON MALTESE

Maltese is a distinct language that is morphologically related to North African Arabic but draws much of its vocabulary, syntax, and idiom from Sicilian.[1] This difficult language is spoken by all classes, but it did not become an official language of the law courts until 1934, when it replaced Italian. As it has only been a widely written language for little more than 100 years, it does not yet have a rich literature.

In order to help the reader with the Maltese names and words that appear in the text, the following is given as a short guide to their approximate pronunciation.[2] In general, vowels have much the same sound as they do in Italian. The following consonants are pronounced as indicated: *ċ*: *ch*air; *ġ*: *g*entle; *g*: *g*ift; *h*: silent; *ħ*: aspirate; *għ*: the *għajn*, is usually silent; *j*: *y*ear; *q*: glottal stop; *x*: *sh*ine; *ż*: *z*ebra; and *z*: boot*s*.

NOTES

1. Joseph Aquilina, *Papers in Maltese Linguistics* (Valletta: Royal University of Malta, 1970), p. 180.

2. For the pronunciation of Maltese consult Joseph Aquilina, *The Structure of Maltese* (Valletta: Royal University of Malta, 1959), pp. 1–17.

Chapter 1

Genesis in the Mediterranean

An elongated inland sea across which people of three neighboring continents long ago began to interact, the Mediterranean is of unique importance to our species. It is associated with many beginnings: megalithic architecture, long-distance marine travel, emergent farming and herding, early empires, and the springtime of Judaism and Christianity. Situated on a part of a land bridge that refuses to sink, the Maltese Islands overflow with stories about the course of life at the center of this sea—geographically, historically, and culturally.

The Mediterranean Basin is made up of many lands in Europe, Asia, and Africa that enclose an inland sea that has given its name to them collectively. Excluding the Sea of Marmara and the much larger Black Sea appendage north of the Bosporus, these lands cluster more exactly around two great basins of water, one eastern and one western. If between the coast of Tunisia and the boot of Italy, one of the shallowest parts of the Mediterranean Sea, water levels were about 600 feet lower, one could walk from mainland Africa to mainland Europe.

The fauna of which such abundant traces have been found in the caves [including even dwarf hippopotami] must have come to the Maltese islands from one or other of the two continents, Europe and Africa, between which they [the Maltese] lie. This would seem to imply the former existence of a land bridge connecting the islands with one or both of these, and the structure of the sea bed in that part of the Mediterranean lends support to this theory. (Evans 1971: 1)

Joining Europe and Africa beneath these shallow waters in the center of the sea, an ancient geological bridge remains which divides the main part of the sea into two large basins. Only slightly closer to the Straits of Gibraltar in the west than to the coasts of Lebanon, Israel, and Palestine in the east, this bridge is most apparent because some areas protrude above the water as islands. At its center, the most notable among these are the Maltese archipelago, Sicily, Pantelleria, Linosa, and Lamedusa. La Favigna, Marettimo, and Levanzo are located at the western tip of Sicily. At the southern end, Tabarka, La Galite, Zembrea, Jerba, and the Kerkenna Islands lie just off the coast of the Tunisian mainland. Remnants of a submerged bridge that few people realize exists, these places defy time, and none are more fascinating and remarkable than those that form the Maltese Archipelago.

This tiny archipelago consists of the islands of Malta, Gozo, Comino, Cominotto, and Fifla, plus a few outcroppings of limestone rock of minute size. Only the largest three of the tiny Maltese Islands are inhabited: Malta with 95 square miles of territory, Gozo with 26 square miles, and Comino consisting of barely one square mile. Though the island of Malta has a maximum length of only 17 miles and a maximum width of only nine, providing it with a total shoreline of a mere 85 miles, over 92% of all Maltese live on this single island. With the exception of a few farmers who dwell on Comino, all the others live on Gozo. Fliegu Channel, which separates Malta and Gozo, with tiny Comino and even smaller Cominotto in between, is only four miles wide. This means that all the Maltese Islands are located quite close to each other.

History reveals no period since the Maltese Islands were settled that they have not attracted attention well beyond the scale of their small size. In fact, these islands have been as important in world culture and human affairs as many lands thousands of times larger. Despite Malta's close proximity to Africa, the birthplace of our species, it was settled relatively late. Maltese, the national language, is the only European language that linguists classify as "Afro-Asiatic," the same huge linguistic family to which languages such as Arabic, Hebrew, Amharic, Hausa, ancient Egyptic, and Aramaic (the language spoken by Christ) belong. Like tiny Monaco and Singapore, Malta is one of the world's most densely populated countries. Resulting from a long history of exporting its redundant population, communities of Maltese heritage are now scattered from Toronto and Marseilles to Cairo and Sydney. Its population of 381,000—long stagnant—is growing again and is projected to increase through 2025 until it peaks at 402,000.

No fossils of Homo sapiens that may be technically classified as "archaic" have ever been found in Malta, not even any of the Neanderthaloids that were at one time widely dispersed around the Mediterranean. The first people to inhabit these islands arrived around 4200 B.C., already evolved into anatomically modern human beings. In other words, they were physically indistinguishable from people in the twenty-first century. These first

Maltese had a Neolithic type of culture, which is to say that they were more accustomed to subsisting on farming and herding than on foraging for wild animals and plants. Trump (1972: 20) has described the situation this way. "They brought with them crops like barley, two primitive forms of wheat, emmer and club wheat, and lentils. Remains of all these have been found at Skorba. Their boats were large and seaworthy enough for the transport of domestic animals, large cattle, sheep, goats, and pigs, doubtless securely trussed to prevent accidents."

Considering that in clear weather, some parts of Malta are visible with the naked eye from Cape Passero on the southeastern tip of Sicily, a place with pre-Neolithic settlement, these first Maltese may have arrived from Sicily. Important similarities exist between the earliest Neolithic cultural phases at Stentinello in eastern Sicily and at Għar Dalam in Malta, especially as revealed in certain pottery types.

On the other hand, in context of the larger Mediterranean, even Sicily was not archaeologically an isolated island. Hawkes's description (1940: 84) of Stentinello culture as having an "archaic Afro-Mediterranean aspect in general" has stood the test of time. In addition to Għar Dalam, the Early Neolithic in Malta is well attested by Grey Skorba pottery dating around 3600 B.C. as well as by Red Skorba finds dating around 3400 B.C.

By the time Malta was settled, various peoples of the central Mediterranean were already in frequent contact with each other and these Maltese were no exception. As the early Maltese engaged in importing obsidian from the Aeolian Islands to the north of Sicily and from Pantellaria, over toward Tunisia's Cap Bon, as well as chert and lava, probably from Sicily, it would appear that they were in contact with a good many of the their neighbors. Maltese archaeology reveals a rather sharp break occurred between the Early Neolithic and Middle Neolithic by 3200 B.C. as reflected in ceramic manufacture and the initial appearance of collective burial in artificially constructed tombs. It is possible therefore that a new wave of immigrants arrived about this time. Though one sees evidence of this transition first at Żebbuġ around 2900 B.C., it is also apparent in Mġarr.

Especially striking in this regard are new cultural influences prior to 2700 B.C. that are associated with the Late Neolithic, perhaps even overlapping the Middle Neolithic. During the Late Neolithic, a number of gigantic temples and stone tombs were constructed, some of the earliest and most magnificent megalithic monuments ever constructed anywhere. Constructed at sites such as Ġgantija on Gozo and Saflieni and Tarxien on Malta until around 2800 to 2300 B.C., they even predate much of the pyramid building in Egypt. Archaeologists have not located structures even vaguely resembling Malta's megalithic temples elsewhere in the world. The absence of plausible technological precedents is underscored by the fact that Egypt's Old Kingdom did not begin before 2575 B.C., Stonehenge not before 2300

B.C., nor the Palaces of Crete before 2000 B.C. (O'Connor 1997: 14; Trump 1972: 28).

Malta reveals evidence of a bronze age from shortly before 2000 B.C. at Tarxien Cemetery and somewhat later at Borġ in-Nadur and at Baħrija. This was a period by which Minoans from Crete had probably set up nearby depots on the coast of Africa to the south of Malta. When Malta's Bronze Age was coming to an end around 1100 B.C., advances in navigation technology had made it possible for a number of peoples to begin staking out long-distance Mediterranean trade routes (in addition to the Minoans, Cyclades, Cretans, Myceneans, and—by the time of the arrival of the Achaeans in Greece—also the Etruscans and Phoenicians). It has been argued that the Phoenicians from the Levantine Coast at the eastern extremity of the Mediterranean reached Nora on Sardinia before 900 B.C. (Negbi 1992: 599–615). It is even possible that they had already founded their colony of Gades (Cadiz) in Spain a couple of centuries prior to that time.

Given the central location of the Maltese Islands and their excellent harbors, it seems certain that the Phoenicians made contact with the Maltese at an early stage. Moreover, through African intermediaries, Phoenicians from settlements close to Malta on the coast of Tripolitania or northwestern Libya established trading links across the Sahara Desert as early as 1200 B.C. Further to the west, a somewhat longer route used by the Phoenicians and their intermediaries led southward from Figuig and Jebel Bani in southern Oran to Zemmur, the Mauritanian Adrar, and Dhar Walata, to Tondia, near Gundam on the Niger. While through the Garmantes and others, the Phoenicians imported precious stones known as carbuncles, gold, and other commodities, as well as even some slaves, they may have supplemented this overland trade to the interior with gold that they imported from western Africa by sea (Bovill 1958: 68; Law 1978). The most powerful early Phoenician settlement near Malta was at Carthage or "New City"—established in the north of modern-day Tunisia around 814 B.C. (Iliffe 1995: 31).

In Malta, archaeologists have unearthed Phoenicians who were buried during the eighth and seventh centuries B.C., and there exists some archaeological evidence that Phoenicians made contact with Maltese as early as the ninth century B.C. (Blouet 1967: 38; Bradford 1971: 72; cf. Evans 1968: 23). However, why the Phoenicians first came, in exactly what numbers, and to what degree they may have exercised any significant political control or cultural dominance remains unknown. Still it is clear that not long after 814 B.C., when according to Punic tradition Carthage was founded on the African mainland opposite Malta as the seat of Phoenicia's maritime empire, the Maltese also had significant contact with the Phoenicians (Bonanno 1990: 209–217).

These rather historically uncertain centuries—really an extension of Maltese prehistory—are known to us largely through many rock-cut tombs that have yielded Phoenician grave goods such as pottery and lamps. Whatever the relationships between the Maltese and the Phoenicians around this time, these did not prevent the peoples of Malta from also maintaining commercial relations with the Greeks, with whom the Phoenicians were very much in competition.

In the long run, the Phoenicians did not fare particularly well in their intense rivalry with the Greeks and the Etruscans over rights to trade and resources in the central and western Mediterranean. Even in the east, Phoenician fortune plummeted in 524 B.C. when Tyre and Persia entered into an alliance that recognized the hegemony of Persia over the Phoenician homeland. Though this effectively marked the end of the Phoenician cities as an independent force in the eastern Mediterranean, Carthage—founded as a Phoenician colony in what is now Tunisia—was by that time becoming the dominant political and commercial force in the western Mediterranean.

While during the sixth century Carthage was consolidating its hold on Sicily, Sardinia, and the Gulf of Sidra, which cuts hard into Libya, it also began to exercise some degree of control over the Maltese Islands, which lay in the center. Though the Maltese apparently continued to enjoy more liberty than was characteristic for residents of other Punic satellites, Carthage's dominance had the effect of continuing the infusion of Phoenician-Carthaginian culture into the islands (Evans 1968: 24).

From 406 to 367 B.C., eastern Sicily was a part of a Greek empire under Dionysius I of Syracuse while the Carthaginians were in control of the western part of the island. The Carthaginians were even more firmly entrenched in Malta, for in 218 B.C. when the Romans finally defeated the Carthaginians at the beginning of the Second Punic War, a garrison of 2,000 Carthaginian soldiers was captured here (Crawford 1900a: 270). The existence of a large garrison in Malta's small territory, coupled with Diodorus Siculus's later statement that the islands had previously been "Phoenician colonies," suggests that the impact of Phoenician-Carthaginian culture in Malta during these centuries was appreciable (Busuttil 1968: 32–33; Busuttil 1971a: 305–307; Busuttil 1971b: 308–310).

During the century-long rivalry between Carthage and Rome, the Romans often used a tactic to undermine their rival by befriending various Berber leaders opposed to the Carthaginians. After the decisive destruction of Carthage in 146 B.C., Rome began an occupation of northern Africa that would last for some 600 to 650 years. As this occupation began, Rome organized the former possessions of Carthage into the Province of Africa, with its capital at Utica, an ally of Rome in the last Punic War. The subsequent conquests of Cyrenaica in 96 B.C., of Egypt in 30 B.C., and of Morocco (then known as Mauritania) in 40 A.D. had the effect of completely encircling Malta by a Roman Empire.

Cicero, who lived from 106 to 43 B.C., delivered a speech against Caius

Verres in the Roman Senate that indicates the Romans of his day knew Malta for its capital city, its cloth, its honey, and its tendency to attract pirates. References to huge ivory tusks in certain Maltese temples also suggests the Maltese sometimes traded with Africa. Shortly after the assassination of Julius Caesar in 44 B.C. the Sicilians were granted Roman citizenship, and the Maltese may have been treated similarly (it has not been possible to confirm this). In any case, the political involvement of the Romans in Malta did not bring an abrupt end to Maltese Punic cultural connections.

Certain temples founded by the Carthaginians experienced an increase in their international importance until the beginning of the Christian era, with some even being expanded (Evans 1968: 24, 26). Punic-style tombs with Punic pottery remained in vogue for a long time after Roman encirclement. Also well into the Christian era, Punic goods are found mixed with grave goods identified as Greek and Roman.

Early in this Christian era, a church was established in the eastern Mediterranean at Jerusalem with James, the brother of Jesus, as its leader. As reported in Chapter XV of Acts of the Apostles, the first church council in history was held to decide the conditions under which non-Jews might be allowed to enter Christianity. In the northwestern expansion of the movement, Caesarea Philipi and Antioch to the north and Athens and Corinth to the west were among the earliest cities where new branches became established.

The security of imperial roads and waterways under the Romans helped the diffusion of the new religion despite much opposition to Christianity in the Roman Empire, in large measure because early Christians threatened the status quo and were viewed as political radicals. After being arrested in Jerusalem on charges of causing a riot and spending a couple of years imprisoned, Paul claimed his rights as a Roman citizen to a trial in Rome, a trial that would inadvertently bring him to Malta. We know from Chapter XXVII of Acts that on his voyage to Rome aboard a boat that had left from Alexandria he became shipwrecked here in A.D. 59 or 60. In this way Christianity arrived in Malta at quite an early time via an apostolic connection.

As the Bible documents that the Maltese were *barbaroi*, we know that they spoke neither Greek nor Latin. Though circumstantial evidence suggests that the Maltese probably spoke Phoenician or Punic, other possibilities exist as both the Romans and the Phoenicians dominated large empires partly in Africa, partly in Asia, and partly in Europe that linked polyglot peoples of many ethnic backgrounds. Though Greek and Latin were important international lingua francas during the early Christian era, rival languages did not everywhere suddenly disappear. Though the early Christian bishops in northern Africa had to learn Punic in order to carry on their missionary work, even there the language died out only in the 400s.

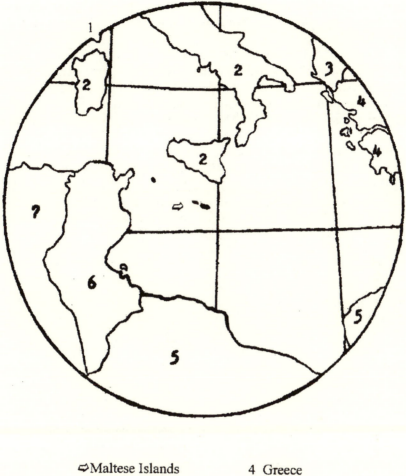

⇨ Maltese Islands   4 Greece
1 France (Corsica)   5 Libya
2 Italy   6 Tunisia
3 Albania   7 Algeria

Maltese Islands in geographical context (within approximately 450-mile radius of Malta).

Tiny Malta is a striking anomaly, however. Many people conversant in Greek and Latin visited or settled in Malta, including Jews and Christians. Others frequently moved in and out of Malta in the course of traveling between Rome and her African colonies. After all, Rome eventually became dependent on Africa for labor, for two-thirds of its grain, and for most wild animals used in its public spectacles. Despite being surrounded by the huge Roman Empire where Latin eventually was dominant, the Maltese did not linguistically succumb. It is nothing less that an enigma of cultural history that Malta has throughout much of its life-course maintained some type of linguistic apartness.

By the time fire destroyed much of Rome in 64, it had become clear to the emperor Nero that Christians were distinct from Jews, and he arranged to have numerous members of the new religion killed as scapegoats. Despite such setbacks, Christianity gained a foothold in northern Africa at an early time, spreading from one Jewish community to another, and gradually among non-Jews. In fact, Northern Africa was considerably more important than Rome in the development of theology within the early church; as Malta was located immediately off the coast of Carthage, it was greatly influenced. In 115 and 116, a revolt by Jews in such widely scattered parts of the Mediterranean as Cyprus, Egypt, and Libya resulted in repression so severe that in some places, such as in Alexandria, Jews were almost wiped out. From the cities of Leptis Magna and Cyrene, many Jews fled into the interior of Libya and Algeria, while others probably joined co-religionists already settled in Malta.

It is sometimes difficult to imagine that people traveled so widely at such an early time and not just because of religious conflicts; but throughout the ages peoples have crisscrossed the Mediterranean going from one continent to another. In 172, for example, such large numbers of Africans were moving from the province of Mauritania (now Morocco) into Spain that the Roman emperor Marcus Aurelius felt compelled to send the general Septimius Severus to restore order.

Carthage, the closest part of Africa to Malta, was a major settlement both for Jews and Christians. In fact, the first church father to write in Latin as well as Greek was Tertullian, a Carthaginian born around 160, a period during which it was still common to persecute Christians throughout the Roman Empire. Already by 180, the church in northern Africa had produced its first twelve martyrs, who were beheaded in the town of Scilli, and the throwing of Christians to lions was also practiced. Even the Roman emperor Septimius Serverus, a Berber born in Leptis Magna in 197, persecuted Christians in Carthage, including Saints Perpetua and Felicitas who were martyred there in 203. He also specifically forbade Jews from undertaking any type of missionary activities.

Despite such hardships for Jews and Christians, Christianity was by this time more firmly established in Tunisia and the northeastern corner of Algeria than in most European countries north of Malta. In 240, for example, Tertullian wrote that in Carthage, Christians were nearly the majority in every city. We know moreover that Christianity was widely established in northern Africa by the fact that when the Council of Carthage convened in 225 or 230, bishops of 70 African dioceses attended. As Malta was never a core area within the Roman Empire, early Maltese Christians probably experienced less persecution than early Christians in neighboring lands; still it seems unlikely that they were unaffected.

Christians were widely distrusted because they were messianic and refused to worship the Roman emperor, to worship the gods whose favor many believed to have brought success to the Empire, and to follow certain pre-Christian customs related to the cult of Iris. They often became convenient scapegoats for any number of reasons, and periodic persecution of them was often severe in imperial cities as widely scattered as Rome, Jerusalem, Alexandria, and Leptis Magna.

In 249, Emperor Decius even proclaimed an edict designed to eliminate Christians by legal means, and a year later he had Pope Fabian killed. Under the same emperor, Cyprian was bishop of Carthage from 249 until his own martyrdom there in 258. The persecution of Christians probably reached its apex under co-emperors Diocletian and Galerius. Diocletian wished to be worshipped as a god. Shortly after certain political usurpers appeared in Egypt during his reign, he caused so much persecution to rain down on local Christians that the calendar of the Egyptian Church starts from 284, marking both the beginning of his reign and the Era of Martyrs (Wellard 1970: 53–54).

Around the same time, a Greek-speaking theologian in Alexandria began to espouse Arianist doctrines according to which Jesus was not of the same substance as God, but only the best of created beings. This doctrine was intended to further exult the one true God by subordinating Christ to a secondary position in which "he was neither truly God nor truly man." It eventually became a prime cause of discord in the Iberian Peninsula of Europe between the Teutonic Christians, on the one hand, and Romanized Iberians, on the other. As the Teutonic Visigoths were especially attracted to Arianism, doctrinal disputes divided Christians into factions there and similar developments existed elsewhere in the Mediterranean world.

When from around 284 to 306, Diocletian allotted Maximian the western part of the Roman Empire, Malta was west of the dividing line. Roman power in Africa was already beginning to decline due to external attack, internal unrest, and spiraling inflation. Christians in places like Sicily, Carthage, and Malta experienced considerable instability as local rebellions began to undermine Roman political hegemony. Though Malta was influenced by Rome without ever being assimilated into the mainstream of Roman culture (Aquilina 1970a: 197; Blouet 1967: 39), from around 217 B.C., it was influenced by the instability associated with Rome's political disintegration.

That numerous Romanesque architectural ruins and artifacts have been discovered in Malta does not mean that adherence to Christianity was universal throughout the islands during this difficult period. Malta has rather extensive catacombs dating to the late fourth and fifth centuries, most notably at Rabat; perhaps used only for burial, it is also possible that these were places of refuge. That they provide inscriptions and symbols identified as pagan as well as Jewish and Christian is also significant (Luttrell 1975: 20). There exists little evidence of Christianity from Gozo during Roman times. In fact, the island yields some evidence of emperor worship between the first and early fourth centuries, and little that is demonstrably Christian is found there before the fifth century (Buhagiar 1997: 114, 116–117).

After the Edict of Milan of 313 introduced the concept of religious tolerance, Christianity began to become the official religion of the Empire under Constantine the Great. Its diffusion throughout various sectors of the Empire, however, was not uniform, and the direct impact on Malta is uncertain. It is noteworthy that in 330—the same year that Constantine transferred the capital of Christendom from Rome to Byzantium (later known as Constantinople)—270 African bishops attended a Donatist Council at Carthage, just off the coast of Malta. Equally indicative that Christianity did not diffuse evenly where the influence of Rome was strong is reflected in the fact that it did not become the official religion in Egypt until 78 years after the Edict of Milan.

With the death of Constantine in 337, the empire was divided for about thirteen years among his three sons portending that the Universal or Catholic Church would have difficulty remaining unified. One of the major doctrinal disputes that threatened its unity throughout the fourth century, especially in parts of Africa located close to Malta, had to do with Donatism. Originally a type of religious fundamentalism, Donatism eventually gave rise to a rival clergy. The hero of the orthodox against Donatism was St. Augustine, a father of the church who had been born on the African mainland not far from Malta in 356. Though St. Augustine triumphed over Donatism by having it officially branded a heresy and driving out its clergy, its survivors continued to stir up desert-dwelling masses against the Christian establishment well into the sixth century.

Another development was even more ominous for Christian unity during the lifetime of St. Augustine. In 395, Emperor Theodosius divided the Empire between his two sons, with Honorius reigning over the western division and Arcadius reigning over the eastern or Byzantine division. Shortly after St. Augustine's death in 430, moreover, another long simmering doctrinal dispute erupted within Christendom that caused another split.

This had to do with whether or not the nature of Christ was Monophysite, that is, of a singular nature with no distinction between his divinity and his humanity (Wellard 1970: 42). In contrast to certain Christians who believed in the tripartite nature of Christ, Monophysite Christians viewed Christ as having a single divine nature, which during a period had merely taken on a human form. As a direct result of this belief and their rejection of the findings of the Council of Chalcedon that convened in 451, there was division. It was this division that led to the emergence of the five Monophysite or Coptic churches: the Syrian Orthodox Church of Antioch, the Syrian Orthodox Church of Malabar, the Armenian Church, the Egyptian Coptic Church, and the Ethiopian Coptic Church.

By 428, migratory Teutonic Vandals that had swept from the Balkans across Poland, Germany, and France were holed up in Spain under the leadership of Genseric. Then a rebellious Roman official asked for their help in constraining the Berbers on the southern flanks of Rome's African colonies. On this invitation, some 80,000 restless European Vandals crossed into Africa where they quickly began assimilating with residents of the coastal cities and towns. It was only a matter of time before these forces joined in common cause against Rome. In this way, Teutonic people, in league with anti-Roman elements from Africa, helped undermine the tethering Empire from the south much as they had earlier begun doing in Europe.

Faced with this threat from the south, Rome tried to buy longevity by recognizing claims of the anti-Roman Vandals to areas of northwestern Africa that it had previously controlled. However, such offers involved too little and came too late to pacify the rebels (Bovill 1958: 55–56). From their African kingdom with its capital at Carthage, the Vandals and their allies conquered Sardinia and Corsica, launched raids on Italy and Malta, and in 455 even sacked the city of Rome as the era that historians of Europe often refer to as "the Middle Ages" rapidly approached (Brown 1975: 71–72; Luttrell 1975: 21; Oliver and Fagen 1975: 57).

With the final fall of the Roman Empire in the west around 476, many parts of the central Mediterranean, including Malta, were caught up in competitive struggles among Romans, Byzantines, Vandals, and others. Toward the end of the fifth century, Malta probably came under the control of the Ostrogothic rulers who succeeded the Vandals in Italy (Brown 1975: 72–73; Luttrell 1975: 21). Even as the Byzantines eventually moved into the void recreated by the fall of Rome and the instability brought by the Vandals, their takeover would prove tenuous.

By 535, domination of Sicily by the Vandals was eventually brought to an end through the victories of Emperor Justinian and Belisarius, his general. A few years later when Byzantine troops under Belisarius arrived on the African mainland to challenge the Vandals, they were welcomed by the masses as a force of liberation. A number of Christians fleeing this turmoil in Africa reached Malta in 544, and sometime between 533 and 592 Malta's first bishop was established (Brown 1975: 73–77; Luttrell 1975: 21). Though Belisarius defeated the Vandals in Corsica, Byzantine control in many of these areas was not destined to endure both because of ongoing rebellion and doctrinal intolerance. As early Christianity exhibited more doctrinal intolerance, it was time and time again faced with new rebellion which fed on itself thereby causing more doctrinal intolerance.

Even as power that was formerly concentrated within the Roman Empire shifted eastward, doctrinal controversies such as had characterized Christianity since at least the third century continued to unfold. New dissentions, rivalries, and atrocities occurred as various factions identifying themselves as Christian aligned themselves against each other, using charges and countercharges of heresy to seek the elimination of each other. So intense was the doctrinal hostility toward Egypt's Monophysite Christians during the sixth-century reign of Byzantine Emperor Justin II that it resulted in the massacre of possibly as many as 200,000 Christians as heretics. Faced also with hostility from Rome, Monophysite Christendom separated from both Roman and Greek Orthodox communities (Wellard 1970: 118) and preoccupied itself with sending missionaries into the African interior.

Out of political expedience shortly before losing Syria, Palestine, and Egypt to Islam, the Byzantine emperor Heraclius made a desperate effort through a new religious doctrine known as Monotheletism to compromise with the very Monophysite Christians whom Rome and Byzantium had previously treated as heretics. This offer bore little fruit. Between 543 and 580, in fact, Christianity obtained it largest reach ever in northern Africa and the Mediterranean Basin and, yet, was made its most vulnerable because of unresolved doctrinal infighting.

Chapter 2

Islam and Realignments

By the time the Prophet Mohammed died in 632, he had established a Muslim state in a large part of Arabia, including some areas that had previously been Christian. Barely 30 years thereafter the orthodox caliphs in Arabia had been succeeded by the first dynastic caliphate with its base in Syria. By this time preexistent alignments throughout the Mediterranean Basin based on power, economic arrangements, religion, demography, and language—though always fluid—were challenged by fundamental change. As realignments occurred through the region, Malta was impacted irreversibly.

By the mid-seventh century so much hostility had been showered on Egypt's Monophysite Christians by Greek Orthodox and Roman Catholic Christians that when early waves of Arab converts to Islam entered Egypt in 640, a segment of Egypt's Christians welcomed them almost as liberators. This situation had not much changed by 641 when Muslims took control of Babylon, and replaced it with a new Egyptian capital slightly to the north, one now known as Cairo. The Muslim capture of Egypt had taken place under the second caliph, Umar bin al-Khattab, who was generally reluctant to sanction military adventures across vast bodies of water. Under a third caliph, Uthman bin Affan, this policy was reversed and Islam surged forth in a number of directions.

Within two years after Muslims had captured Egypt, they were advancing to its west. Though during the next 30 years internecine quarreling slowed Muslim expansionism (as the new religion developed its own schisms having to do with succession to the Prophet as well as some doctrinal controversies), Islam's advance never really stopped. In 649, for example, a Muslim armada under Muawiya invaded Cyprus off the northeastern coast of Egypt without capturing it. However, when they again attacked it five years later, they left behind a garrison of 12,000 troops. Though Christianity is presumed to have been well established throughout the Maltese Islands by this time, its status in Gozo as late as the early 600s is largely unknown (Buhagiar 1997: 119).

The influence of Muslims in the Mediterranean would not be limited to the realm of religion, as they would also become a force influencing government, commerce, and numerous areas of culture. Converting to Islam was only one of several options that the Muslim vanguard made available to non-Muslim populations it encountered. Other relationships included coexistence more or less as equals, imposition of restrictions, paying tribute, engagement in war, vassalage, and enslavement.

In the Muslims' expansion west of Egypt in 642, they encountered Father Gregory, the Byzantine governor in northern Africa who had declared himself an emperor independent of Byzantium. After the Muslims' defeat of Gregory at Sufetula in Libya, the Byzantine Empire was rendered essentially impotent in northeastern Africa though its naval superiority permitted it to remain a force to be reckoned with in Asia Minor, the Balkans, and the central Mediterranean.

Faced with the prospect of a Muslim push across Africa that might change the Mediterranean Basin culturally, politically, and demographically in profound and irreversible ways, the Byzantines undertook to use their naval advantage in a way calculated to better protect their heartland in Asia Minor and the Balkans. Essentially, this involved preventing encirclement by building up defenses in the central Mediterranean. Seals found on Malta and Gozo dating to the seventh or eighth century suggest the presence of some types of Byzantine military or naval officers, possibly as early as 637 (Brown 1975: 76–78; Luttrell 1975: 21).

Constans II left Constantinople in 662 with naval reinforcements intended to shore up Byzantine control in southern Italy, Sicily, and nearby islands such as Malta. However, this did not prevent a Muslim raid on Sicily in 667. Though Constans was assassinated in Syracuse the following year, the presence of a strong Byzantine navy in this central area was destined to limit Muslim activity nearby to mere raids and temporary conquests for a long time.

It was around 670, or almost two centuries before Muslims would take over Malta, that they arrived nearby in Ifriqiya, an area of Africa south of Malta that had previously been under the control of Berbers, Carthaginians, and Romans, as well as Byzantines. This was the period during which a number of populations at the northern end of trans-Saharan caravan routes were embroiled in strife that destabilized trade between Malta and her African neighbors. By 678, Muslim forces, newly arrived in Ifriqiya under the leadership of Ukba bin Nafi, began to threaten this western flank of Byzantine power.

As the arrival of Ukba's forces in this area was part of a western expansion by Muslims, and as they passed to the south of Malta heading in the direction of the Atlantic Ocean, they called the area they were entering Maghreb, meaning "the west." Hence, at essentially the same time that Constans II was attempting to protect the Byzantine heartland in the Balkans from Muslim advances, Muslims were moving into and across Byzantine-controlled Ifriqiya, in fact across the whole of Maghreb. The Muslim conquest of Maghreb did not take place unchallenged however, neither by the Byzantines nor by various African populations of the region.

Unable to take Carthage from the Byzantines before continuing their sweep to its west, the forces of Ukba bin Nafi founded the city of Kairwan as a military base some 90 miles to its south. Malta and Sicily were most impacted by these developments in 693 when Carthage finally fell to the Muslims and numerous Byzantine and Berber refugees fled northward (Ahmad 1975: 3). The closeness of Malta to these events is underscored by the nearness to it of Aspis-Clipea on Cap Bon where the great Kelibia fortress is located. The Kelibia fortress is where in 698 the Byzantine army made its last stand in northwestern Africa before finally taking flight to the island of Pantelleria located midway between the northern tip of Cap Bon and the westernmost part of Sicily.

Following a large number of attacks and counterattacks by Muslims and Byzantines in the central and western Mediterranean, the Muslims succeeded in firmly occupying Pantelleria in 700 and proceeded to carry out raids on the Balearics, Sicily, and Sardinia. Meanwhile when the Muslim vanguard Ukba reached the Atlantic in 710, he is reputed to have triumphantly spurred his horse into its waves to show that his conquest of Maghreb was complete (Bovill 1958: 57).

The Muslim occupation of the northern littoral of Africa quickly transformed the islands of the Mediterranean into southern outposts of Christianity and increased their vulnerability to attack. In fact, Muslims ventured ashore on Sardinia in 711 when soldiers under Musa bin Nacair captured the town of Cagliari and some neighboring regions along the shore. Though Muslims had raided Spanish territory in 710 and then withdrew, it was only in 711 that they gained their first lasting foothold on the mainland of Europe.

Accepting an invitation from a Teutonic claimant to the throne in Spain to come to his aid, a Berber named Tariq bin Ziyad led a force of some 7,000 Africans into Europe, evicting all rival Teutonic claimants. Jealous of this phenomenal success on the part of their African auxiliaries, some 10,000 Muslim warriors, mostly from Syria and the Arabian Peninsula, rushed into Spain hard on the heels of Tariq.

While over the next two decades Muslims made numerous raids against such islands as Sardinia, Corsica, and Sicily, and even achieved a brief capture of Constantinople in 716, counterattacks by the Byzantine navy largely maintained a balance of power in the central Mediterranean. On the Iberian Peninsula, in contrast, Muslim warriors fanned out quickly and eventually moved with resolve into France. Finally at Poitiers in 732, they were decisively checked in this advance by Frankish troops under the leadership of Charles Martel.

Following decades of numerous attacks on islands in the central Mediterranean, Ifriqiyan Muslims made serious attempts to occupy Sicily in 740 and 753. However, during both invasions they had to withdraw to attend to serious ethnic conflicts between Arabs and Berbers in Africa. Muslims took most of Corsica between 784 and 810 and essentially maintained it under their control for the next two centuries. By 827, Muslims had occupied large parts of Sardinia, especially in the region of Cagliari, Porto Torres, and Olbia. Pausing momentarily to reenergize their expansionism in the east, they began occupation of Crete in 824.

Since early in the ninth century, a large group of unruly Arabs and Africans living in Ifriqiya had been in rebellion against the Shiite Abbasid Caliphate in Baghdad; this eventually found expression in their establishment of a new dynasty under Ibrahim I bin al-Aghlab, the Ifriqiyan governor, known as the Aghlabid dynasty. From its capital at Karawan, the new dynasty acted rather independently of Bagdad though it nominally recognized the overlordship of the Abbasid Caliphate and agreed to pay it tribute so as not to invite retaliation. At the same time, this position invited some risk on the home front as many Ifiqiyans yearned for a large degree of independence from caliphal authorities in Bagdad.

In order to reduce the threat of being overthrown by either Ifriqiyans or the Abbasid Caliphate as much as to enlarge the domain under its control, the Aghlabids channeled restless energies of Ifriqiyans who constituted its home base into European expansionism, shrewdly rationalized in terms of religion. It was against this background that the Aghlabids eventually encouraged the conquest of Sicily and Malta by a military command led by *qadi* Asad bin al-Furat and other religious officials. In 826, Euphemius, a former Byzantine naval commander at odds with his emperor, arrived in Ifriqiya with a proposal that Muslims conquer Sicily and recognize him as their vassal emperor. Though the Aghlabids found this enticement too inviting to turn down, Sicily's conquest and occupation would not be accomplished rapidly.

Under the Aghlabids the direction of the Arab conquest was from west to east, from Mazara and Palermo eastward. The Arabs fought with varying fortunes for four years until 831. During the next ten years, 831 to 841, they strengthened their hold on the Val di Mazara where they founded their first colonies. During the next eighteen years, 841 to 859 they subdued with much harder effort the fertile Val di Noto. From 860 onwards they seriously undertook the final phase of the conquest, that of the Val Demone, which they finally succeeded in occupying in 902. (Ahmad 1975: 17)

When during the Muslims' final phase of Sicily's conquest, they undertook to also conquer Malta, Malta was an important part of the Byzantine empire that appears "in the official Byzantine episcopal lists or *notitiae espiscopatuum* from the eighth and early ninth centuries" (Brown 1975: 79). Muslim raids began occurring in the central Mediterranean from the second half of the seventh century, yet we find no historical reference to raids on Malta before the ninth century and no reference to its conquest before the late ninth century suggesting that the Byzantines considered Malta to be of strategic importance and provided it with good defenses (Brown 1975: 78, 82).

While Ibn Khaldun states that Malta was captured in 869, and the Cambridge Chronicle posits that this happened on August 29, 870, there also exists evidence for other dates around this time (Brown 1975: 82–85). Led by an Aghlabid prince named Ahmed bin Umar, Malta was conquered by fleets from Ifriqiya, no doubt based in Tunis, Sousse, Sidi Daoud, and Kelibia adjacent to the ancient fortress on Cap Bon. In its center was a *ribat* where ascetics indoctrinated volunteers for the expeditionary corps. Though the Byzantines offered a challenge, they were turned back by reinforcements sent from Sicily by Muhammed bin Khafaja (Ahmad 1975: 15). Though Malta became one of the last European island groups to fall to the Muslims, ironically it would be the place where they would stay the longest and have the most lasting cultural impact. In this sense as well as many others, Malta truly bridges the Mediterranean.

Regarding the bishopric prior to Malta's conquest by the Arabs, Kendal (1999: 3) has stated: "After the Council of Chalcedon in 868, he [the bishop] was unable to return to his see, which was being invaded by the Arabs, and not long after [in 878] we find him in chains in a Saracen prison at Palermo. Of successors of his under the Arabs there are no records, though probably such were appointed." That no bishop of Malta is known between 878 and 1156 suggests some degree of intolerance, at least with respect to religious leadership, during this period (Luttrell 1975: 27). Still, based on linguistic evidence in general and toponymic comparisons between Ifriqiya and Malta in particular, Aquilina (1970a: 194) has speculated that by the time Arab-speakers conquered Malta, they may have lost much of their "proselytising spirit." It is possible that the Arab-speaking conquerors even included a small minority of Christians, as there still was a minority segment resident in Ifriqiya.

Long-standing distortions in the presentation of Mediterranean cultural history have included the projection back into the Middle Ages of the rather fixed lines that we now think of as separating Europe and Africa and the ascribing of too much homogeneity to places and peoples associated with these names. We sometimes rather simplistically assume that wherever the followers of Islam and Christianity came into contact with one another they were implacable foes. We sometimes assume that during the periods that they were engaged in vigorous contests, the situation was much the same on all fronts simultaneously. In reality, war and legitimate trade often took place side by side; both Muslims and Christians often found allies or refuge behind the lines of their opponents.

Miscegenation has always been part of the Mediterranean inheritance, and the extraordinary vitality of the basin over thousands of years may be ascribed in no small degree to this mingling of the races. Europeans, Africans, Asiatics, Persians, and Arabs have all contributed their genetic structures, as well as their cultural inheritance, to the vast pool of human knowledge that is Mediterranean civilization. To call the twentieth century product of all these cultures and comminglings "Western European," as is sometimes done, is to insult the immense contributions of the East. (Bradford 1971: 422–423)

It would be a great distortion of historical facts to pretend that all the Muslims who settled in various parts of Mediterranean Europe during the centuries of Muslim expansionism into Europe were "Arabs." In reality, they were of many African ethnic groups as well as of many populations in Asia. A Mediterranean area where this is particularly well documented is Andalusia or Spain. The heterogeneity of that society is hinted at by some of the social labels that were used. For example, there was a special term *"muzarabes"* that referred to Christians who lived as a minority among Muslims and the term *"mudejares"* that referred to Muslims who lived as a minority among Christians. Jews had arrived from numerous places. Not only is the term saracen used in the literature, but also is the term *"saracen negro,"* which in the context can probably best be translated "black Arab-speaking Muslim."

Prior to having himself declared caliph in Spain in 929, Abd al-Rahman III ordered a princeling in Ceuta to send him as tribute thousands of Africans that included both Berbers and blacks for military service (Rout 1976:14) and as his labor battalions (Lévi-Provençal 1950: 75). Between 961 and 975, Hakam II "drafted and mobilized large numbers of slaves of all races for military service and even established a black honor guard which solemnly paraded on official occasions" (Lévi-Provençal 1950: 177–178). Moreover when Al-Mansur was royal chamberlain, but also de facto ruler of the caliphate between 978 and 1002, he imported Africans who were decidedly black not only for use as soldiers but also as couriers, carrying messages both to and from his armies in the field (Lévi-Provençal 1950: 178). Moreover, the Arabic literature on Spain consistently distinguishes between Almoravids and Arabs (Masonen 1995: 5).

A similar situation in Sicily: "Sicily under the Aghlabids was inhabited by a mixture of many different peoples, races and religious persuasions, Sicilians, Christian and Muslim, Greeks, Lombards, Jews, Arabs, Berbers and even some Persians and Negroes" (Ahmad 1975: 21–22). And history

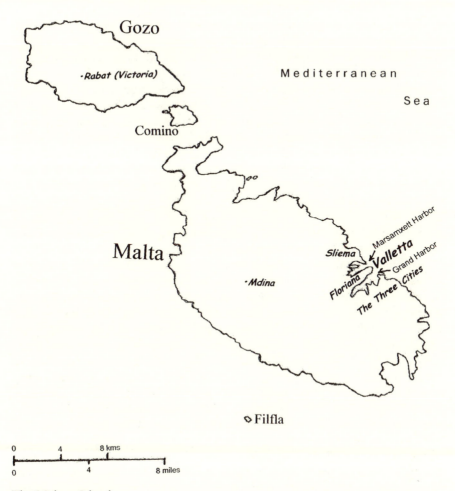

The Maltese Islands.

reveals that the same pattern existed in Palermo, Sicily's largest city, where "Apart from the Arabs, there were Berbers, Greeks, Lombards, Jews, Slavs, Persians, Turks and Negroes" (Ahmad 1975: 40). In fact, the heaviest concentration of Muslims in Sicily was in the western Val di Mazara region of Sicily where Palermo is located. Muslims were somewhat less numerous in Val Demone while in the Val di Noto region, they never outnumbered the Christians. Similarly, in the Maltese Islands, the proportion of Muslims in the population was considerably higher on Malta than on Gozo, where they may never have been the majority (Luttrell 1975: 39).

Based on his linguistic analysis of Arabic-derived place-names in Spain, Sicily, and Malta, Aquilina (1970a: 191) has argued in favor of important communality among the Arab-speakers who settled Malta and the other

two lands. There seems little doubt, moreover, that the Muslims who settled in Malta were also ethnically heterogeneous. As pointed out by Aquilina (1970b: 47), "The Semitic vocabulary of Maltese indicates ethnic
admixtures within the Aghlabid tribe that conquered Malta."

We shall never know the specific ethnic backgrounds of all the Arab
speakers who settled in Malta. We do know however that commerce and
culture flowed rather freely between the various continents that are a part
of the Mediterranean during the late Middle Ages; and hardly anywhere
was this more true than in the center. Even between the end of the eleventh
and the end of the thirteenth century when the Crusades were being waged
in the east, and to a lesser degree in the west, religious antagonisms did
not completely determine the modus vivendi in the central Mediterranean.
In this regard, the poorly known history of what transpired in Malta in
relationship to the Mediterranean region during the four centuries from
870 to 1283 is particularly illuminating.

Considering that there exists little evidence of pre-Arab place names in
Malta, the cultural importance of Muslim penetration, mainly from Ifriqiya, can scarcely be overstated. During this time, numerous Muslims
moved into the islands from Ifriqiya, though others came from Muslim
Sicily, and perhaps from Andalusia, Egypt, Syria, the African interior, and
other places.

To be sure, all Muslims in Malta were not Arabs. From various Maltese
documents dating before 1545, the 500 or more surnames and nicknames
as well as the 3,200 place-names reflect a strong Ifriqiyan Berber influence
(Luttrell 1975: 24). Even in Egypt, Arabicization had proceeded rapidly
only from 832 when Muslims became the majority (Lane-Poole 1968: 38).

Ifriqiya, in contrast, was located in a part of Africa where Berbers and
other African populations remained even more viable demographic, cultural, and political forces than in Egypt despite the fact that many of them
were Arabic-speaking by the ninth century. History knows no period when
people living in northern Africa have been ethnically homogeneous, and
scholars have long recognized the term "Arab" as having a number of
different meanings (Lewis 1969: 3–9; Trimingham 1979: 1–21). Hence, in
what is commonly known as the "Arab Period" of Maltese cultural history,
people of Berber heritage were probably more numerically important than
people who could trace any recent parentage directly to Arabia. In addition
to Muslims that came into Malta, some Muslims were undoubtedly former
Christians who converted to Islam much in the same way as this happened
in Sicily, especially in the Val di Mazara region (Ahmad 1975: 22).

It was predominantly the Kutama Berbers who brought an end to Aghlabid rule in Ifriqiya around 909 and invited in Said bin Husain, a Syrian
imam, who founded the Shiite Fatimid dynasty in opposition to the
Bagdad-based Abbasid Caliphate and was thereafter known as Ubaidullah
al-Mahdi. Though Ubaidullah was probably interested in expansionism as

early as his installment as Fatimid Caliph in 909, it was five years before he succeeded in capturing Alexandria and a couple of years more before he is known to have raided Malta, some other islands in the central Mediterranean, and the Egyptian Delta (Freeman-Grenville 1973: 45). Following Ubaidullah's death in 934, however, his successors succeeded in imposing their rule on Malta, Sardinia, Corsica, the Balearics, and even for a short time Genoa.

As Fatimid rule became increasingly harsh against Sunni Muslims and Kharidjite sectarians in Ifriqiya, Berbers across Maghreb rose up in rebellion against what they considered Arab domination within Islam. One result of this rebellion—mostly between 943 and 947—was the flight of Ifriqiyan refugees into Sicily, and presumably into Malta. That this Arab-Berber ethnic conflict within Islam spread into Sicily (Ahmad 1975: 28), and most certainly into Malta, illustrates that Muslims were not a homogeneous element in the societies where they lived and the impacts of their social diversity were complex.

Neither before nor after this unrest were the Fatimids very interested in the cultural domination of Malta, Sicily, or the Maghreb. Their central policy was the conquest of Egypt. With this goal finally reached in 969, they returned de facto control of western Algeria, northern Tunisia, Sicily, and Malta to the Berbers, and in Ifriqiya, a vassal Zirid dynasty came into being.

Since the Fatimids remained the de jure rulers of these areas, however, the Zirids cited the Fatimid caliph's name in the Friday prayer, placed it on the coinage, paid an annual tribute to him, and made certain that all successions to the governor's office had the approval of a caliph's diploma. In this sense, by 991, the same Fatimid sovereignty which extended over Malta and over Sicily also stretched over an unstable political confederacy that included the Zenate principalities of northwestern Africa and continued eastward as far as the Syrian desert and the Orontes River (Lane-Poole 1968).

In 991, a census of the Maltese Islands, taken by order of the emir, officially counted 14,972 Muslims and 6,339 Christians. The Muslims refortified the old Roman capital and renamed it Mdina (or in Arabic, "Medina"). They constructed some coastal fortifications on the peninsula of Birgu where Fort St. Angelo would later be built. Muslim contributions to what was apparently a prosperous economy probably included the introduction of citrus fruit, an animal-powered device for lifting water from wells onto land (Blouet 1967: 41), and a system for supporting limestone slabs on notches and pilasters that greatly improved roofing techniques (Mahoney 1996: 35). They seemed to have lived more in harmony with the natural habitat than their successors who would gradually harvest so many of Malta's trees that they would create an aridity from which the country would never recover.

Though in the late tenth century, the huge Iberian Peninsula remained firmly under Muslim control, a shift was beginning to take place in Europe's favor concerning the balance of power further east. After numerous attempts to take Constantinople from the Arabs, the Byzantines achieved a short-term success in 964. Infighting among Muslims that was occurring south of Malta in the early eleventh century signaled real weakness in Maghreb while in the northern sector of the central Mediterranean a resurgence was taking place.

In this central area of the Basin, European challenges to Muslim dominance were coupled with increased European interest in trans-Saharan trade. Genoa and Pisa managed to break the Muslim grip on both Sardinia and Corsica and followed this up by establishing their supremacy in the Tyrrhenian Sea north of Sicily. By 1034, they were able to pillage Bône on the Algerian coast. Shortly thereafter with assistance from the Byzantine navy, they seized the island of Pantelleria from Ifriqiya and even invaded Mahdiya in the heart of Ifriqiya, Malta's closest neighbor to the south. As this was still about fifteen years before northwestern Africa would be devastated by bedouin invasions, Ifriqiya was at that time also a strategic terminus for a thriving trans-Saharan trade.

When in 1046, Moizz bin Badis, the governor of Ifriqiya, accepted a fresh investiture from the Sunni caliph, which prompted his Shiite subjects to revolt, instability quickly threatened. To punish Moizz three years later, Al-Mustansir Abu Tamim, the Fatimid caliph in Cairo who was Shiite, invited hordes of restless Arab nomads that he had been containing in Upper Egypt, numbering between 40 thousand and 200 thousand, to plunder Maghreb to their contentment (MacMichael 1967: 146, 169, 173; see also Julien 1966: 70–74; Lane-Poole 1968: 137–138). While permanently changing the demographic make-up of Maghreb and massively destabilizing its political life and trade with Europe and sub-Saharan Africa, this plundering devastated Ifriqiya and weakened its links with Malta. This invasion of the Beni Sulaym, Beni Kurra, and Beni Hilals—who were in alliance with some Berber groups—caused so much instability in Maghreb that the trans-Saharan trade routes, which until this time ran to Ifriqiya, shifted much further to the west. Historians ranging from Ibn Khaldun, Idris, Julien, Goitein, Millet, Bovill, Lombarad, and Hazard have referenced the tremendous importance of trans-Saharan trade to the central Mediterranean prior to these bedouin invasions.

Against this background of internal factionalism among the Muslims in Sicily, Zirid distress in Ifriqiya, and the rupture of important African trading links in the central Mediterranean, Norman mercenary soldiers who had recently asserted their independence from former Byzantine employers around Messina decided to push southward, first into Sicily and next into Malta. In a 30-year struggle that would last until 1091, the Normans eventually wrested control of Sicily and Malta from Ifriqiya. In fact, when the

Normans arrived in the Maltese Islands, one of their first undertakings was to pillage both Malta and Gozo, though they also freed a good number of enslaved non-Maltese Christians whom they allowed to return to their various homelands (Buhagiar 1997: 123; Luttrell 1975: 30). Whether or not indigenous Christianity survived until this time and, if so, to what extent is a matter of uncertainty at the present time. Orr (1992: 146) has suggested that perhaps the Muslim influence on Gozo was less profound or less lasting than on Malta.

In any case, the Norman lunge southward to take over Sicily and Malta had little to do with religion and much to do with an interest in reestablishing profitable political and commercial links with Ifriqiya which was once again beginning to attract trade from sub-Saharan Africa. In fact, a large part of the Norman military consisted of Muslims, and Count Roger consistently resisted ecclesiastical pressure to convert them to Christianity (Ahmad 1975: 54; Johns 1987: 89–101). The Normans, moreover, did not restore the bishopric of Malta (Luttrell 1975: 33).

Neither under the Muslims nor the Normans was the central Mediterranean an implacable region of religious intolerance. That some Christians even remained in Ifriqiya—though surrounded by a sea of Muslims during the very period that Islam was the predominant religion in Malta—suggests their probable survival in Malta as well. Though the restoration of a line of Catholic bishops in Malta has often been alleged to have resulted from the arrival of the Normans, documentary evidence for this is lacking. It is possible that a degree of qualified religious tolerance had existed under the Muslims, and there is documentation that such a policy prevailed under the Normans. The Normans even allowed an emir to remain in power with the understanding that he would pay an annual tribute to them in mules, horses, and munitions.

Although the Knights did not permit Maltese—including even members of the nobility—to become Knights, some Maltese served within their clergy. Gian Francesco Abela, a patrician clergyman who eventually became the Order's vice-chancellor, also laid the foundation for Maltese historiography. Unfortunately, Abela was quite willing to distort Malta's history in the interest of deemphasizing her historic links with Africa and with Islam. Abela's determination that Malta be portrayed as innately European and Christian at all cost eventually incorporated into popular thinking about Malta's history a number of false traditions. In an eighteenth-century effort to strengthen the case for Abela's distortions and misinterpretations, a Maltese priest named Giuseppe Vella even generated forged Arabic documents.

Other prominent Maltese subsequently contributed to popular folklore and legends which held that Muslims of African origin had never inhabited Malta in large numbers, including Domenico Magri, also a priest (Luttrell 1975: 1–3, 9; Luttrell 1977: 105; Smith 1998: 51–52). As these distortions bore fruit and circulated within the general populace, numerous Maltese became convinced that their Semitic tongue could only have come from illustrious and pioneering Asiatic Phoenicians and not under any circumstances from neighboring Arab-speaking Africans who for reasons having to do with religion, national pride, and "race" the Maltese were more comfortable viewing as implacable enemies and inferiors. It is not coincidental that one of the most prestigious hotels in Malta is a grand edifice in Floriana named "The Phoenicia" while the country is without a hotel anywhere called "The Arabia." Though recent scholarly opinion in Malta is virtually unanimous that Malta's linguistic and demographic connections are much stronger with her Arab and Berber neighbors than prehistoric Phoenicia, once out of a "Pandora's Box," legends die hard.

[T]he outlines of the story have been distorted by a number of false traditions which are strongly rooted both in the existing historiography and in popular lore, and which often involve matters of national sentiment, religious dogma or political dispute. Whether the Maltese are "European" or "African" and whether Maltese Christianity has a continuous history have, for example, long been questions affecting the identity of the Maltese people. (Luttrell 1977: 105)

Though by the end of the fifteenth century all Maltese Muslims would be forced to convert to Christianity, they would still be in the process of acquiring surnames as required in European tradition. Ingeniously, they often used their father's personal Arabic names as the basis of surnames, though there was a consistent cultural avoidance of extremely obvious Arabic and Muslim names, such as Muhammed and Razul. Also, many families disguised their Arabic names, such as Karwan (the city in Tunisia), which became Caruana, and some derived family names by translating from Arabic into a Roman form, such as Magro or Magri from Dejf (Wettinger 1999: 341).

Although many students of cultural history in the central Mediterranean have assumed the existence of a continuous intolerance between Muslims and Christians throughout most of the Middle Ages, documentary evidence for such interpretations is simply lacking (Luttrell 1975). Though it was only four years before the first Crusade that Count Roger I established his overlordship of Malta, what was occurring in Malta, as in Sicily, was rather in the spirit of fluid coalitions and gradualism than crusading zeal.

Such minimal support as Count Roger gave to Christianization in Sicily lay in enslaving Muslims who rebelled against him and in encouraging Christians from other parts of Europe to settle there, perhaps knowing that some of the European immigrants would eventually vie with Muslims for land (Ahmad 1975: 70). By contrast, given that in Malta there was much less land to attract immigrants, a larger proportion of resident Muslims, and an emir in charge of day to day governance, Norman support of Christianization must have been nil.

Though navy personnel under Roger II—the son who eventually succeeded Count Roger—was predominantly Greek, it was Muslims who made up the backbone of his army. It was also to Muslims that he tended to entrust the financial management, though Muslims, Normans, Byzantines, and Jews held important positions in his civil administration. People from throughout the Mediterranean Basin, including Jews, Muslims, and Christians, were involved in regular trade, communication, and cultural exchange in the central Mediterranean Basin in the early 1100s. No fixed line of demarcation separated these peoples, and it was probably only in response to Sicily's attempt to expand its sphere of influence in Africa that Pisan and Genoese fleets withdrew from the African city of Mahdiya in 1104.

Idris, the ranking geographer at the Sicilian court of the Normans—probably born in Africa at Ceuta and educated at Cordoba in Europe—traveled widely in Spain, Asia Minor, and Africa north and south of the Sahara. Information transmitted to Roger II about the abundance of gold in Ghana time and again led Roger to try expanding his kingdom into Africa (Bovill 1958: 61, 81–82). Even in 1130 when Roger's kingdom had grown to include Sicily, Reggio Calabria, Apulia, and Malta, the acquisition of Malta was part of a larger policy for a southern expansion in the direction of Ghana. In keeping with this policy, Roger wrestled the island of Jerba from the Zirid rulers of Tunisia in 1134. And even after being defeated by the Zirid Hasan bin Ali the following year, Roger's attempts to reach Ghana only temporarily ended in 1137 when he was checked in the Battle of Cape Dimas.

Roger II's takeover of Malta, like his attempts to expand his Norman empire into Africa, was more motivated by lust for gold than by religion. Neither in Sicily nor Malta did he attempt to force Muslims to convert to Christianity. Given his overall policy in the central Mediterranean, Malta's strong ties to Africa and to Islam were a bridge, an asset. In addition to Roger's strong dislike of the Frankish rulers of Jerusalem, he chose to play no part in the Second Crusade, in part because of his religious tolerance and in part because Muslims remained a majority in Sicily and Malta in 1145. Hence, even as a so-called Age of Crusades was unfolding in the eastern Mediterranean, it left the day-to-day lives of Maltese essentially unaffected.

Roger II resumed his campaign to gain a foothold in Africa by taking control of Mahdiya in 1148. By 1160, he controlled a stretch of northern Africa extending from Tripoli in Libya to Bône in Algeria, with few holdouts except for Tunis, Kelibia, and for a time Sfax. These conquests coupled with his control of Malta secured his control in the strategic straits around Malta and south of Sicily. Against this background, he had few scruples about allowing Malta—still a predominantly Muslim and Arabic-speaking archipelago—to remain the strong cultural tie to northern Africa which it had been at least since 870. Even in Sicily, it was only shortly before the end of his rule in 1154 that Roger II placed mild pressure on Muslims and Jews to convert to Christianity (Ahmad 1975: 71).

Around 1149, or only 50 years after the fall of Jerusalem to Crusaders, the Normans were able to extend their conquests in Sicily and Malta to include possessions from Tripoli to Cape Bon and south to Kairwan and the island of Jerba. This is indicative that power struggles and cultural exchange involving forces based north and south of Malta were continuing on a large scale. Gradually, however, the accompanying instability began to wear down many of the African contenders, including the Zirid dynasty in Ifriqiya (Amari 1937–1939; Brett 1969; Idris 1962; Julien 1966; Lane-Poole 1968).

Although the Almohads succeeded in expelling the Normans from Africa after only a 10-year stay (Smith 1968: 29; Wright 1969), considering its long-term consequences for Islam, it was in some respects a pyrrhic victory. At least in Sicily, two of its results were the disarming of some Muslims not in the military and retaliation against resident Muslims on the part Norman and Lombardi barons sufficient to cause many to hide in the countryside. Though from 1068, many members of Sicily's Muslim elite began to emigrate, it is equally significant that others opted to stay. It is also significant that no order to deport Muslims outside of Italy was ever issued (Ahmad 1975: 71, 75).

According to Wright (1969: 86), the "Almohads [including the Hafsids] refused to trade with Europe, until Genoa won a concession to send ships once a year to the Maghrib ports. The profits and customs dues to be collected from trade were effective in eroding religious scruples on both sides of the Mediterranean, and Pisa, too, was granted commercial rights in several ports, including Tripoli." As of 1169, when Fatimid rule ended in Egypt and the Ayubids came to power under Saladin, his major foreign policy opposed the Christians on all fronts. Saladin was consistent in confronting Crusaders in the Holy Land and African Christians in Nubia, as well as Christian commercial interests in the central Mediterranean Basin. In fact, during 1172 and 1173, he undertook the capture of the African littoral from Barca in Cyrenaica to Gabes in Tunisia, and from the Muslim Hafsids so as to curtail the trade between the northwestern coast of Africa and Christian powers in Europe. Significantly however, his hostility was not directed at Malta, presumably because Malta was still predominantly Muslim.

When the bishop of Strasbourg passed through Malta in 1175, he recorded that it was inhabited by Muslims (Blouet 1967: 43; Luttrell 1975: 32). We know from Idrisi that much African trade reached Sicily via Malta in the twelfth century. It was undoubtedly lust after lucrative commerce rather than religious animosity that led a Pisan captain to seize a richly laden Tunisian ship at Malta around 1184 and throw its crew overboard (Luttrell 1975: 31–32).

By the period when Tancred was king of Sicily between 1189 and 1194, general anarchy increased in large measure because of Muslim unrest coupled with intolerance toward Islam. Although in Sicily, cultural symbiosis which included Arab elements sharply declined during this period, the fact that the population of Malta included a larger proportion of Muslims than that of Sicily did not yield exactly the same result. For example, while government documents began to be recorded in Latin to the exclusion of Arabic in Sicily, this did not happen in Malta.

Although Sicily was faced with unrest on the part of an oppressed and rebellious Muslim minority who were vying to be power brokers, the fact that Muslims remained a clear majority in Malta apparently spared it comparable instability. The Third Crusade, which tangentially impacted Sicily when Richard the Lion-Hearted occupied Sicily's port of Messina, left Malta unaffected. Sicily again felt of the impact of the Crusades when in 1215, Frederick I of Sicily and Frederick II of Germany—based on his marriage to Yolanda, the hereditary heiress to the Latin Kingdom of Jerusalem—assumed the title of King of Jerusalem.

During approximately the same period, or more precisely from 1205 to 1222, Malta had an uncharacteristic and short-term brush with the Crusades. This came about when under the authority of the rulers of Sicily, a corsair with more interest in piracy than crusading in 1203 acquired the title of Count of Malta and used Malta as his principal base to intermittently trade with, and fight against, various Muslim powers in Africa and the Levant. This episode essentially ended in 1221 when Henry "Pescatore," this Count of Malta, was elevated to Admiral of Sicily, and transferred his base of operations largely to Sicily. Hence by 1222 Malta was again on the sidelines of the Crusades (Luttrell 1975: 35).

By 1223, Christian intolerance of Islam and Muslim rebelliousness had reached such a point in Sicily that a decision was made by King Frederick to send a large segment of the Muslim population to a part of Italy north of Sicily. He established a colony at Lucera near Italy's Adriatic coast, far north of Islam's stronghold in Africa where many of Sicily's Muslims were sent. In fact, at least some from Malta eventually were sent there as well.

This occurred between 1207 (when the Almohads made the Hafsids autonomous in Ifriqiya) and 1237 (when Egypt once again granted trading concessions to the Italians). It was during these three decades that major African trans-Saharan trade routes that had shifted westward due to the chaos caused by marauding bedouins in the eleventh century now shifted east toward the central Mediterranean again. That Sicily and Malta were home to many Muslim residents contributed to this realignment in commercial ties between Europe and Africa. According to Wright (1969: 86), it was during the thirteenth century that medieval trade between Italy and

Africa was in fact at its maximum. Not surprisingly, the African ports near Sicily and Malta were the busiest ones along Africa's entire northern littoral, and most of the trade shipped out of these ports was of sub-Saharan origin.

Against this background, there seems little doubt that Malta was an important link in an economic and cultural chain that stretched from King Duname's thirteenth-century empire of Kanem adjacent to Lake Chad northward to the Mediterranean Sea and on into Italy, and probably Malta. In Sicily, an important cultural symbiosis that included Arab and Berber elements declined sharply by the end of the twelfth century. In contrast, a similar cultural symbiosis in Malta was still alive during the first half of the thirteenth century, a period when a cultural renaissance was also occurring in Ifriqiya.

In keeping with the renaissance's outreach to Europe under Abu Zakaria Yahya I after Ifriqiya regained its independence in 1228, Zakaria relocated his capital northward from Kairwan to Tunis and exhibited a new openness to Europe. He signed commercial treaties with Genoa, Pisa, Venice, and Sicily and extended his control to Bougie and Algiers. This Ifriqiyan sultan even encouraged trade with Aragon and the Italian maritime states. Though he initiated construction of the Zituna mosque—which would eventually evolve into the leading center of Islamic learning in Maghreb—his patronage of scholarship and the arts crossed religious lines. Given that between Ifriqiya and the rest of Europe, Malta is a geographical bridge and that Malta had well-established cultural links with Ifriqiya, including a common language, it seems most unlikely that Malta would not have been greatly impacted.

Unlike some other parts of the Mediterranean Basin during what is usually thought of as the Age of the Crusades, Malta was hardly at the center of major Muslim-Christian conflict. As it still had an Arab-speaking majority and possibly a Muslim majority, it largely maintained close cultural ties with its neighbors in Africa. During the time that Ifriqiya prospered, Malta seems to have profited, from both a flourishing trade and numerous advancements, especially in agriculture (Blouet 1967: 43).

The establishment of an Italian colony for Sicilian Muslims at Lucera on the Italian Peninsula beginning in 1223 has led to much speculation that there must have been a general expulsion of all Muslims from Malta in 1224. However, it is virtually impossible to reconcile this viewpoint with a report of 1240 or 1241 by Gilibert to Frederick II of Sicily to the effect that in that year Malta and Gozo had 836 families that were Saracen or Muslim, 250 that were Christian, and 33 that were Jewish. Moreover, Ibn Khaldun is on record as stating that some Maltese Muslims were sent to the Italian colony of Lucera around 1249 (Luttrell 1975: 37).

A lasting connection with Arabic is indicated by the fact that it is not until the fifteenth century that we encounter a literary work sufficiently different from Arab to be considered Maltese, this a poem entitled "Cantilena" written by Pietro Caxaro. Given the linguistic continuity in Arabic per se in the thirteenth century, either the number of Arab-speaking Christian families was much larger than reported by Gilbert in 1241 or a large proportion of the Arab-speaking Muslims accepted conversion to Christianity and remained in Malta (Wettinger 1984: 22–37; Wettinger 1999: 333). It is most unlikely that Christians again become the majority of the Maltese population or owned the majority of wealth until around 1244 (Aquilina 1970b: 58; Aquilina 1970d: 177–178; Blouet 1967: 43).

Even the proportions of an often-alleged expulsion of Muslims from Malta claimed for 1244 is highly suspect. It is probably based on a false assumption that virtually all Muslims refused to convert to Christianity and hence that virtually all people who had once been Muslims were expelled, but this assumption raises several problems. First, the rulers in Sicily never ordered Muslims deported from Italy, although some Muslims were eventually deported from Sicily to other parts of Italy. Second, since a larger part of the population in Malta was Muslim than in Sicily, a general deportation of a majority of the population would have depleted Maltese society more than is documented, even assuming some immigration into Malta from Celano. Third, Frederick signed a truce with the ruler in Tunis in 1231 "which stipulated that the island of Pantellaria should be governed by a Muslim nominated by the emperor" (Ahmad 1975: 86). Four, the thriving commercial relations between Ifriqiya and Pisa, Genoa, Venice, and Sicily in the 1230s, and those with predominantly Muslim Egypt when in 1237 it once again granted trading concessions to the Italians, would seem improbable in the face of a massive deportation of Muslims.

Additionally, even when Frederick undertook an unauthorized crusade around 1240, his motivations seem to have been as much political as religious. In fact, he had already been excommunicated from the church on claims that he was too friendly with Muslims and too tolerant toward them. Not only did his retinue on his crusade include some Muslim pages and ladies—dressed somewhat like Muslims and guarded by eunuchs—it even included a number of Muslim soldiers (Ahmad 1975: 85). It has sometimes been easy to graft onto Maltese cultural history more confrontation with Muslims during the Age of Crusades than can be justified by local developments. The kinds of circumstances cited here do not suggest that any general expulsion of Muslims from Malta took place in 1244.

During some periods the Maltese Islands were incorporated with Sicily and during some periods they were not, instead being reduced to a mere fief of some aristocrat or another. Even Sicily after 1194 became but a single peripheral region in a succession of large empires and by 1250 lost the cultural impetus that had made it a leader in literature and science among the Italian states. When in 1250, the reign over Sicily and Malta of Frederick I (also known as Frederick II of Germany) ended, it would be only a matter of time before Malta would again become a rotating fief of European royalty living elsewhere.

Malta, in 1266, was turned over in fiefdom to Charles of Anjou, brother of France's King Louis IX, who retained it in ownership until 1283. During the rule of Charles of Anjou, faltering religious pluralism still existed in the sense that Orthodox Christians, Jews, and Muslims still constituted a substantial minority of the population (Dunbabin 1998: 151). Eventually religious coexistence became precarious in both Sicily and Malta under Charles, however, for he had a genuine intolerance of religions other than Roman Catholicism. In Italy, he exerted strong pressure on the Muslim colony at Lucera to convert, most especially after their resistance to him in 1268 and 1269. He even forced some Muslim men to leave their families in Lucera and settle in other parts of his realm. Though Charles was also interested in the conversion of Jews for fiscal and political reasons, he oppressed them less than Muslims and even employed some as physicians and translators (Dunbabin 1998: 152–153, 158).

It was not until 1270 when Louis IX, the brother of Charles of Anjou, chose Tunis as the destination for the Eighth Crusade, that the Crusades really landed on Malta's doorstep and posed a large-scale test for religious coexistence in the islands. Though when the plague broke out Louis and many of the Crusaders died, Charles of Anjou (even with some Muslims among his troops) went on to defeat the Hafsid army in Tunisia. As Charles maintained large garrisons both on Malta and Gozo manned mostly by Maltese, the Maltese were most certainly involved (Dunbabin 1998: 174).

A curious result of Charles's victory over the Hafsids was that the emir of Tunis became his vassal, a fact that caused Charles I of Anjou to moderate his hostility toward small remnant populations of Italian Muslims (Dunbabin 1998: 153–154). That peace was quickly restored between the Spaniards and the Hafsids of Tunis even following this Eighth Crusade shows that it was mostly a brief flare-up in what were rather even relations. In fact, the Hafsids of Ifriqiya were trading as usual with Aragon, Pisa, and Venice by 1271. By the next year, moreover, trade was restored between Ifriqiya and Genoa.

That in 1275 a Moroccan government delegation was received in Spain on friendly terms is a further indication that religious differences seldom prevented neighboring Mediterranean peoples from civil interactions with each other long-term. This was only a year before Peter I of Sicily (also known as Peter III of Aragon) became the first in a succession of Aragonese tyrants exercising feudal control over Malta.

In the wake of a massive 1282 rebellion against the rule of Charles of Anjou in Sicily—known as the Sicilian Vespers—Charles's empire began to crumble (Dunbabin 1998: 89, 169). However, it would not be until the turn of the fourteenth century, when his son Charles II was in power, that Islam would finally be banished from the Italian Peninsula. It was only at this time that the last Italian Muslims were forced to convert, including apparently those at Naples, Girofalco, Nocera, and Lucera (Ahmad 1975: 84, 106).

From Count Roger's conquest of Sicily, and eventually Malta, through the reign of Manfred, strong Muslim institutions at the Sicilian court only gradually gave way to influences that were Christian and European (Ahmad 1975: 64–67, 87, 92; Chalandon 1907). Against this background, it is only in the narrowest sense of titular feudal ownership that a claim may be made that Malta's Muslim period of cultural development lasted but 220 years. Of greater cultural significance, the demographic and economic dominance of Muslims continued for at least another century and a half after which forced conversions undoubtedly permitted many former Muslims to remain.

The likelihood that many Muslims in Malta eventually converted to Christianity rather than leave seems indicated by parallels in Sicily as well as by the fact that there is linguistic evidence suggesting that "there was a time when the church of Malta was fed by Christian Arabs" (Aquilina 1970b: 46). Luttrell (1975: 40) is also on record with the argument that "the persistence of the spoken Arabo-Berber language" in Malta can probably best be explained by eventual large-scale conversions of Maltese Muslims to Christianity. Even when Islam had completely been erased from the Maltese landscape, Arabic remained, especially as represented by colloquial dialects of the language as spoken in Libya, Tunisia, and in medieval Sicily.

In the words of Aquilina (1970b: 45), "The Arabs are linguistically the most important people that ever managed the affairs of the country . . . for there is no doubt that, allowing for a number of peculiarities and erratic developments, Maltese is structurally an Arabic dialect." Sicilian historians commonly consider the period under Norman kings and their Hohenstaufen descendants (at least through the reign of Frederick I), a time of great cultural effervescence, involving a mixture of Arab, Berber, Latin, and Greek Sicilian inputs (e.g., Norwich 1967; Runciman 1958; Smith 1968). While a similar blossoming of culture probably also took place in Malta, some notable differences between Malta and Sicily did exist.

First, Malta did not have a Greek infrastructure comparable with that of Sicily. Second, Muslims never formed as large a part of Sicily's overall population as they did in Malta. Third, beginning with the Hohenstaufen dynasty, there was more discontinuity of feudal rule in Malta than in Sicily, with Malta frequently being handed over from one European noble to another.

In contrast to the Muslims who settled in Malta mostly from nearby northern Africa, the Normans came to Malta as rulers rather than as colonizers. In fact, they seem never to have been Malta residents in large numbers. Malta's links with Africa remained strong until the beginning of Malta's Spanish rule in 1283. While many other European countries were engaged in waging religious crusades against Islam, Malta was essentially a nonparticipant. It was not so much Norman control that eventually brought an attenuation of Afro-Asian cultural influences in Malta as it was Roman Catholic religious orders. Though some religious orders began to become established in Malta as important disseminators of European culture as early as the thirteenth century (Blouet 1967: 44), for the most part they came later.

An attempt in 1364 to attract the Benedictines of Catania to set up base in Malta was unsuccessful. . . . The Benedictines of San Nicolo d'Arena, although they had been bequeathed land in Malta, refused to undertake pastoral work on the island on the pretext of inherent dangers and their ignorance of the Maltese language. It was only during the course of the fifteenth century that a number of religious Orders permanently established themselves on the island. These included the Augustinian friars who arrived in 1413, the Franciscan Minors in 1442, the Carmelites in 1450, and the Dominicans in 1473. (Thake 1996: 23)

Though Malta's Spanish control under the authority of Aragonese monarchs between 1283 and 1410 was one during which Malta's economy did not prosper, it was nonetheless during this period that important cultural changes took place. This period witnessed "the rise of Christianity to take a central place in Maltese society, the creation of a nobility, the development of local government (i.e, *some Maltese-based government*), and the influx of migrants, particularly from Spain and southern Italy" (Blouet 1967: 46). The extremely weak Malta-based government entailed the recognition of Malta as a *Università* or commune with two officials annually elected from among the Maltese by the *Consiglio Popolare* for final approval of others.

The fact that Christianity in the larger Basin experienced a severe setback in 1461 when Athens fell to the Turks tended to ratchet up the hostility toward Islam in predominantly Christian lands everywhere, and most especially in the Mediterranean. One result was that by 1487, the long arm of the Spanish Inquisition extended directly into Malta and Sicily. The cultural ramifications of this may be imagined from the magnitude of "suspect" cultural survivals still to be found in this part of the Christian world. In describing Sicily in the fifteenth century—where the Muslim impact had been less than in Malta—Smith (1968: 98) described the situation this way. "Away from the coastal cities the peasants had been accustomed for centuries to extreme conditions of either anarchy or semi-slavery. Some of them dressed and spoke like their Arab forebears."

The role of ecclesiastical authorities as great landholders in Malta goes back at least as far as this period of Spanish control in Malta, and the Spanish Inquisition was but an additional means by which the church and state were harnessed together (Smith 1968: 107, 164). By the beginning of the fifteenth century when much of Europe was more interested in embryonic secular nationalism than with Crusades, the Maltese Islands remained a fief that was internally constricted by feudalism and externally constrained by the foreign policy of Spain. Moreover, the people were able to give expression to their political yearnings primarily in religious terms for even with their *Università* the Maltese learned that their islands were still a fief that could be sold at whim.

Assuming some broad parallels between the experiences of Malta and Sicily during the Spanish period, civil authority and control of taxation remained in the hands of the nobility and the bishops, and there was no real development of a middle class. Moreover, resources were depleted in large measure to pay for ambitious political schemes of the Spanish. These schemes included efforts to regain Granada from Muslims, to counter the expansionism of the Ottoman Turks, to capture Naples, and to gain a foothold along those parts of the coast of northern Africa known to attract lots of sub-Saharan gold.

The extravagant religious pilgrimage of Mali's Mansa Musa to Mecca via Northern Africa in the fourteenth century and the writing of Ibn Khaldun had contributed to a European assumption that much of the wealth of the African interior was to be found in Mali. It was not coincidental that by the turn of the fifteenth century when Europe was suffering from a shortage of precious metals that on the island of Majorca and in some other parts of Catalonia, Europeans were moved to attempt mapping the interior of Africa with greater specificity. Nor was it coincidental that their crude maps almost invariably attempted to locate Mali.

Even as the Portuguese were establishing *fronteiras* along the Africa's Atlantic coast, the Spaniards were establishing themselves in the *presidios* along her northern littoral, at least until they eventually found themselves checked by the Ottoman Turks. This was the same dynasty of Turks to whom Constantinople would fall in 1453. As Turkey was also interested in expansionism, Malta's association with Spanish schemes in Africa had the effect of turning her strategic location in the central Mediterranean into a liability of exposure. There were almost continual raids on Malta by Muslim powers throughout the fourteenth century, followed by raids of still greater severity in the first half of the fifteenth century, a time when the Maltese also suffered several natural calamities such as droughts and plague.

That the events of this period contributed in no small way to the proverbial "Maltese siege mentality" seems beyond question. In fact, present settlement patterns on both Malta and Gozo reflect this quite well (Blouet 1967: 89–98; cf. Smith 1968: 140). Moreover, this was a period of negative population growth and considerable economic dislocation, when the Maltese did not fair well as a rotating fief of European aristocracy.

That some religious diversity continued to exist in fourteenth-century

Malta is attested by documentation that King Fredrick III granted a piece of land at Tabia to the Universitate Judeorum, that is, the Jewish community, for a cemetery in 1372 which was located at Ghariexem, near Marfa (Wettinger 1985: 6). Most probably, the often alleged expulsion of Muslims from the islands in the 1240s involved only some Muslims who refused to convert to Christianity. Malta remained an archipelago with cultural influences from many parts of the Mediterranean Basin throughout much of the fifteenth century.

The penning up in Granada of the Iberian Muslims and the upsurge in Spanish nationalism through the uniting of Aragon and Castile under Ferdinand and Isabella toward the end of the fifteenth century afforded the Spaniards a real opportunity to strike at the African mainland. With Malta in the firm grip of a resurgent Spain and the Spanish Inquisition, non-Christians were finally expelled from the islands in 1492. Using Sicily as a base, and presumably Malta as well, Spain proceeded in annexing the Tunisian island of Jerba in 1497; and she added Oran in Algeria and Tripoli in Libya in 1510. Due, however, to the strain of holding onto territories in the central Mediterranean Basin at this time, Spain opted to retain control of Sicily but eventually heeded the Pope's admonition to give Malta and Tripoli in fiefdom to the Hospitallers of St. John of Jerusalem.

Although Malta and Tripoli, at least in theory, remained attached through feudal vassalage to the rulers of Sicily, in fact, Malta was never directly governed from Sicily after 1530. While much of Europe experienced the Age of Crusades roughly from the late eleventh to the late thirteenth century, it was well after that period that the Knights of St. John imported into Malta a way of life based on crusading. Although the medieval conception of "the Universal Church, uniting Christendom into one great theocracy governed by the impartial wisdom of the Vicar of God" (Runciman 1958: 87) was thought by the Holy See to be applicable far beyond the shores of Malta, perhaps nowhere else was this legacy destined to have so much impact on the cultural history of an entire people as in these islands.

Chapter 3

Knights and Revolutionists

The Knights of Malta had their conception in the Order of St. John of Jerusalem, an eleventh-century lay brethren of nobles founded to offer hospitality and medical care to Christian pilgrims traveling in the Holy Land. Around the same time, the Byzantine Empire—hard pressed by Muslim Turks—appealed to the Roman papacy for assistance despite the ecclesiastical schism that divided them. Responding to this appeal, Pope Urban II launched the Age of the Crusades in November 1095 and the order became a military force. It remained headquartered in Malta from 1530 until ousted by Napoleon in 1798.

As Europeans returned to their homes in victory after the First Crusade conquered Jerusalem in July 1099, the fame of the servants of the Benedictine abbey of St. Mary spread far and wide. As a consequence of this fame, noble families from many countries endowed it with numerous properties scattered throughout Europe. In time, the order that began with but a simple hospital in Jerusalem was transformed into a rich international organization with hospitals spread along numerous pilgrim routes. This rapid expansion led Pope Paschal II in 1113 to issue a bull providing it with a charter of incorporation (Sire 1994: 3–4).

The group of noble hospitallers with a simple Jerusalem hospital eventually acquired many daughter houses and under a papal charter was transformed into the Order of St. John of Jerusalem (Bradford 1971: 355, 358). The Order's papal charter implicitly recognized its military disposition by providing that it was not allowed to enter into any type of alliance with one European power against another. Already by 1148, the Order was in the military forefront of the Second Crusade.

The Knights Templars, or "Poor Knights of Christ and of the Temple of Solomon"; the Teutonic Knights; and the Knights of the Order of Saint John of Jerusalem; these were the three great orders which sprang out of the Crusades and whose names are indissolubly linked with this period of history. In terms of the Mediterranean, however, the one which carries the deepest and longest association is the Order of St. John. (Bradford 1971: 353)

Muslim forces that overpowered the last Christian stronghold of Acre in 1291 left only seven members of the Order of St. John surviving. Only 10 years later, however—urged on by the Pope and the Genoese—the Order found a new home for itself by capturing Rhodes from the tottering Byzantine Empire. By the middle of the sixteenth century, Christian expansionism in the eastern Mediterranean on the parts of European powers was encountering opposition from an increasingly powerful Muslim power also interested in empire-building, the Ottoman Turks.

At the beginning of 1522, the Ottoman's Suleiman the Magnificent ousted the Knights of St. John from Rhodes. As Turkish expansionism surged, only seven years later, Barbarossa, a vassal of the Ottomans, captured the Spanish fortress of Peñón on the Algerian coast in the western Mediterranean. When during the following year, Suleiman launched a serious effort to conquer Vienna, the concern turned into desperation on the part of some Christians, including the Pope and Spain's Charles V, whose suzerainty also extended over Sicily and Malta.

Meanwhile after losing Rhodes, members of the Order of St. John—with a reputation as resolute warriors—were searching for another Mediterranean home to use as a base of operations to fight against Islam. Charles V, head of the Holy Roman Empire as well as Spanish monarch, heeded the Pope's appeal to offer the Knights a base of operations in the central Mediterranean. Hoping that the Knights would stop the Turkish advance at the strategic straits in the center of the sea thus protecting Sicily and Spain, Charles offered the Order a fiefdom over the Maltese Islands in the center of the straits and Tripoli on the African mainland.

As the Knights were still intent on returning to Rhodes, they were not initially interested in the offer of this fief. They were not favorably impressed by the fact that it had a small population, few natural resources, essentially no industries, was not self-sustaining, and would likely be difficult to defend. With considerable reluctance in 1527, they voted to accept this fief from Charles V whose suzerainty they would annually acknowledge with a gift to him and his successors of one falcon.

Because of further dissension caused largely by nationalist feelings on the part of French members, the Knights did not actually move to occupy their new fief until 1530. Their misgivings were not ill placed as there were continuous raids against them, directed especially at Tripoli and Gozo (Vella 1975: 364). Gozo lost much of its population in Muslim raids and the Knights only managed to hold on to Tripoli—which they planned to use as their main headquarters—for 21 years until a Turkish admiral named Sinan Pasha successfully expelled them. Shortly thereafter, Sinan's forces went on to capture and enslave most of the inhabitants of Gozo. Though for the nine years the Knights—under Grand Master La Valette— periodically tried to retake Tripoli, they were not successful (Vella 1975: 380–381).

The Knights tended their wounds, and they consolidated their paternalistic control over the Maltese archipelago, the only part of their fief that they still controlled. However, they chose not to settle in Malta's large and centrally located major town of Mdina. As it was a seafaring organization, it settled instead in the port of Birgu on Malta, then only a tiny fishing village. Here, the Order was divided into eight language-based *langues* corresponding roughly to the parts of Europe from which various knights originated: Aragon, Auvergne, Castile, England, France, Germany, Italy, and Provence.

Meanwhile, Darghut, a Greek captain who had become a Turkish pirate, was named governor of Tripolitania in 1552. As one of Darghut's central concerns was the reopening of trade relations with the sub-Saharan kingdom of Bornu, the Order and the Turks for a while turned in different directions. In Malta, the Spanish Inquisition had been made inoperative when the Knights arrived. The Inquisition of the Holy See would not be established for another three decades—a sufficiently long time to permit Lutheranism to begin spreading in some elite circles due in large measure to the cosmopolitan atmosphere that accompanied the arrived of the Order (Cassar 1988: 65–66).

Not all Maltese liked the theocratic military oligarchy influenced by French and Spanish absolutism that the Order of St. John introduced into the islands. In fact, some resident nobles, who were especially disappointed at seeing Malta's oldest and most prestigious *Università* in Mdina lose much of its political power, left the islands rather than be ruled by the Knights. On the other hand, Gozo—which had been severely depopulated—began to be resettled around this time (Fiorini 1986: 203–244).

The Knights (European noblemen never likely to reign in their own countries) elected their own Grand Master who then became ruler of both the Order and Malta. This Grand Master was subject to the ultimate authority of the Vatican, which had legitimated the Order's charter, and the Pope's principal representative in the Islands was the Maltese Inquisitor. The Knights effectively undercut preexisting institutions of government, and such feeble expressions of nationalism as existed tended to find voice only through the Maltese clergy and nobility, the latter of which remained largely holed up in the city of Mdina.

The government that the Knights imposed, though paternalistic, had significant checks and balances, a number of which lay outside the islands

(Earle 1970: 102). One check was the King of France who had influence because over half of the Knights were French and also because many of the lands elsewhere that supported the Order were located in France. Moreover, Malta under the Knights was not self-sufficient in her food supply. Whoever was ruling in Sicily (whether the King of Spain or the Bourbon Kings) could exert considerable influence on the Knights, as much of the country's corn and wheat was imported from Sicily. Almost from the beginning, more attention was given to keeping Malta on a war footing than on producing food sufficient to feed a rapidly growing population.

The first Inquisitor arrived around 1565 and after this time, theocratic rule in Malta was somewhat triadic, with the authority of the foreign Knights sharply contested from time to time by both a foreign Inquisitor and the local clergy headed by a foreign Bishop. Hence although factionalism existed, it was among various factions somehow representative of the Universal Church. The viability of this type of economic and governmental arrangement was early put to the test when in 1565 the Ottoman Turks, after a 30-year period of Mediterranean expansionism, felt emboldened enough to lay siege to Malta.

In a siege by over 200 vessels, during which Turkey threw between 30,000 and 50,000 men into battle against the tiny islands, it remains a remarkable feat that so few knights, some 5,000 Maltese, and 4,000 others, many of whom arrived as reinforcements at the very last moment, were able to fight off this major power. Fortuitous for Malta, Darghut Pasha, an outstanding military strategist, fell mortally wounded in battle (Bradford 1961). To this day, this defeat of the Turks in the Great Siege is celebrated as a national holiday in Malta.

The Great Siege—coupled with the 1571 Turkish defeat in the Battle of Lepanto in Greece, aimed at keeping Cyprus in Christian hands—did not completely stop Turkish expansionism. Still, its importance in boosting European morale and convincing the Turks to stay away from Malta for a long time can scarcely be overstated (Sire 1994: 71). On the other hand, Turkey's defeat in Malta, coupled with the work of the Inquisition there, left the Turks in no mood to be tolerant toward the final remnants of a Christian community in northwestern Africa with roots going back to such early church fathers as Cyprian, Augustine, and Tertullian.

Until this time, at least a few African Christians had managed to survive in nearby Africa during some 15 centuries, though they were now surrounded by a sea of Muslims. However, when the Ottomans in 1583 took over Tunis from the last Hafsid sultan, who had withdrawn to his capital under the protection of a guard of African Christians, the Turks determined that those last Christians west of Egypt would either convert or die. It was in that year that history records the final disappearance of indigenous Christianity in northwestern Africa.

During the next four years, the African coast opposite Malta was formally divided into three regencies, with capitals at Algiers, Tripoli, and Tunis (Clissold 1977: 26–27). This new positioning corresponded with an upsurge in piracy and enslavement on the Mediterranean, where pirates and corsairs operated out of numerous ports both in Africa and Europe. Important among these African ports were Tripoli, Tunis, and especially Algiers, as well as several others in Morocco and the European ports of Majorca, Toulon, Marseilles, Genoa, Pisa, Leghorn, and Malta's Grand Harbor.

In addition to exploiting the labor of slaves, the Maltese, like the Africans, made handsome profits in commissions and ransoms from the turnover of slaves. While from the 1500s "race" increasingly became the rationale for enslaving Africans destined for transport to the Americas, by contrast, religion more than race was used as justification for enslaving a wide array of peoples in the Mediterranean Basin, even into the late 1700s. As a consequence, Mediterranean slavery ensnarled in bondage many people of Europe, Asia, and Africa. In fact, as honorable trade declined on the Mediterranean Sea during the early seventeenth century, piracy, slavery, and the *corso*—a type of licensed robbery on the high seas—became more rampant, and Turks, Africans, and Europeans were deeply involved both as aggressors and as victims. The prevalence of piracy, the *corso*, and enslavement not only imperiled shipping on the Mediterranean, but also made it dangerous to live along the coasts in many places.

In 1614, for example, a large Turkish raiding party landed in Malta at Marsa Scala and ravaged as far inland as Żabbar before being driven off. Not long afterwards, raiders carried off most of Gozo's population. Many of the present settlement patterns in the islands, as well as the locations of most fortifications, are directly related to vulnerabilities made manifest during this period. On both Malta and Gozo, it is not a mere coincidence that nucleated settlement patterns are the norm, with populations living near fortified areas. Moreover, there still exist lookout towers scattered across Gozo, as well as near localities such as Marsa Scala, Mellieħa, Naxxar, and Żurrieq on Malta.

From the second half of the seventeenth century onward, Malta was as involved in piracy as was the regency of Algiers, the most important headquarters for piracy among Malta's African neighbors. The only European slave market that could rival it in size was Leghorn. So well organized was the *corso* in Malta, in some other ports of Europe, and in northern Africa that it issued permits of safe conduct that were internationally recognized. In fact, in the late 1660s, an estimated one-fifth of all Maltese men were engaged in the *corso* (Earle 1970: 122).

Piracy declined more in the eastern Mediterranean than in other areas beginning the latter half of the seventeenth century. This reduction came about partly because the sector of the Basin in which the Knights were willing to wage war shrank considerably. In fact, their last land engagement in the eastern Mediterranean took place in 1707, and their last expedition against the Turkish navy was shortly thereafter in 1716. After this time, the Knights rarely ventured into the Levant and were engaged mostly in contests close to their home base of Malta.

In the central and western Mediterranean, however, the Knights continued to wage holy wars, engage in piracy, and capture slaves even as they pursued such benign activities as providing escort services and engaging in ordinary trade. The Knights did this even as they imported foodstuffs not only from Sicily but also from lands populated by people they considered to be enemies. According to prevailing practices in northern Africa, when ships from European countries such as Malta were in Maghreb for legitimate trade, their sails and oars were ordered removed to prevent Europeans enslaved there from escaping on board (Earle 1970: 84).

Still, it was largely due to constant uncertainty and danger associated with violent contests between the Knights and their opponents that the Order was motivated to invest so heavily in Malta. Throughout the entire stay of the Knights in Malta, they remained committed to the improvement of fortifications. Profits that the Order earned from piracy, from the textile trade, from levies on the Knights, and from the Order's properties in many parts of Europe infused much capital into Malta. This capital permitted the Order also to spend lavishly on building shipyards, ordnance establishments, elegant villas, Baroque palaces, and urban improvements and infrastructure that were generally reflective of the highest known standards in design and technology.

The Knights positioned themselves at the top of a rigidly stratified social order with particularly high material standards for themselves. Maltese were not allowed to become Knights, not even members of the Maltese nobility, although some did serve in important positions with the Order's clergy. The Knights were highly dependent on the Maltese masses and naturally a portion of the Knights' wealth trickled down to the masses who worked in a whole range of service capacities. Numerous Maltese were even drafted to work on projects for which they were denied pay as *corvée* laborers.

Though the maintenance of a large war machine primed development by creating new service industries and gave the Knights access to cheap slave labor as well, continuing warfare proved very costly for economic development in the long run. For one thing, it resulted in the Order's paying inadequate attention to food production and in its accumulation of significant international debts. The lack of natural resources and scarce water supplies had a negative impact on manufacture. Even the gains from cheap slave labor tended to be short-term and had little multiplier effect on development.

Widespread Mediterranean slavery had important ramifications nonetheless. In fact, the selling and ransoming of slaves became businesses with its own own rules that were recognized throughout the Basin. European consuls stationed in Maghreb sometimes gave the color of law to slavery by ratifying ransom transactions involving Europeans in bondage.

Many European cities, provinces, lay and religious institutions had their own ransom organizations or contributed with collections and bequests to those organized by others. Certainly the most active of the religious organizations directly involved in this business was that of the Redemptionist Fathers, a medieval order that was interested not only in alleviating the hardships of Catholic slaves but also in discouraging them from becoming renegades (Clissold 1977: 107–122; Earle 1970: 86). Both Christian and Muslim captives were tempted by apostasy, that is, converting to the religion of their captors (Clissold 1977: 86–101; Earle 1970; Lane-Poole 1970). Others became renegades for profit or mere adventure. In fact, a French naval commissary once advised a French ship captain not to allow his sailors from Provence ashore in northern Africa less they "put on a turban as easily as a nightcap" (Earle 1970: 93).

At considerable risk to themselves, some renegades like Malta-born Osta Mameto Guivara, who fled Tunis in 1661, returned home even after changing their religions. Before this flight from Africa, he even succeeded in carrying on an international business in partnership with a brother who remained resident in Malta. An English renegade was issued a permit of safe conduct to travel from Alexandria to Malta in 1663 after promising the Knights a bribe that he no doubt hoped would aid his acceptance back home. As these cases illustrate, the walls that separated Muslims and Christians in the central Mediterranean were quite pervious and flexible at times.

That ransoming was often a brutal, heartless, and inhumane business is illustrated by the actions of a Maltese sea captain in 1651. He paid the ransom for another Maltese sea captain who was captive in Tunis with the stipulation that the latter had to repay him with 25% interest within 15 days after returning to Malta (Earle 1970: 89). This was in line with prevailing practices whereby ship owners sometimes carried freed slaves back to their homelands on credit as a business arrangement that paid well and made use of existing commercial contacts between Islam and Christendom.

Slavery was not an anomaly in the world during the period we are discussing. Not only were slaves who were captured in the Mediterranean Basin sometimes forced to propel huge galleys in the manner of human machines and used as beasts of burden on laborious construction projects, they also worked at numerous other jobs. Some Christian slaves in Africa eventually rose to positions of considerable prestige and importance, and most especially if they became renegades.

Armenians, Jews, and Greeks often acted as middlemen who crisscrossed religious frontiers along the Asian, African, and European coasts of the Mediterranean in order to ransom slaves for commissions; history records that Egyptian Arabs, Maltese Christians, and others were involved in such pursuits (Earle 1970: 88–89). On occasion, slaves were permitted provisional release to return home to seek to raise their own ransoms, sometimes sending family members or fellow townspeople to be held hostage to guarantee their good faith. In Leghorn there even existed a "bonded warehouse" maintained by the grand duke for slaves released from Africa which operated on the principle that if they did not raise their ransoms in a stipulated time they would be returned to their captors (Earle 1970: 90).

Although Malta absorbed significant numbers of immigrants from Italy and the Greek island of Rhodes during the seventeenth and eighteenth centuries, some Knights contributed marginally to population increase in violation of their vows of celibacy. During certain periods, even prostitution was tacitly encouraged. With Malta's population being so small, it was very sensitive to demographic change. Moreover, a fraction of the population was made up of Jews, Muslims, and renegades.

Though slaves did not constitute as large a proportion of the population in Malta as they did in northern Africa, they were of great demographic importance. In fact, the Maltese slave market under the Knights was extraordinarily large by contemporary European standards. Though this market placed much emphasis on rapid turnover through selling and ransoming, it can not be discounted that a significant proportion of the population in slavery—mostly from northern Africa and Turkey—possibly contributed to population increase in Malta (Earle 1970; Blouet 1967). Unlike European renegades in northern Africa, Muslim renegades in Malta found it extremely difficult to ever be trusted to leave the country.

Among those who stayed and were assimilated, was Fatima, daughter of Mamet Mustaf of Tunis. In 1604 when a Maltese named Leonardo Mansico attempted to ransom his daughter who was enslaved in Tunis for an Arab woman named Fatima who had been taken to Malta, Fatima refused to return as she was apparently happily married to a Maltese (Earle 1970: 91). In 1644, the Knights captured from a Turkish galleon esteemed prizes in the persons of the wife and son of a Turkish sultan. Following the death of the mother, the Grand Master took it upon himself to rear the son up at his own expense. This Turk eventually became a Dominican priest in Malta with the name Father Ottoman (Laspina 1971: 139).

Another Muslim who stayed and was assimilated was Mustapha Pasha, a high ranking Turk of Rhodes, who arrived in Malta in 1784 on a boat where Christian slaves had mutinied. Because of his high station, he was allowed to live luxuriously in Malta. When eventually offered his freedom in 1749, he declined to leave, subsequently became a Christian, and married a Maltese woman (Laspina 1971: 145). Similarly, some Maltese refused to return from Muslim lands.

Ideologically and economically, Muslim and Christian corsairs were quite similar. Renegades could be found on both sides, and both Muslims and Christians considered those of other religions whom they regularly challenged and threatened to be "infidels." Both Christian and Muslim slaves sometimes mutinied. Moreover, the economic operations of pirates and corsairs on the two sides depended on exploitation of a common trophic niche in ways that were largely identical.

In Malta, however, regulations usually required free Muslims, renegades, and slaves to sleep away from the general population. Still, the enforcement of such regulations varied from period to period and were more strictly enforced for slaves than for the others. Slaves, in fact, participated in many sectors of the day-to-day economy, a situation which required social contacts and the interchange of culture.

Even slaves who worked at the hard tasks of propelling the Knights' galleys sometimes worked as merchants from their own rented stalls and shops in Malta between trips. While during times of trust these shops were likely to be in the main square of Valletta, in time of distrust they were more likely to be under the walls of one of the slave prisons. Slaves participated in the economy through construction projects; others worked for private individuals, and history records the presence in 1740 of an Ethiopian slave who worked as a barber (Earle 1970: 176–177).

In general, slaves and renegades found assimilation into society more difficult in Malta than in northern Africa, though in the first half of the eighteenth century, many of Malta's regulations that required social segregation between slaves and Maltese were loosely enforced. This situation was quickly reversed in 1749 when news of a conspiracy by slaves planning to revolt leaked out, resulting in repression, restrictions, surveillance, and even a few executions.

Although a very significant improvement in living conditions under the Knights contributed to population increase, it can hardly account for the fact that it increased by 50% in the first 60 years. Similarly, improved living conditions can not explain a fivefold increase in population from 20,000 to 100,000 over the period of merely 268 years that the Knights were in control. At the end of the eighteenth century slaves still accounted for 2% of Malta's population, a very high rate by European standards.

While European historians typically put an end bracket on the Middle Ages at about 1450, Malta in some ways experienced an extension of the Middle Ages during much of the 1530 to 1798 period that the Order of St. John ruled Malta. At the very time that a number of other European countries were engaging in commerce without religious scruples, internal nation-building, and external expansion in the spirit of an evolving globalism, the Maltese would be destined to live out almost three centuries of debilitating holy wars.

This order of knights, owing allegiance only to the Pope and dedicated to eternal war against Islam, was an institutional anachronism during much of its stay in Malta—although this fact became most glaring in the eighteenth century. In some ways, learning and technology associated with the

Renaissance had negative repercussions in Malta in that ancient trans-Mediterranean trade routes began to lose out in competition with new oceanic ones to sub-Saharan Africa, the Indies, and the Americas. Still, pluses and minuses characterized economic and political development of Malta under the Knights.

The Knights made important contributions to Maltese economic development by continually infusing large amounts of capital into the islands, a situation which made possible the construction of a wide variety of public works, including fortifications, port facilities, and shipyards for the outfitting and repair of vessels. In keeping with an inbred sense of grandeur and adventure, they engaged some of Europe's most renowned architects to design churches, villas, public spaces, and towns. They also nursed a turnaround in the cultivation of cotton in the seventeenth and eighteenth centuries and instituted quality control in 1773 in order to maintain the international reputation for cotton exports. As the Knights became less involved in religious wars in the second half of the eighteenth century, Malta prospered as an important entrepôt for transshipment, especially for the French, "rather similar to what Leghorn was for the English and Zante was for the Venetians" (Camilleri 1996: 6; Earle 1970: 100).

In 1592, hardly more than a half century after the Knights arrived, they made an important contribution to education through the founding of Collegium Melitense—a college run by the Jesuits—which Grand Master Pinto, who ruled from 1771 to 1773, transformed into a university. It was in the seventeenth century that there first emerged a written tradition in a language distinct enough from Arabic to justify having its own name. Between 1722 and 1736 Grand Master Antonio Manoel de Vilhena spearheaded the revitalization of Mdina, and he also introduced a new code of law largely reflective of prevailing practices in continental Europe. Emmanuel de Rohan-Polduc, who became Grand Master in 1775, was fond of reading such French philosophers as Rousseau, Voltaire, and Montesquieu, and he further updated the code put in place by de Vilhena,

As a result of the unceasing building activities of the Knights, which led to the erection of palaces, fortifications and churches, Malta was changed from a "barren rock" into a treasure-house of fine baroque art and architecture. The local population lived on subsistence-farming, fishing, and cultivation of cotton. Besides, there was also employment in connection with the Order's building-activities and ship-construction as also the opportunities for sailors and soldiers. The Order had made Malta rich and it was not only the Knights themselves who stood to gain, but certain groups of the population as well because many profited from the jobs and patronage yielded by the Knights. (Koster 1983: 301)

Among the negatives that revealed themselves toward the end of the Order's reign, Grand Master Pinto alienated many segments of Maltese society through his despotism, including especially the local church. Also, he was succeeded by Grand Master Ximenes who offended the Maltese by diminishing the residual rights of the *Università*. Grand Master De Rohan, who was elected to his position in 1775, stymied political aspirations by abolishing the long-established *Consiglio Popolare* as well as imposing many French customs on the Maltese. By the end of their reign, many of the Knights turned away from their vows of celibacy and engaged in debauchery. Small wonder that between 1760 and 1775, there were at least six uprisings against the Order (Camilleri 1996: 9), the last of which was widely alleged to have been plotted by a number of clergy.

The Knights were European—they were not Maltese—and under their rule, indigenous nationalism was not allowed to develop in a natural manner. "We also find, in this period of Maltese history, episodes in which the racial animosity displayed by some members of the Order of St. John towards the Maltese was of such intensity that, quite often, the two communities found themselves on the brink of violent confrontation" (Pirotta 1994: 104). Moreover, the Knights "gradually extended their rule until government embraced whole departments of political and social life. In the late 1700s, the Order controlled or financed the water supply, public works, hospitals, charities, education, and similar social institutions" (Price 1954: 1–2).

Malta's thin soils constitute a natural challenge to agriculture, and efforts to bring marginal lands into production were never successful for the most part. Problems were exacerbated during the seventeenth and eighteenth centuries, a period during which population was growing most rapidly and the Knights and the religious institutions remained owners of most of the land. The feudal distribution of this scarce resource left most Maltese landless with somewhat more bitterness against the Knights than toward the religious institutions.

French influence in the islands had been strong under the Knights as three of the eight *langues* into which they were divided were of French heritage. In the late eighteenth century, Malta's commercial relations with France were more important than those with any other country (Orr 1992: 168–169). In fact, there existed such good relations between France and the Order in 1765 that France granted the Maltese the status of French nationalized subjects. A more tumultuous French influence that began to permeate Malta in the late eighteen century, however, was ideology related to revolutionary Republicanism.

As Republicanism evolved in France, it was directed especially against the higher clergy and the nobility, that is, against the so-called First and Second Estates. In addition to being distinguished from the masses by social rank, hereditary, property, and privileges, the members of these estates were tainted by lots of corruption. However, the movements of religious skepticism, anti-clericalism, and political radicalism in France and other parts of Europe had no mass following in Malta. Moreover, no dissemination of knowledge by rationalists resulted in any Maltese challenge to the church's domination of education nor to its exclusive authority in areas such as baptism, registration of births, registration of deaths, and the performance of marriages. In other words, there was no social movement demanding the complete separation of church and state in Malta.

Though Malta prior to the French Revolution was as feudal as France, it was still in many respects quite different. Between 1778 and 1788, the French Revolution had a rather devastating impact on the income of the Knights. And as the Maltese economy was heavily dependent on the external wealth of the Knights, changes in French law that removed almost half of the wealth of the Order were not popular in the islands. Eventually, similar anti-Order measures were taken in other European countries that Napoleon would conquer (Koster 1983: 307).

In 1789 when a French National Assembly replaced the Estates General, endorsed a "Declaration of the Rights of Man," and declared church properties in France to be at the disposition of the French nation, Maltese were alarmed. By 1792 when the French National Assembly withdrew the citizenship of all members of any order of chivalry based outside of France, this alarm turned into panic. Moreover, the escape of numerous French Knights from France to Malta became a drain on the decreasing resources of the Order at a time that the Assembly had already placed it in an economic bind.

While this was occurring, expansionist interests that had existed in France at least since the 1770s—in good measure because of a convergence of nationalism, rivalry with Britain, and Masonic enthusiasm for Egypt—were mushrooming (Bernal 1987: 184). By 1797, these interests were transferred into state policy as France decided to expand her sphere of influence in the Mediterranean and attempt to control a strategic trade route between Britain and India, the wealthiest colony in her growing empire. The French were also concerned that a destabilized and no-longer neutral Order of St. John might lead Malta into the fold of Great Britain or Russia.

It was on September 13, 1797, that Napoleon Bonaparte first suggested an expedition to Malta and Egypt in a letter to Talleyrand, Foreign Minister in the Directory. After noting that he had personally had all the possessions of the Knights in Italy confiscated, Napoleon added: "With the island of St. Pierre, which the King of Sardinia has ceded to us, Malta, Corfu, etc., we shall be masters of the Mediterranean" (Lloyd 1973: 10). It was against this background that by a secret decree dated April 12, 1798, the Directory authorized Napoleon Bonaparte to seize Malta on his way to conquer Egypt in order to prevent its falling into enemy hands (Lloyd 1973: 12). On May 19, 1798, under the leadership of Napoleon, France's Army of the East departed from the port of Toulon.

On June 4, the Knights in Malta received from their ambassador, who was attending a conference in Austria, their first warning of an imminent French attack in a letter dated May 18, but largely due to ambivalence on the part of French Knights, no defenses were readied (Lloyd 1973: 15). Exactly three weeks after Napoleon's departure from Toulon, his army of 38,000 men in 472 ships appeared off Malta. The Knights' obsolete naval forces consisted of only two sixty-cannon ships of the line, one frigate, four galeottes, and four galleys. While there were 17,282 men under arms and 332 Knights—a good number of whom were in no condition to fight— that so many were French also made the leadership of this defending force unreliable (Camilleri 1996: 30).

With large-scale defections shortly after the French were ashore, within days the Maltese soldiers mutinied at the Cottonera Lines. When a delegation sued for a cessation of hostilities, the terms imposed by the French were harsh. Bonaparte himself spent but one week in Malta, but the revolutionary impact of his presence was long lasting. For example, although the last Inquisitor had left Malta two months before his arrival, Napoleon abolished the tribunal of the Inquisition and confiscated its landed estates (Ciappara 1976: 54). Although Napoleon distributed the benefices of the foreign clergy whom he expelled from Malta among Maltese clergy, his short stay in Malta was more notable for many Draconian decrees which were intended more to benefit France than Malta.

In addition to ordering that the Knights quickly depart Malta and surrender all but their personal property, Napoleon demanded those from countries he deemed to be at war with France to leave almost immediately. His decree that Greek ships be sunk and Greeks allied with Russia executed served France's interests. Other pro-French decrees with little relevance to Malta provided only French Knights would be given a pension by France and that only French Knights would be allowed to return to their native land. The French decreed that the Order's hospital should be devoted to their military and closed to Maltese. They ordered all Maltese, including ecclesiastics, to wear a knot of ribbon in the red, white, and blue national colors of France (Lloyd 1973: 22–24).

Napoleon's distrust of the Maltese was obvious. He ordered that the public be disarmed and that Maltese troops be drafted into France's Army of the East heading for Egypt or be sent to Corfu—to be replaced at home by 3,000–4,000 French troops under Vaubois as French commander-in-chief and only a small Maltese National Guard (Gaillard 1997: 200). That they were to be recruited from the upper and middle classes is ironical from a Republican perspective. Requiring that 30 boys from the richest families be sent to study in Paris at their parents' expense seemed more to serve French than Maltese interests at the same time that it was elitist. Moreover, a further requirement that a like number of boys from wealthy families accompany his Army to Egypt as volunteer guides fell into the same category.

Faced with radical Republicanism heavily colored with French chauvinism, arrogance, and even elitism, the Maltese found the transition from the
eighteenth to the nineteenth century both abrupt and traumatic. Its "*Ancien
Régime*" was uprooted virtually overnight through the imposition of numerous decrees that reordered central institutions. The feudal privileges of
the nobility along with their titles and status symbols were nullified.

Some decrees affected religious orders, such as restricting each order to
the possession of a single house and preventing members of minor orders
from wearing the cassock. Other interference was more general, such as
decreeing that religious vows could only be taken by those over 30 years
of age and forbidding the ordination of priests until all those already ordained were employed. One order forbade priests from seeking remuneration for their services while another decree provided for the expulsion from
Malta of all ecclesiastics of foreign heritage. By providing for civil registration of births, for civil marriage, and for civil administration at the local
level by justices of the peace and the abolition of the office of the Papal
Inquisitor, the French also altered the traditional balance between civil and
religious authority.

So basically did the new rules strike at central social institutions and
reward France at the expense of Malta that after less than three months of
French control, there occurred the first ever nationwide uprising against an
alien conqueror. The immediate developments that incited this insurrection
had to do with national pride and church interference. Especially incendiary
were actions undertaken to enrich French coffers by robbing important
churches of treasures such as gold, silverplate, precious stones, and tapestries. When on September 2, 1798, this pilfering spread to some of the
convents at Rabat and Mdina, the population rebelled.

The next day—less than three months after French seizure—Mdina was
recaptured by Maltese insurgents with many French soldiers being massa-
cred. Within hours, revolt spread across the countryside. Battalions from
many parts of Malta assembled at Mdina and—no doubt influenced by
Revolutionary events in France—formed a national council or assembly to
combat their French oppressors. It is noteworthy, however, that this rebellion did not occur until the Maltese had learned of Nelson's devastating
defeat of Napoleon at Aboukir in Egypt (Frendo 1992: 80; Gaillard 1997:
200).

By September 4 the insurgents held the countryside while the French
along with about half of Malta's population remained cloistered behind the
defensive gates of fortified areas adjacent to the Grand Harbor. On the
sister island of Gozo, the French were compelled to barricade themselves
in Fort Chambray and in the old Castle of Gozo (Laspina 1971: 211). The
arrival of British troops, under the command of a General Graham, established the British as the ultimate power, and Ball exercised veto power over
all policies developed by the joint revolutionary leadership, which he con-

vened on a regular basis to map out strategy. Though the Maltese were very poorly armed, they carried the brunt of the fighting. While no British life was lost in the confrontation with the French, Maltese casualties have been estimated as high as 20,000 (Orr 1992: 173).

With Portuguese and British ships blockading the harbors, the Maltese controlled the countryside, assisted only by some Neapolitan reinforcements and a few British officers. Unlike their armed compatriots on the island of Gozo, the French on the island of Malta were in serious danger of starvation by the summer 1800. Events fared as poorly for Napoleon in Egypt as they did for his troops in Malta. When no relief for the beleaguered French was able to penetrate the blockade by September 5, a capitulation was signed, allowing the humiliated troops to leave Malta. After ousting the French, the Maltese invited the British to establish a presence in their islands.

Most chroniclers of these events point to the attack on religious institutions as the raison d'être of the general rebellion against the French. It is plausible however that accumulated economic injuries were almost equally important. The French refused, for example, to pay indemnification to the Maltese for war damages they had caused; they refused to pay allowances promised to Maltese sailors, soldiers, and their dependents; and they refused to continue the distribution of free bread to poor women. Though they installed a government commission with a Maltese majority, this commission controlled the official pawnshop and grain imports in ways that proved harsh. It also precipitously imposed new taxes and foreclosed on the land of many farmers.

When the French in 1798 abolished slavery in Malta, this deprived the Maltese of a form of free labor at a time when Europeans did not generally consider it inhumane nor anachronistic to enslave people, especially if they adhered to religions other than Christianity. It was only in 1803, that is five years later, that Denmark became the first European country voluntarily to outlaw slavery. To put the situation in broader context, slave dealing was not abolished by Great Britain until 1808 nor made a felony there until 1811. Holland outlawed slavery only in 1814. It was only in 1815 that the last Muslim slaves were liberated in Sicily. Although Morocco forbade privateering in 1817, a hypocritical France did not finally get around to making the slave trade illegal until 1818, that is, two decades after it ended slavery in Malta and 21 years before Pope Gregory XVI issued his bull *In Supremo* condemning slavery (Freeman-Grenville 1973: 143–155).

Even as major European powers claimed to be increasingly repulsed by slavery, they were less repulsed by slavery per se than by the enslavement of Europeans who were Christians. In any case, not long after the French had abruptly brought slavery and piracy to an end in Malta, major European powers were becoming ever more comfortable with depriving people of their freedom through a new system, one which in time would be known as global imperialism.

Before turning our attention to how Malta would fare in this system of global imperialism, it is well to note some parallels between what had happened and what would happen. More precisely, when the Knights came to Malta in 1530, they were not so much interested in staying as in having a base from which to reconquer Rhodes. When Napoleon came to Malta in 1798, it was largely as a stopover on a mission to Egypt. Similarly, when the British gradually began to take control of the islands from the French in 1798, they were drawn less by interest in Malta than in constraining the French. In fact, the British originally intended to honor the terms of the 1802 Treaty of Amiens, according to which Malta was to be returned to the Order of St. John.

It was global imperialist scheming and tremendous jealousy about French advances in northern Africa, rather than a deep interest in directing the cultural development of the Maltese people, that convinced the British that they had to stay in Malta. No sooner had the French been chased out of Malta, than the British followed Napoleon to Egypt to make certain that he would be chased away from there as well. As the British became more established in this place that could help secure their trade with the Levant and serve as a vital link in their global empire potentially stretching toward Egypt, they realized Malta was of too much strategic importance to honor the Treaty of Amiens. International recognition that Britain was already in possession of Malta came with the signing of the Treaty of Paris in 1814 that marked the final defeat of Napoleon at Waterloo; hence, the British actually maintained control of Malta for a full 150 years.

Chapter 4

Urbanization in Miniature

Urban sociologists have long made a distinction between urbanism and city living, for one is not contingent on the other. In Malta, the concepts of city, town, village, and parish converge and overlap in ways that make any strict placement of nucleated settlements along a demographer's rural-urban continuum impossible. In many Mediterranean countries such as Greece, Morocco, Bosnia Herzegovina, and Egypt, many city residents were born in rural areas. In Malta, on the other hand, urbanism impacts everyone.

The first villages and towns in the world are generally thought to have been creations of people who became sedentary due to farming. Remnants of villages dating back to the fourth millennium B.C. are still visible in Malta today as are also the remains of fortified villages dating to the second millennium B.C. (Blouet 1967: 29). For the Maltese to begin living in such nucleated settlements, they only needed to accumulate a surplus or to settle long-term near each other—perhaps for mutual protection or maybe because of the availability of water or of fertile land or choice grazing locations. As in Greece, where cities emerged at an early time, Malta has soils that are thin and rocky as well as sparse and meager natural resources.

Though the first people who settled Malta were already familiar with the domestication of plants and animals, nomadic pastoralism was not possible given the small size of the islands. A type of transhumance or sedentary pastoralism was apparently important in the founding of the earliest villages. That *raħal*, the word referring to a village in Maltese, is derived from an Arabic word referring to a resting place or station more than to a permanent settlement points in this direction (Aquilina 1970a: 191). However, Wettinger (1975: 183) has pointed out that while *raħal* is not the usual

Arabic word for village, it was used in medieval Sicily, the Balearic Islands, and southern Spain in just this way.

Early nucleated settlement patterns in the Maltese Islands have characteristics that are both typical and atypical within the context of the region. Malta is a small and homogeneous land where space has a sacredness and intricacy of meaning that do not translate easily to larger places. Whereas in many countries, countryside and urban areas are articulated by means of towns of intermediate size, all Maltese cities are towns with respect to absolute numbers, and at the same time, all Maltese towns are city-like with respect to their population densities. Trends in Malta's urban development are germane to understanding many other aspects of its culture. Moreover, they provide in miniature a case study of processes underway in some other parts of the Mediterranean.

"The greatness of the past is easy to exaggerate," according to Hawley (1971: 32). "Actually . . . [ancient] towns were comparatively small. Athens at its peak embraced but 612 acres of land, less than one square mile. In Rhodes there were 125 acres; in Antioch, 325 acres; Carthage, 721 acres; Damascus, 532 acres. Nineveh, Babylon, Byzantium, Alexandria, and Rome were the giants. But only the latter exceeded 5 square miles in scope."

Unlike prehistoric ancestors who constructed megalithic temples in places that looked out at the sea, Maltese who developed nucleated settlements of size tended most often to be drawn to fortified highlands well removed from the sea. During the sixth century B.C. when Carthage was engaged with ancient Rome in a contest to control the central Mediterranean Basin, Carthage at times exercised some degree of control over the Maltese Islands. To the extent that such control concentrated troops in Malta, it contributed to nucleated settlement. Of a certainty, some nucleated settlement can be assumed before the beginning of the Second Punic War in 218 B.C. when a Roman defeat of the Carthaginians caused the Maltese Islands, with a resident garrison of 2,000 Carthaginian soldiers, to be taken over by Rome.

The next 17 years are rather unclear about outside influences on Malta's settlement patterns. However some Roman soldiers likely replaced the Cathargian soldiers that were expelled by Rome in 218 B.C., much as at the same time, the Roman navy was stationed at Panormus on Sicily. It can not be assumed that the Romans were firmly entrenched in Malta before 201 B.C. at the earliest, when a decisive defeat of Hannibal in Italy compelled his troops to return to Africa. That such a small place as Malta housed an organized group of 2,000 troops, probably the equivalent of at least one fifth of its total population, certainly points in the direction of early nucleated settlement. As quoted from Laspina (1971: 17), Livy references the existence of a town as follows: "The Consul passed over from Liliboeum to the island of Melita which was held by the Carthaginians. On his arrival, Hamilcar, the son of Gisgo, the commander of the garrison, together with little less than two thousand soldiers, and the town and the island, were delivered up to him."

Roman baths, villas, and other structures scattered across the islands are material testimony to important Roman influences. Given Malta's strategic location at the center of the Roman Empire, an irony of its history is that it was never made into a major colony of Rome. By around 146 B.C., the Roman Empire was established in Tunisia, to Malta's southwest, as well as in Sicily, to Malta's north. Moreover, by the death of Augustus in A.D. 14, Rome controlled the northern African littoral stretching from Egypt into a corner of Algeria while Mauritania, an African client state, extended Rome's influence to the Atlantic Ocean. Considering that by 45 Caligula had even incorporated Volubilis in central Morocco into the Empire, it is quite clear that Rome's impact was not as great on Malta as in Africa (Aquilina 1970a: 197).

Latin was spoken in Roman Africa as well as Roman Europe, and Roman influences probably came into Malta as much from the south as from the north. Many of the Jews diffused throughout the Empire moved into Malta from nearby areas of Africa where they were well established: Egypt, Carthage, Cyrenaica, certain parts of Algeria and Morocco. In 23, according to the Roman historian Tacitus, there were two Roman legions stationed in the colony of "Africa" just off the shores of Malta in addition to the two stationed further east in Egypt. Even Malta's connections with Christendom during the period of the Roman Empire linked it as much with lands to its south as to its north. Even as late as the third and fourth centuries, Christianity was more broadly established in Tunisia than in Sicily, Spain, France, Germany, or the Italian Peninsula.

Given Malta's small size and centralized location within the ambit of the Empire, it is a marvel of its marginality and cultural assertiveness that during at least two centuries when Roman influence was significant, Malta's Punic temples continued to draw pilgrims from outside the islands. It is also a marvel that the Maltese continued to speak their own language, which was quite different from Latin. Under Augustus, Roman imperial coinage was reformed, enlarged, and probably imposed on Malta. There exists no material evidence that Malta issued its own coinage under Roman hegemony. Still, through trade and other contacts with the Roman Empire, there seems little doubt that Malta would have been influenced by urban development in nearby areas.

No lesser Roman cities than Paris, Vienna, Cologne, Mainz, and London had started as semi-permanent military encampments and open areas. The city of Rome, within the wall named after Servius Tullius dating from the middle of the fifth century B.C., was about one mile by two miles, and some eight and a half centuries later it was only about three miles by three miles within the walls constructed by Aurelian through Honorius. During the

period of greatest Roman influence in Malta, city life centered largely upon
a fortified centralized plateau known at that time as Città Notabile, where
there is some evidence of settlement extending back into prehistory.

When Paul of Tarsus was shipwrecked in Malta on his way to stand trial
in Rome, the fact that according to Acts 28: 7 of the Bible he and 275
fellow travelers were received by a chief or governor of some kind named
Publius and entertained with hospitality for three days suggests some type
of centralized control. The earliest documentary evidence of Città Notabile,
a city also known as Melita, dates back to the second century A.D. when
Ptolemy, a Greek geographer of Alexandria, recorded its precise longitude
(38.45 degrees) and latitude (34.40 degrees) in his *Geographia* (Thake
1996: 2).

That Maltese might have been privileged to exercise some important political rights as a part of the Roman Empire is plausible in view of the fact
that the inhabitants were called "*Soci*" and their Islands referred to as
"*Fœderata civitas.*" Moreover, the fact that between 117 and 138, during
the reign of Hadrian, Malta as well as Gozo was recognized as a "*municipium*" implies that each island enjoyed some self-government, possibly
including the right to send ambassadors to Rome. In fact, for Gozo, the
evidence is even stronger than that for Malta (Buhagiar 1997: 119; Laspina
1971: 248–249). It is unlikely that either island would have been recognized
as a *municipium* had its people not achieved some considerable degree of
town development. This was a period during which the Roman chronicler
Diodorus Siculus spoke of Malta as having some stately buildings and
wealthy citizens (Thake 1996: 2).

In any case, the dissolution of the Roman Empire in the fifth century
marked the decay of cities in western Europe for approximately 600 years.
Virtually throughout western Europe, "the fall" contributed to a situation
where cities and towns, becoming more isolated than previously, had to
become self-sufficient to survive. In time, local lords offered peasants protection from outside raiders in return for serfdom, a type of slavery or
helotry.

The city of Gaulos occupied the north corner of a plateau in the centre of the island
to which it lent its name. It consisted of a lower town and an acropolis that rose
over 30m above it. In the course of the Middle Ages, a citadel, known as the Gran
Castello, was built on the ruins of the acropolis and a residential suburb, called
Rabat, sprouted naturally on the plateau below. It is difficult to determine with
precision the extent of the Roman city. (Buhagiar 1997: 115)

That Città Notabile, Malta's major city during the Roman-Byzantine era,
shrank considerably in size thereafter may have had to do with instability
in the area and the need to make it more defensible. This reconfiguring of
Città Notabile may be associated with a wave of new Arab-speaking settlers

who penetrated Malta in the second half of the ninth century largely from northern Africa. Though they did not greatly disturb existing settlement patterns overall, the Città Notabile of the Roman and Byzantine period took on the name of Mdina under Arabic-speaking Muslims and the fortified town in the center of Gozo was named Rabat—to be later renamed Victoria in 1897. While the presence of the Arab-speaking Muslim settlers was very significant on Malta, we have fewer details about their stay on Gozo (Buhagiar 1997: 123–124).

The settlers came mostly from a part of Africa which—under the hegemony of the Carthagians and Romans—had experienced city life. They had more recently also experienced city life within Ifriqiya largely under the control of urbanized Arabs (Bovill 1958: 58–59). While making an indelible imprint on technology and language, these newcomers also contributed to greater social complexity in places such as Mdina and Gozo's Rabat through the infusion of new social and ethnic heterogeneity. The size of the Muslim cemetery just outside the walls of Mdina suggests that Mdina's Muslims were rather numerous, while the contrasting degrees of ornamentation on their tombstones suggest the existence of significant socioeconomic differences among them (Luttrell 1975: 27; Thake 1996: 6).

Such stratification in an area of dense settlement is consistent with what one would expect in a city setting. That there was some considerable degree of religious tolerance seems indicated by the fact that in 1991, over a century after Muslims arrived, a census of the Maltese population ordered by the emir recorded 6,339 Christian as well as 14,972 Muslim residents. As this is a slightly larger population than the 20,000 persons who would be resident in the islands four and half centuries later, this situation, moreover, is consistent with a picture of relative prosperity during Malta's Arab-Berber period.

Already by this time, the architectural character of Malta's Mdina, and to a lesser degree Gozo's Rabat, as defensible places, contrasted with open areas—which were undefended places, still partially forested. A pattern of partitioning farming plots with "rubble walls" by meticulously placing limestone rocks one upon another was already established. Moreover, terracing used in the farming of sloping areas was no doubt apparent when one scanned open areas compared to those that were built up. Though the area enclosed within the walls of Mdina became more restricted under the Arabs, the walls were fortified and a suburb named Rabat began to develop next to this ancient city. In addition to making changes close to the central plateau where the historic capital was located, the Muslims also built fortifications on the end of the peninsula known as Birgu, where Fort St. Angelo is now situated.

When Count Roger at age 60 led Norman knights in taking titular control of Malta from the Ifriqiyans in 1091, it was his capture of Città Vecchia (another name for Città Notabile or Mdina) which determined the fate of the Maltese Islands as a whole as we know from accounts by Amari in *Storia dei Musulmani de Sicilia* (Crawford 1900b: 248). We also know that thousands of Muslims from both Sicily and Malta later fought under his standard. Hence, the pattern of heterogeneity and ethnic tolerance that was probably a part of Maltese life under the Ifriqiyans, especially in its towns, apparently continued.

Roger not only protected the Muslims in their religion and allowed them to have tribunals of their own, he also actually discouraged their conversion to Christianity and punished some Muslims for converting (Crawford 1900b: 248–249). The emir in Malta was not deposed, and half a century after the king of Sicily had become the titular overlord, Gilibert reported to Frederick II of Sicily in a 1240 census of Maltese families that 836 were Muslim, 250 Christian, and 33 Jewish.

Maltese medieval towns and villages, at least when they were fortified, tended to be densely populated with narrow street and alley systems. These systems evolved informally in maze-like configurations where passageways seemed often to bend, to start, and to stop haphazardly. Where space was more generous, and in nonfortified settlements, this pattern was less pronounced or absent. Contrasting growth patterns for towns corresponded to other variables, including how various towns functioned, in what periods they developed, and in what physical settings they emerged.

The Maltese have probably always had fishing villages, but these were vulnerable places that they tended not to fortify. During emergencies, access to fortified places was important to people who ordinarily lived in exposed areas. So, Maltese fishermen and farmers in these islands have preferred from an early time to live in nucleated settlements rather than live scattered defenseless across the land. In contrast to Mdina, none of the hamlets or villages had fortifications that were still in use by the 1400s (Wettinger 1975: 184).

Activities supportive of settlement for trading and fishing in the coastal town of Birgu are documented from an early time, and early Maltese Christians probably worshiped primarily in houses (Buhagiar 1975: 163). Congregation for Christian worship during later times was easier in places like central Gozo and Malta's Città Notabile than in scattered hamlets. Birgu served as the seat of a governor, or at least a representative of the ruler of Sicily, virtually from the time that the Normans arrived, and it has chapels dedicated to St. Anne and St. Lawrence, which are among the oldest known in Malta, dating back to the end of the eleventh century. It was also in Birgu that the Normans constructed a fortress known as Castrum Maris or Castle by the Sea, possibly using foundations built by Muslims (cf. Luttrell 1975: 29).

Castrum Maris may have functioned as much to protect commerce as to ward off enemies. There was much trade, communication, and cultural exchange in the central Mediterranean Basin in the early 1100s when the

Normans arrived. We know from Idrisi, the Moroccan geographer who spent most of his life at the Palermo court of Roger II, that settled life and prosperity existed in an array of Maltese towns and villages in the twelfth century. In fact, he described the situation this way: "Malitah [Malta] rich in everything that is good and in the blessing of God . . . well peopled, possessing towns and villages, trees and fruit" (Blouet 1967: 41).

The Normans did not deal harshly with the Muslims when they took titular control of Malta in the name of the king of Sicily. But they nonetheless gradually began a process whereby the Muslims began to lose power at the expense of European nobles over the next century or so. These nobles largely from Sicily and the Iberian Peninsula had surnames such as De Nava, Gatto, Falzon, Alagona, and Inguanez that were quite distinct from the Arabic-derived names of the masses. As increasing numbers of this gentry settled in Malta to be close to their feudal estates, they were especially drawn to Mdina as their place of residence. Over time, they were granted some institutional privileges that provided them with a measure of autonomy. Some evidence points to the existence of four-person town bodies for the privileged from Frederick I's reign between 1197 and 1250 (Laspina 1971: 48). By 1230, moreover, a centralized *Consiglio Popolare* had emerged. In the sphere of religion, as in the secular sphere, Malta was set on a path to evolve for many years in subordination to Sicily.

In contrast to a village which could be recognized as such by the presence close together of members of a large family or group of families, a Maltese town traditionally has been marked by its religious status as a parish. Although some towns may have a number of churches and chapels, the most important for its status as a town is invariably the parish church. In fact, the history of a town is largely the history of its parish church, while pride in one's locality is largely manifested in the extent to which one supports the parish church and pays homage to its patron saint.

Hagiolatry, or the veneration of the saints, has been a feature of Christianity from the earliest time (Bowen 1972: 106) and it is widespread in the Mediterranean. In fact, it often gives rise to a cult around a particular saint, including places associated with the saint—perhaps an earthly home, a tomb, or even some relic of the body of the saint. Many Maltese believe that even after death, saints may bestow blessings if intercession is sought in appropriate ways such as through prayer, alms-giving, pilgrimages, and processions. Environmental conditions intersect with religious and local conditions to produce a ritualization of time and place that goes back at least to Malta's earliest settlements since its conversion to Christianity. This ritualization, associated with hagiolatry, is often entwined with local expression, pride, and a feeling of belonging, as all parishes in this country have patron saints.

Urban continuity and urban transformation are symbolized by the continuing process whereby a new Maltese parish branches off from a previously existing one, and, a new locality from an older one. Though until 1436, Birgu and Mdina were the only two parishes on Malta, it was always Mdina that was the headquarters of the Maltese church. It was in Mdina, for example, that many major religious functions were conducted for the entire country. Moreover, a special prestige was associated with Mdina because a good proportion of its population consisted of landed nobility as opposed to Birġu, a more humble seafaring community.

Between 1207 (when the Almohads made the Hafsids autonomous in Ifriqiya) and 1237 (when Egypt once again granted trading concessions to the Italians), major trade routes between Europe and Africa, which had shifted eastward after the bedouin invasions of 1049, again followed their previous course toward Malta, Sicily, and mainland Italy. In fact, medieval trade between Italy and Africa reached its maximum in the thirteenth century (Wright 1969: 86).

As thirteenth-century Malta was under the suzerainty of the king of Sicily and possessed a Muslim majority, it seems most unlikely that this commercial upsurge surrounding it could have bypassed its towns. Town-life in Malta was likely impacted further by a cultural renaissance that took place in Ifriqiya between 1228 and 1249 that intensified relations with Europe. Though most of the early towns in Malta had been situated inland, this upsurge in international trade probably supported some settlement adjacent to harbors. In 1241, a representative of the king of Sicily was residing in Birgu, in the House of the Castellan, or Captain's House. According to tradition, this fortified house withstood Aragonese attacks during a sustained assault on Malta in 1282.

Though by the end of the fourteenth century the masses in Malta remained firmly in the grip of private lords and Malta as a whole remained a rotating fief of European royalty, by a privilege approved on November 27, 1397, a *Università*, or town commune, was established in Mdina. This system did not end such feudal abuses as the *corvée* or forced labor system. It did, however, place in the hands of a resident oligarchy some autonomy with respect to enforcing price controls and issuing decrees on numerous issues having to do with security and town management. Shortly after a *Università* was established on Malta, one was also established on the island of Gozo.

These *Universitàs* were in some ways the equal of contemporaneous Sicilian communes in Palermo, Messina, and Catania although there is some doubt that, like those in Sicily, they were provided the privilege of sending ambassadors to the Sicilian parliament. In 1441, King Alfonso was sufficiently respectful of privileges bestowed on the nobility that he limited the jurisdiction of his representative in the islands to Fort St. Angelo on Birgu and ordered the Giurati and captains of the Casali to observe the decisions of Malta's *Consiglio Popolare* (Laspina 1971: 251). Though these institutions in no way freed the masses from feudal abuses, they did sometimes function as mechanisms through which some residents living in towns were able to exercise degrees of autonomy.

One thing that could not be taken for granted as villages, towns, and cities were emerging in Malta was security. By the 1400s, only Mdina offered its residents relative security by means of its fortifications, though some other localities probably obtained a measure of security from their proximity to Mdina, including especially its suburb of Rabat. In reality, already in the fifteenth century, Mdina was losing population, and much of its housing stock was in a state of decay (Wettinger 1975: 199).

Of the 30 villages that disappeared on the island of Malta before 1419, the vast majority were near the coasts, in the southeast as well as west of Marsamxett Harbor near where Sliema and St. Julian's are now located (Wettinger 1975: 192). Even during this period before 1419, when 43.3% of all disappearances of medieval villages took place on Malta and many people abandoned the coasts for fear of pirates, they were attracted by the services and the security of living near each other in large villages such as Rabat, Naxxar, Birkirkara, Siġġiewi, Żebbuġ, Qormi, and maybe Żejtun (Wettinger 1975: 184–185, 190, 201).

While some people found security in living close to each other away from the coasts, others found security in locations where the geography presented obstacles to invaders (Wettinger 1975: 191). An example of a city in this last category is Siġġiewi. In contrast to the Citadel on Gozo and Mdina on Malta, Siġġiewi was a rather open area that blended in organically with the surrounding farmlands and which was never constricted within fortifications.

By Maltese standards, Siġġiewi is also the considerable distance of three miles from the fortifications of Mdina. Like the medieval town of Qormi, Siġġiewi is neither adjacent to a major port, nor located on a central plateau. Still, direct access to it was made challenging for raiders by the fact that it was located on an elevated ridge 600 to 800 feet high, which drops to the sea in cliffs, limiting ingress on the south to Wied iz-Żurrieq or Għar Lapsi (Cave of the Ascension), two miles to the west.

Siġġiewi evolved through the aggregation of several once discrete fiefs and hamlets. While many Maltese lived in small hamlets at risk of being captured and enslaved, life even in large settlements such as Siġġiewi was not risk-free (Guillaumier 1972: 432–444). Though a major raid from northern Africa on Malta and Gozo in 1429 laid waste to the countryside and numerous towns, many of the damaged villages were soon rebuilt (Wettinger 1975: 193).

By 1436, Malta's earliest two parishes, Mdina and Birgu, had been joined by a Siġġiewi parish and a number of others at rather widely scattered localities, including Żejtun, Gudja, Żebbuġ, Hal-Tartarni—not far from the Dingli Cliffs, and even Mellieħa in the sparsely settled northwest. That many village of this period did not fare well is reflected in the fact that between 1419 and 1545, 15.4% of disappearance of medieval villages and hamlets in Malta occurred. Though the parish of Mellieħa and several others had disappeared by 1500 (Wettinger 1975: 189), a rudimentary diocesan structure consisting of twelve parishes was in place when the Knights arrived in 1530. However pastoral care was provided primarily in the principal two urban parishes: Mdina-Rabat and Birgu (Koster 1983: 302).

With lots of vernacular architecture, Malta's medieval towns tended to contain a space, if not several, which acted as a market, and in Mdina it was not uncommon for commerce to flourish close to a town gate. Though fortification was sparse in medieval Malta, commerce thrived widely, including in the medieval *parivs* or plaza in front of every major church. Given limited segregation of functions typical of this period in Europe as well as northern Africa, trade and commerce could take place throughout a locality in both closed and open areas (Morris 1994: 102).

Squalor was doubtlessly commonplace in medieval cities throughout the Mediterranean and far beyond, with chickens, donkeys, and even wild animals sharing muddy or dusty passageways with pedestrians who darted in and out of cul-de-sacs. In 1438, wolves even ate fourteen Parisians in the heart of their city. Though such towns revealed a concern for spatial organization and aesthetic unity, global organization through methodical overall planning was missing. They tended to be compact with houses encroaching into streets and open areas. In some parts of Mdina that strongly reflect medieval patterning, some houses were even built directly into the fortified wall of the city.

At the same time that other localities were growing, Mdina continued to function as Malta's capital and most important city. It was between 1480 and the 1492 expulsion of non-Christians that Mdina reached its peak population with around 1,150 residents, equaling 5% of Malta's total population (Wettinger 1985: 7–8). This was a period during which Mdina was probably home to Sicilians, Muslims, Greeks, Jews, Spaniards, and others. Between one-forth and one-third of Mdina's population during this period was Jewish, especially in a northern neighborhood where a synagogue was located (Thake 1996: 10; Wettinger 1985: 7).

Between 1492 and 1530 three major developments occurred that would have extraordinary impact on the future direction of Maltese urban development, though none of them was controlled by the Maltese. First, under the influence of Ferdinand and Isabella in 1492, the Spanish Inquisition expelled non-Christians from Malta, thereby depriving towns of much of their vitality. Second, privileges granted through the *Università* and *Consiglio Popolare* gradually began to be ignored in Sicily, thereby depriving the nobility ensconced in Mdina of some of its autonomy. Third, when Knights of the Order of St. John came to Malta and initially settled in the coastal town of Birgu rather than in the capital city of Mdina, they set in motion the decline of cities, towns, and hamlets not located close to the Grand Harbor, including Mdina.

Although the Knights did not directly usurp the authority of the resident nobility and ranking ecclesiastics, their decision not to settle in Mdina had far more than a symbolic impact on urban and social development in Malta. On taking office, all Grand Masters of the Order followed the custom of going to Mdina to promise before its *Università* and the Bishop to respect the old customs and rights of the Maltese. By rather consistently failing to keep these promises, they actually contributed to the decline of Mdina and its nobility. Even as they followed a course of undermining the status and authority of the *Università* both in Mdina and on Gozo, in 1538, Grand Master Juan d'Omedes established an additional *Università* at Birgu.

In contrast to the church and the nobility, which found security largely away from the shores, the Order of St. John had a long, close association with seafaring and sought security on the coast. Birgu, where the Knights settled, adjoins the medieval town of Bormla, already established before the sixteenth century, and Bormla also connects to the peninsula where the medieval town of Isla is located. Prior to 1530, Isla was an area so open that it could still be used for hunting, and Bormla was mainly an unprotected village associated with fishing and commerce. At that time, Grand Master Sengle issued a permit to allow Isla to be fortified, after which time it rapidly began to attract new residents (Guillaumier 1972: 417–432). Bormla was the last of these three towns that the Knights began fortifying, not long, in fact, before Turkey's Great Siege of Malta in 1565.

The victory of the Knights in the Great Siege notwithstanding, it proved a wrenching experience for them and revealed to them some important weaknesses in their defenses. Responding to the situation, they made five decisions that would profoundly impact the course of future urban development, not only for the next 232 years that they would remain in power, but well beyond.

First, Grand Master La Valette convinced the Order that it should remain permanently in Malta. Second, the Knights decided to greatly strengthen the fortifications around Birgu, Isla, and Bormla. Third, they built a new urban, fortified headquarters for themselves on the opposite side of the Grand Harbor, on the seaward end of an undeveloped peninsula known as Mount Sceberras. Fourth, they constructed a citadel in Victoria to better protect Gozo. And fifth, implicitly rather than explicitly, they decided that physical maintenance of fortifications and buildings at Mdina, though Malta's largest city, did not deserve a major investment on their part.

This decision to essentially turn their backs on the inland citadel of Mdina, though in part motivated by their lack of real control there, was probably taken as much because of limited resources and higher priorities. The seafaring interests of the Order made Mdina ill-suited to play a major role in its policies. Moreover, Malta's vulnerability from the sea, coupled with the Knights' aggressive intentions to engage in holy war with Islam, caused them to combine their interest in defense and urban development through the construction of an extensive network of fortified towns adjacent to the Grand Harbor. This policy would first involve "The Three Cities," and soon thereafter extend to the other side of the Grand Harbor.

Taken together, the localities of Birgu, Isla, and Bormla are known as The Three Cities, for they are contiguous and are linked in history. For most Maltese, the survival of Malta and the salvation of the Grand Harbor are inseparable, and in this regard, The Three Cities are fabled above all others because of their importance during the Great Siege. In fact, to honor the bravery that The Three Cities exhibited in turning back the mighty forces of Suleiman the Magnificent, they were renamed after that battle. Birgu became Vittoriosa, Isla became Senglea or Invitta, and Bormla became Cospicua.

As fortune and good will showered the Order in the aftermath of the Great Siege, La Valette moved quickly to lay the foundation stone for the Order's new fortress capital in March 1566. The Pope generously engaged the famous engineer Francesco Laparelli to undertake its design. In March 1571, the Knights moved from Birgu (now Vittoriosa) to the new city that was still in the process of being constructed. Five years later, the *Università* that had been established by Grand Master Juan d'Omedes at Birgu was relocated to the new city, Valletta (Laspina 1971: 258).

Eight months later, construction work on the new city slowed, as many Knights sailed off to check the Turkish challenge to Christian control of Cyprus in the Battle of Lepanto. Despite a Christian victory in this battle, heavy losses presented the Knights with a challenge to the ambitious construction underway in Malta. Additionally, other distractions arose such as laxity on the part of some Knights.

Designed to be impregnable, Valletta was outfitted with ramparts, bastions, and artillery on all sides. With land connections to the rest of Malta through triumphal gates and magnificent bridges that would span huge ditches, Valletta was conceived also as a city of Baroque magnificence that would reflect the most progressive ideas in town planning as applied to glorify the powerful. Its fidelity would be to notions of an ideal Renaissance city rather than to preexistent settlement patterns associated with medieval living.

Just as the Knights earlier built Fort St. Angelo to protect the peninsula that was Vittoriosa, they constructed Fort St. Elmo to protect Valletta— named after Grand Master La Valette—at the point of Mount Sciberras. Like historic Mdina, the new city was bisected by its main street, its Strada Reale. According to regulations, its streets were not to be encumbered and no farming was to take place within its borders. As aesthetic coherence was a major concern, no courtyards or external staircases could abut the streets. Moreover, in a radical departure from medieval urban form, streets would be patterned according to a rectangular grid, resulting in blocks. This grid system conformed to the Renaissance aesthetic of uniformity, facilitated travel by carriage, and contributed to efficiency in land division. Important corner buildings were even to be decorated by craftsmen selected by a commission.

"Any study of the Renaissance," according to Zimmerman and Weissman (1989: 9) "is, by implication, a study of its emerging urban character." A Renaissance European city was conceptualized as a planned city where urban habitat would affect culture, religious rituals, and social structure, preferably compartmentalizing social strata in different parts of the city. However, this part of the theory was often difficult to implement, whether in Paris, in Rome, or in tiny Valletta (Ackerman and Rosenfeld 1989: 39–46; Blouet 1967: 102). Valletta was intended to be "a city for gentlemen." Though popular protests dissuaded the Order from enforcing a part of an original plan that would have segregated the Knights from other residents in their new capital city, land still was allocated largely according to social rank. Some sites were reserved for palaces and many regulations were put in place that generally made it difficult for people of modest means to erect homes there. Moreover, Valletta was conceived as a city that would be built according to comprehensive plans and that would operate according to enforceable regulations.

Typical of regulations enforced when Valletta was being constructed were the following. After a building site was acquired, construction had to begin within six months and the building had to be fit for occupation within one year. Moreover, building commissioners operating under the authority of the Knights determined how much money was to be spent on each building and monitored to make sure that the full expenditure they decided upon was made within three years (Blouet 1967: 103). Some regulations first adopted for Valletta later set urban standards in other Maltese towns, for example, that each house should have a cesspool that would connect to a public sewer and should have a cistern that would capture rainwater.

With few exceptions, Valletta evolved into the city where most of the important religious, administrative, and military offices of the Knights would be located. Over time, the *auberges* or hostels of all the Order's eight *langues* relocated from Vittoriosa to palatial edifices in the new capital as did the conventual church of the Order, the grand Cathedral of St. John the Baptist, named after its patron saint. In addition to other churches, magnificent buildings included the Grand Master's Palace, the Magistral Palace, and the Holy Infirmary. Valletta, as planned and developed, would house all major institutions of the Order of St. John.

The fact that the headquarters of the Order was in Valletta and the focal headquarters of the Maltese church was in Mdina did not prevent these institutions from competing with each other. Though both were ultimately responsible to the Pope in Rome, territorial and jurisdictional contests surfaced with some frequency. As Valletta in all its splendor began to assume more importance and Mdina began to lose population, including even some of its nobles, the contests often evolved into disputes requiring the intervention of authorities outside of Malta to bring resolution. As a result of one such dispute over ecclesiastical jurisdiction in Valletta that was referred to the Holy See, a papal Inquisitor was dispatched to Malta. With this new center of power added to the mix, jurisdictional disputes and jealousies between the Grand Master, the Bishop, and the Inquisitor caused even more power and territorial bases to be pitted against each other.

In a sense, Mdina was the Bishop's city, Valletta was the Knights' city, and the Inquisitor's office was located at Vittoriosa, though his summer palace was eventually constructed in Siġġiewi. The Inquisitor oversaw an ecclesiastical court charged with reporting to the Order all persons found guilty of heresy, a charge equivalent to high treason against both God and king. The Inquisitors assigned to Malta were confident in their authority and tended to be greatly feared. In fact, 25 of them became cardinals, and two eventually popes.

Regulation of defense, supervision of architecture as related to defense, control of public streets and squares, as well as the day to day civil administration of the islands, all fell under the Knights' authority. A particularly sensitive situation arose in the late sixteenth century when some officials from the Inquisitor's office were accused of plotting against the life of the Grand Master. The Bishop and the Cathedral Chapel were supposedly outside the control of the Order. Still, it was clearly not possible for the Grand Master, the Bishop, and the Inquisitor to operate completely independently of each other as each of them had some authority that reached throughout the islands. Although the Bishop had a palace in Mdina, after being initially rebuffed by the Order, he was also allowed to build a residence in Valletta. As most religious orders, though headquartered in or near Mdina, operated throughout the islands, they constituted an additional, though less autonomous and less centralized, power base.

Whereas Mdina had been home to Malta's only grammar school in 1471 when the Jesuits arrived in Malta, by 1592 they established a Jesuit college in Valletta. Although this college was established as a result of an appeal by the Bishop to the Pope, it was apparent to even Bishop Gargallo by this time that Valletta and The Three Cities had far surpassed Mdina and her suburb of Rabat as population centers of importance.

Many people were drawn to the Grand Harbor for the protection that its fortifications offered against pirates. Some were attracted by its centrality in the political and status system, others by new economic opportunities ranging from shipbuilding and construction to domestic service and the *corso*. The result was a mass exodus from the major city at the center, and even from many villages and hamlets, toward the Grand Harbor. In contrast, Gozo's major population center continued to be at its core rather than adjacent to a harbor (Bowen-Jones et al. 1961: 139–140).

Even after the founding of Valletta, much money continued to be spent on The Three Cities to make them lavishly appointed in the aristocratic tradition of the Order. Though Cospicua was not laid out according to a gridiron pattern, Senglea, Valletta, and Floriana were. That was a direct reflection that town-planning ideas associated with Renaissance urbanism diffused into Malta. As the new city of Valletta along with The Three Cities evolved into the cultural, political, and population nucleus of the island of Malta, the fortifications and buildings of Mdina slid more into disrepair. Moreover, every new threat of invasion caused more resources to be devoted to the repair and expansion of the fortifications of the inner harbor area.

It sometimes happened that the Bishop had to appeal to the Order for permission to build in a particular location or to have a particular type of architecture approved because of defense considerations. Also, in 1645, the Bishop successfully persuaded the Order to reverse its decision to withdraw its artillery from Mdina. On the other hand, at the turn of the eighteenth century, there were strained relations between the Bishop and Grand Master regarding whether the latter would be allowed to place his insignia on the façade of the Mdina Cathedral. Ultimately, the Cathedral Chapter, convened at the request of the Grand Master, ruled that the Grand Master could not. On Gozo, by contrast, the façade of the Cathedral bears both the coats of arms of Grand Master Perellos and that of Bishop Cocco Palmieri.

Though by 1681, a total of 35 parishes existed in the islands, no new ones would be established for another 150 years (Koster 1983: 303) as people continued to leave other parts of Malta to move close to Valletta or *il-Belt*. Beginning in 1722, under Grand Master Vilhena, the Order made a concerted effort to extend the reach of its authority into Mdina, and four years later, when Rabat's parish church was officially consecrated, Vilhena authorized the simultaneous remodeling of adjacent St. Publius Church, then under the control of the Order. Just two years later in 1728, he succeeded in a campaign with the Holy See to have his secretary of French affairs appointed by the Pope as the new Bishop of Malta at a time when there was a dispute going on about whether or not a new seminary should be constructed in Mdina or in Valletta. Ironically, however, the new Bishop supported the cathedral chapter's view that it should be constructed in Mdina.

During the seventeenth and eighteenth centuries, the wealth that fed The Three Cities came largely from piracy, and it was here that the slave prisons were located. To incorporate together The Three Cities and the St. Margherita Hill, just east of Vittoriosa, the Margherita Lines were constructed. Though work on this project began in 1633, and three bastions were finished at that time, it was not completed until between 1716 and 1736. Additional outer fortifications known as the Cottonera Lines, which incorporated eight bastions and two semi-bastions, were built between 1670 and 1680.

Senglea became so densely populated at times that the Knights found it necessary to outlaw additional settlement. By the beginning of the eighteenth century, Kalkara Creek to the east of Vittoriosa had become overcongested with shipping, and a dockyard was built adjacent to Senglea. This industry attracted new workers to the locality and certain sections became overcrowded and unsavory. From this time, technical workers attached to the dockyards began to be an important part of Senglea's population.

Valletta was such an attractive place that it quickly had more residents than were originally projected. In this development lies the genesis of Floriana, a town which developed as a suburban extension of Valletta, with which it shares the same peninsula. In fact, one can only reach Valletta by land by passing through Floriana. Pope St. Pius V procured Francesco Laparelli to design Valletta and provided some of the funding along with the kings of France, Portugal, and Spain. Similarly, a later appeal by Knights to Pope Urban VIII resulted in the 1634 arrival in Malta of Pietro Paolo Floriana to advise on the design of Floriana—its suburb (Guillaumier 1972: 72–96).

A gun powder factory was moved from Valletta to Floriana as early as 1665 because it was found to pose a hazard to the densely settled population of Valletta. In 1639, the Floriana Lines were begun on the side of Floriana away from Valletta. However, this work was discontinued between 1638 and 1640 so that the Margherita Lines around The Three Cities could be completed.

The situations of Siġġiewi and Mdina are especially well documented among the cities, towns, and hamlets across Malta that lost population to the new localities of the inner harbor area. Despite the presence of St. Paul's Cathedral and the adjacent residence of the Bishop in Mdina, the city gradually became almost abandoned due in part to the Order's neglect. By 1680, it was home to a mere 327 inhabitants (Thake 1996: 53–57). However, because Siġġiewi was so important in food production in a way that Mdina was not, the two cities did not fare in exactly the same way.

By the time the Knights arrived, Siġġiewi had a population of approximately 1,500 and about 300 dwellings. The extensiveness of Siġġiewi's farmlands never permitted it to be surrounded by great defensive works, and it suffered a particularly grave assault in 1554 during which many residents were carried off to be enslaved. The many large fortified houses along its Triq il-Kbir (or Main Street) are material testimony to the insecurity to which local residents had to adapt themselves.

Though the Siġġiewi area had been home to some 46 chapels in 1575, by 1646 the number of residents in town had declined to 1,494 and the dwellings to 295. There was an increase to 1,774 persons and 640 dwellings by 1667. The parish church of St. Nicholas was constructed in the center of town between 1675 and 1696. In contrast to Mdina, Siġġiewi was simply too important to food production to be deserted.

During the quarter of a century following the 1693 earthquake which caused considerable damage in Mdina, there were valiant investments in the city's reconstruction by the church and some religious orders. Among their architecturally grandiose projects was the building of a new imposing Baroque cathedral and an adjacent Bishop's Palace. Unfortunately this reinvestment by religious organizations was not sufficient to reverse decline in the city's population. Reversing of its previous neglect of Malta's ancient capital, the Order by the early eighteenth century began to take interest in playing a more significant role in the city. Along with a growing interest in protecting the inner countryside as well as coastal areas, it adopted a more positive view of Mdina's defensive potential.

There exists some irony in the fact that this changed view of Mdina's defensive importance did not occur when Malta was most vulnerable to attacks and counterattacks by pirates. Rather it came at a later time when piracy was on the decline. The Order's disposition to invest in Mdina did not begin to bear fruit in a major way until Vilhena became Grand Master in 1722. In undertaking lavish building projects in Mdina, it is likely that Vilhena was likely guided by more than military considerations. Of equal or even greater importance, he seemed intent on expanding the Order's influence in the city in keeping with its grand and absolutionist projection of itself.

Another of Vilhena's projects between 1722 and 1736 included the construction of a number of warehouses in Floriana in an area that fronted on the Grand Harbor. By 1766, hardly more than twenty blocks of this new suburb had been completed. However, it had already been determined that its settlement pattern would accommodate spacious gardens, public squares, and elegant malls. While from the very beginning this appendage of Valletta attracted a population that was urbane and diverse from a socioeconomic perspective, it is ironic that this last great town that would be built by the Knights ended up further sealing Mdina's fate as a depopulated "silent" city. Instead of new residents being drawn to a physically rehabilitated Mdina, they were more attracted to the new town of Floriana. With the drastic decline in piracy by this time, they also began to be attracted to outlying towns such as Siġġiewi.

Territorial contests and intrigues that played out between the Order, the Bishop, and the Papal Inquisitor in a variety of local settings were still running their course in 1798 when Napoleon entered on stage and removed both the Order and the Inquisitor from the scene. Against the background of the new modus vivendi, and since no diocese is allowed to have more than one cathedral, Pope Pius VII elevated St. John's Cathedral in Valletta—formerly the conventual church of the Order—to the status of Co-Cathedral in 1816. In this way much of the symbolic rivalry between two of Malta's most important cities was ended.

The Knights had arrived in Malta at a time when the medieval city form was giving way to that of the Renaissance and when the city-state throughout the Mediterranean Basin was collapsing and the territorial state was emerging (Braudel 1972a: 339–340). Though their mission of continuously waging holy wars with Islam would eventually prove anachronistic, for a long time they managed to hold their own as a theocratic micro-state while the large secular territorial state was emerging. At the same time, moreover, they contributed in significant ways to urban development in the Mediterranean Basin.

Within 110 years after they first established themselves adjacent to the Grand Harbor, at least a third of Malta's entire population had settled nearby. From that time onward, there began to be towns located on the shore that were extremely important, and at least on Malta, surpassed in importance others that were inland. In fact, it was during the period between 1545 and 1800 that 15.4% of Malta's lost villages and hamlets were abandoned (Wettinger 1975: 190). Though the small size of Malta would never permit it to become a territorial state, except in miniature, The Three Cities as well as Valletta were illustrative of important new directions in its urban development, beginning in the sixteenth century.

Under the Knights, the Three Cities quickly became densely populated settlements occupying various compartments of a vast network of fortifications, magnificent architectural monuments to the military nature of the Order, to the noble background of the Knights, and to the insecurity of the age in which they underwent their major development. Within a relatively short time, there existed no open areas of significance within The Three Cities, as Senglea, Cospicua, and Vittoriosa were completely built up.

So densely populated did Senglea become at times that the Knights found it necessary to ban additional people settling there to guard against plagues such as the one in 1676 and to maintain a high quality of life. By the beginning of the eighteenth century, a dockyard was built adjacent to Senglea. As the dockyard attracted new workers, the city became overcrowded, and such sections began to be unsavory even before the expulsion of the Knights.

With a focus on centralized colonial control, neither the French nor the British who succeeded them, were particularly interested in the empowerment of localities. By the time Great Britain began to govern, Malta had a number of different types of nucleated settlements, and it is not always easy to classify them. In Patrick Brydone's 1774 book about his tour of Sicily and Malta, for example, he noted from his British perspective: "The island is covered over with country houses and villages, besides seven cities, for so they term them; but there are only two, the Valletta and the Città Vecchia [Mdina], that by any means deserve that appellation" (Brydone 1774: 340).

Sometimes it simply seems easier to refer to all Maltese cities and villages as towns. In 1544, Senglea had been originally designated Città Senglea by Grand Master Claude de la Sengle. Certain Grand Masters, especially during the eighteenth century, followed him somewhat in designating certain localities as cities in an honorific way. Grand Master Pinto in 1743, for example, gave Qormi the name Città Pinto; Grand Master De Rohan elevated Żebbuġ to the status of Città Rohan in 1777; and Grand Master Ferdinand von Hompesch gave Siġġiewi, Żabbar, and Żejtun the status of Città Ferdinand, Città Hompesch, and Città Beland respectively.

When in 1802 representatives, deputies, and lieutenants of villages and towns presented to the British a "Declaration of Rights of the Inhabitants of the Islands of Malta and Gozo" in which they requested political representation in a general congress, they did so by means of a historic document that listed some localities as "cities" and others as "villages." The five places they listed as cities were Notabile and Casal Dingli (essentially Mdina and certain surroundings), Valletta, Vittoriosa, and Cospicua. (That no cities or villages were listed for Gozo is probably a reflection that the revolutionary document was drawn up by activists on the island of Malta.) The document leaves us to ponder what those Maltese patriots considered to be the essential differences between a city and a village (for example, Siġġiewi, Birkirkara, and Qormi). It is also curious why the representation proposed for various localities was so out of line with the way Malta's population was then distributed.

Both outside and inside *il-Belt*, the peace secured under Great Britain stimulated population growth. By 1830, the population of Siġġiewi reached 3,202. Despite a slight decline in the first half of the nineteenth century, it surpassed 5,000 in the second half of that century. Floriana also grew rapidly though its population peaked in 1871. The population of Senglea would not peak until 1931, however, as a very intensive period of British naval activity from 1800 to 1841 drove its economy.

Under British protectionism, people began to settle in new inland locations long too insecure to attract settled life. Perhaps they were still mindful that only four years after Fort St. Luciano had been completed, a Turkish assault occurred that left much destruction in Żejtun as well as where Marsaxlokk is now located. Even long after 1610 when Fort St. Luciano had been built in the area, few people settled where Marsaxlokk is located. Rather most of the fishermen who worked out of its harbor lived in nearby Żejtun and traveled back and forth to the shore.

It was around 1846 that some of the fishermen whose permanent housing was in Żejtun decided to settle directly on the bay. For several decades even after this time, Marsaxlokk remained an offshoot of Żejtun in that the fishermen regularly traveled back to Żejtun to be with relatives and friends, to sell their catches, and to attend church. By 1926, however, Marsaxlokk became a parish, meaning that a permanent settlement of size had been established alongside the bay. As in Marsaxlokk, outlying fishing villages in St. Paul's Bay, Birżebbuġa, and Marsa Scala also eventually evolved into towns and gained parish status, most of them with less compact configurations than had characterized more insecure older towns.

Northwestern Malta, largely barren and devoid of fishing harbors, has always been thinly populated. Beginning around 1840, however, large stretches of this area were divided into geometrical blocks and "given to farmers on long-term leases which stipulated that the holding had to be developed and brought into cultivation" (Blouet 1967: 179). Though some of these areas were later deserted, in others the tapping of ground water made irrigation possible and helped to sustain permanent settlement. Even prior to the late twentieth-century mushrooming of tourism in this region, towns such as Manikata, Żebbieħ, Mellieħa, and Mġarr sprang up.

While in the context of the Americas or Australia, suburbs, often have their whole life cycles chronicled in decades, Maltese suburbs are sometimes centuries old. Mdina, for example, was in symbiotic union with its suburb of Rabat even in the ninth century. During the era of British colonialism, a tremendous relocation of population began to take place from old cities to modern suburbs. Even Malta's newer suburbs more often than not have their genesis in the late nineteenth century. Sliema, long a city in its own right, was in 1833 only a village suburb of mostly summer homes for residents of Valletta.

Many residents began to move to suburbs away from the Grand Harbor as Valletta's population peaked in 1861 and Floriana's ten years later. Near The Three Cities, Paola (also known as Raħal Ġdid or "New Village") grew from a population of 488 residents in 1861 to 14,793 in 1948 (Blouet 1967: 178–179, 182). On the other side of Valletta and Floriana—the side which looks away from The Three Cities—is Marsamxett, a body of water as large as the Grand Harbor. Along the shores of Marsamxett, a string of suburbs stretching to Sliema developed through much of the nineteenth century continuing into the 1900s. This unbroken chain of suburbs later stretched even further until it reached Paceville. Because of their physical and demographic continuity with *il-Belt*, they form part of a conurbation.

The heavy bombardment of Malta during World War II was an important factor impacting population distribution. Prewar Senglea, for example, had a high concentration of Malta's most prosperous and illustrious families. Due to heavy war damage, many of its residents were evacuated and at war's end, never returned. While many Maltese localities are socioeconomically diversified with a large educated elite, the recovery of Senglea's socioeconomic balance after the war never occurred. The situation was complicated by the fact that public funds for the reparation of war damage were accompanied with restrictions on rent increases. These restrictions on rent made Senglea more attractive to working-class people than to others, and this locality is now rather homogeneous in this way.

The Maltese Islands are quite culturally homogeneous despite a long history of socioeconomic complexity. Cutting across and adding to this complexity even at the local level is a very intricate religious and secular social organization. In fact, much of the factionalism that is associated with ethnic differences in many other parts of the Mediterranean plays itself out in these islands between localities and parishes as they compete fiercely with each other for status, and for splendor in celebrating the feast days of their patron saints. Because of Malta's small size, however, rival localities or parishes often adjoin each other or are perhaps only a few hundred yards apart (Boissevain 1969b: 27). Each parish has its own parish priest who has traditionally been a patron, a guardian, a confessor, and until recent years, almost a type of unofficial mayor going back even to the time of the Knights.

Prior to the strengthening of the diocesan organization in Malta in the late 1500s, all parish priests would annually pay homage to the Grand Master in a Candelmas ceremony on February 2 (Koster 1983: 304). In all localities, virtually everyone is a member of a parish priest's flock. Most parish priests are assisted by at least one curate, and in all parishes a network of people is organized around the upkeep of the parish church, the planning of parish *festi*, and related activities.

Adding to the character of each locality are various religious organizations—known as lay apostolate associations and devotional societies which have semiautonomous divisions at the parish level although they are organized by the Malta and the Gozo dioceses. These societies tend to be run by local priests who are responsible to the parish priests with the notable exception of the Society of Christian Doctrine (also known as *tal-muzew* or MUSEUM). MUSEUM is better represented on Malta than on Gozo, but it is everywhere a very strict lay apostolate association which supports parish priests and the church hierarchy (Boissevain 1969b: 19–21). Diocesan religious organization at the local level also includes third orders, a number of lay counterparts of religious orders such as the Franciscans and Carmelites. A number of groups are more loosely organized such as the Association of Christian Mothers and the Holy Name Society and Circulo Maria Bambina, the local women's section of a national Catholic Action Movement (Mizzi 1981: 214).

Each parish has at least one confraternity, and all the confraternities in Malta have local autonomy and are dedicated to a particular saint. Many of these confraternities trace their origins to medieval towns. They have functioned in a variety of ways over the centuries, including as mutual aid organizations, trade guilds, groups that offer prayers for dead members, and groups whose uniformed male members sometimes participate in public processions (Boissevain 1969b: 21–22, 45–46, 61, 74–91). In many localities there exist more than one confraternity and more than one band club, meaning considerable factional rivalry often exists locally. This intra-locality rivalry exists quite in addition to the considerable rivalry that exists between localities.

Keeping track of the status of various parishes can be a complicated matter and has sometimes led to rather serious disputes. One dimension of status for a parish is derived from its seniority, of which younger parishes obviously have less and older parishes more. Relative seniority can sometimes be difficult to establish where a particular parish has disappeared only later to re-emerge under its previous name or a new one. The title *Matrici* bestowed on the church at Naxxar also carries a type of special seniority with it since it implies that this church is an ancient one from which others developed.

Another type of status that some parishes have is that of being a Collegiate Chapter, a status that requires papal sanction. On Malta, there are Collegiate Chapters in Senglea, Vittoriosa, Cospicua, Rabat, Birkirkara, and Valletta, while on Gozo, they are found in Għarb, Nadur, and Xagħra. A parish church where there exists a Collegiate Chapter will have exalted status, sometimes being considered a basilica, and some of its priests will be canons and have special titles such as monsignors.

Only in a few localities have size and prestige converged in such a way that a Maltese locality has attained the unusual status of having more than one parish within it. Exceptional in this way on Malta are Valletta, Marsa, and Qormi which are divided into two parishes, and Sliema, which is divided into three. Similarly, on Gozo, Victoria (still known popularly as Rabat) is divided into two parishes. In localities where this kind of structural pluralism exists, social organization is made more complex.

Though in some ways both the church and the state have tended to be centralized in Malta, traditionally it was the state more than the church that was centralized. The church in Malta has long had a fully elaborated local organization. While the church was represented at the local level in numerous ways, the institutional presence of the state was until recently mostly reflected through the police, public works, dispensaries, utilities, postal service, public transportation, sanitation, and public education.

Apart from some semi-social clubs sponsored by political parties, there was no formal political apparatus at the local level until 1993. Except for a brief experiment with regional government on the island of Gozo that ended prior to 1971, local authority was more religious-centered than government-centered. Until 1993, local boundaries recognized by the Central Office of Statistics were largely those of the various parishes.

By the early 1990s, two processes were converging that would alter this balance between church and state presence in localities. On the one hand, Malta's state government—in a society without a long history of clear boundaries between church and state—was demonstrating more assertiveness in extending control at the local level. On the other hand, Malta's participation in international associations with other European countries increased awareness that its essential lack of secular government at the local level made it look odd and inhibited certain kinds of international cooperation at the local level.

Not surprisingly, the Maltese Parliament adopted in 1993 the Local Councils' Act, an act modeled on the European Charter of Local Self-Government (Council of Europe Publishing 1997). It provides for limited statutory local government for the first time in the modern era. Currently, 67 local councils are in existence. While the average territory in a municipality is 4.38 square kilometers, the mean average population per locality is 5,111. Along with the national government, local councils have some concurrent authority with respect to social welfare, housing, and town planning, as well as environmental and public sanitation matters. In very limited ways, the councils also share with the national government authority relating to transportation and traffic planning and to cultural, leisure, and sports activities. Males and females have equal rights to be elected as local councilors, and 15 or 20% of councilors are women.

Local population densities vary considerably, not only between Gozo and Malta but also from one part of Malta to another. Despite some considerable decentralization of population that began to take place under British rule beginning in the early nineteenth century, a disproportionately large part of the national population still lives close to the inner harbor area, not far distant from where the Knights first settled in 1530. Densities sometimes vary considerably between neighborhoods within the same towns. While Siġġiewi contains a land area of 6.659 square miles (approximately 1/18 of all the territory of the entire country), Floriana contains only 0.341 square miles, and Senglea a mere 0.057, making it the most densely populated locality in Malta. The present population density of Senglea is approximately four times greater than that of the overall population in the five boroughs of New York City. However when Senglea's population peaked in 1931 with 7,683 residents, the density was almost six times higher than that in present-day New York City.

Most Maltese towns have one or more band clubs loosely affiliated with some political party, and each band club has a meeting place where the band practices and where various social events take place, an important dimension of local factionalism. Moreover, this type of devotion to different parties often has religious parallels in devotion to different saints and often gets played out quite publicly in ceremonious ways (Boissevain 1994: 271–283). Although church and state are anchors to which many social organizations are attached at the local level, these institutions do not totally account for factionalism within localities, pride at the local level, nor rivalry among localities.

For example, the regatta held on September 8 in the Grand Harbor to celebrate Malta's victories during the Great Siege of 1565 and World War II is a kind of water carnival where local rowing teams from the cities bordering Grand Harbor such as Valletta, Vittoriosa, Senglea, Kalkara, Cospicua, Marsaxlokk, and Marsa—strongly supported by their fans—compete against each other with dogged determination. Though the football clubs of some larger localities similarly generate considerable civic pride, the individual players often do not have strong roots in the localities for which they play, a cause of frequent shifts in the allegiance of fans to local teams.

Mobility and virtual mobility—by means of new advances in telecommunications—are altering the significance of local boundaries in Malta, one of the world's most urban countries as well as one of its most densely populated, a development that is also occurring in many other lands. As Malta forges ahead with its patterns of urban adaptation, it will inevitably establish precedents many of which will predict developments beyond its shores.

Chapter 5

National Emergence and the Modern Age

One finds some megalithic temples older than Egyptian pyramids, bronze-age archaeological sites, Phoenician inscriptions, and catacombs contemporaneous with those of ancient Rome in tiny Malta. Special emphasis and pride are associated with societal development since Christian conversion. Though keenly aware that peoples of many nationalities have at times contributed to the culture and gene pool, Maltese are fiercely independent and proud.

Among the many peoples that have contributed to the population and culture that we know as Maltese are Romans, Greeks, Arabs, Berbers, Normans, Sicilians, Swabians, Aroganese, Castilian, French, and British. It is the people of nearby Northern Africa who more than any other contributed the foundation of the Maltese language. That these people tend to be non-Christian, however, contributes to a strong tendency to view the emergence of Maltese nationhood in opposition to them. While exhibiting great pride in European ancestors, readily speaking of supposed Phoenician forebears, even acknowledging the contributions of Jews, Maltese claim little knowledge of the Turks and Africans who became Maltese.

This tendency not to be celebratory about African and Muslim contributions to Maltese heritage probably results less from current antipathy toward Africans and Muslims than from the fact that Maltese nationalism has been molded in a status-conscious world where Europe is globally esteemed. Within the complex blend of ingredients that get fused into nationalism are religion, language, geographical closeness to Africa, European identity, and a strong drive toward economic betterment and political autonomy. While such ingredients often reinforce each other, they are sometimes at the roots of contests within Maltese nationalism.

Malta's embrace of Europe's modern age was reluctant, though courtly. Knights of noble heritage dwelling in Baroque palaces were still occasionally waging holy wars from Malta as late as the founding of the United States and after the beginning of England's Industrial Revolution. Printing was not undertaken on Maltese soil until quite late by European standards, not until 1642 when it was introduced on a very limited scale. The Grand Master initially reserved to himself and the Inquisitor the right of censorship but "when the Bishop protested that he had been excluded, the Holy Office excluded the Grand Master as well" (Koster 1983: 305). As conflict over the matter was continuing in 1746, an ordinance issued by Pope Benedict XIV made it clear that any local printing could be censored by three authorities beholden to the Holy See; first the Bishop, second the Papal Inquisitor, and finally the Grand Master of the Order of St. John (Clair 1969: 15). With the possible exception of a single book, publishing in Malta thereafter was discontinued for a century.

Widespread nationalist pride is associated with feelings that during many centuries Malta was on the frontlines helping to protect Christian Europe from Islamic expansionism. The importance of religion as an ingredient of nationalism is enhanced by the fact that from the late 1700s to the late 1900s, numerous Maltese ecclesiastics emerged as nationalist heroes. In 1673, there almost took place a rebellion against the Knights that was instigated by the secular clergy and the Bishop. Also, a priest named Gaetano Mannarino was the leader of an abortive revolt against the Order of St. John in 1775 (Koster 1983: 306, 310). A mere 13 years later, Canon F. S. Caruana emerged as one of the three most prominent leaders in the insurrection against invaders from revolutionary France, an uprising which not coincidentally was in large measure a spontaneous defense of nation and pride in the local church.

It is significant that this insurrection was in part a rejection of an all-too-abrupt encounter with the modern age by a society that was in many respects still feudal and where a separation between church and state remained to be worked out. In fact, religion is largely inseparable from nationalism in the context of Maltese cultural history.

From 1156, the Diocese of Malta became a dependent of the Metropolitan of Palermo and except under Charles of Anjou in the thirteenth century (who caused Maltese prelates to be appointed), the Bishop of Malta was commonly a Sicilian. No Maltese was allowed to become a Knight in the Order of St. John, probably to prevent the development of a *langue* of Knights that would be especially favored by the general population. There was appointed, however, one Maltese Bishop under the Spaniards and a Bishop whose heritage was half Maltese under the Knights. Ecclesiastical grades under the Knights were open to Maltese, however, and we find the names of three Maltese who were grand priors at various times (Kendal 1999: 3). Since 1808, all Bishops of Malta have been of Maltese nationality.

Religion was even a factor in the first general insurrection against a foreign ruler that occurred when the Maltese rose up against invaders from revolutionary France at the end of the eighteenth century. It is all the more remarkable that this insurrection occurred at a time of great economic uncertainty, in fact at a time when Malta was deprived of the external wealth to which it became accustomed while it remained under the rule of the Order of St. John. It was also a time when Spain, to which Malta had been exporting most of its cotton, had enacted a prohibition on the importation of foreign cotton. This prompted the Maltese to embrace Great Britain as a new patron following their routing of the French.

Had Maltese at this point been interested primarily in mere symbols of nationalism, they probably would have welcomed back the Order of St. John as provided for by the 1802 Treaty of Amiens. This treaty, after all, provided that the Knights of the Order would have to establish alongside the other *langues* into which it was organized, one based on the Maltese language. It also required that one half of all municipal and administrative jobs would be set aside for Maltese.

Though these conditions symbolized a dramatic enhancement in the international recognition of Malta as a nation, the fact that the Maltese roundly objected to the treaty provisions for the return of the Knights was a complex response based on a range of self-interest factors which went well beyond symbols. On the one hand, the Order of St. John had been deprived of most of its wealth. British patronage, on the other, brought the prospect of economic assistance as well as military protection. As anticipated, there was an upsurge in trade after 1806, and by 1813, the British had made available a total of £433,000 in loans (Price 1954: 3). Moreover, Maltese leaders widely assumed and hoped that British protection would be compatible with the enjoyment of certain of their rights that they considered traditional. As interpreted locally, these rights were ancient ones, some of which it was claimed went back as far as privileges granted by ancient Rome.

Throughout the period of British colonialism, a feeling that self-government would automatically solve social problems (Price 1954: 22) would frequently surface as an important ingredient of nationalist expression. As early as 1802, some Maltese nobles and gentry—whose national pride was insulted by the idea of an outright British takeover of Malta as a mere colony—petitioned for a legislative assembly on the grounds that only in 1782 had the Grand Master illegally suppressed the *Consiglio Popolare* (Blouet 1967: 169; Price 1954: 21). They were greatly disappointed when the British refused to reconstitute the *Consiglio Popolare*, a body which though hardly a representative legislature had existed as a lofty historic symbol that could be portrayed to the masses as one around which they should rally (Blouet 1967: 173; Smith and Koster 1984: 39).

Manifesting at least a modicum of concern about national sensitivities in their new possession, Britain instructed the early commissioners "to give the Maltese 'as large a share of civil liberty as is consistent with the military circumstances of the island' " (Blouet 1967: 169). Early British administrators tended more often than not to view Maltese wanting to be involved in government as extremists, and the governor was to be advised by a committee of local citizens only if he wished (Blouet 1967: 171).

Though the sense of nationhood evolving in early nineteenth-century Malta was not a secular one, it was based on a struggle for respect and self-determination as a unified people. In this sense, Maltese nationalism has roots older than that of many of Malta's neighbors. Libya, Algeria, Morocco, and Italy were not united in the early 1800s, nor did unified modern nations exist in the Balkans where the two dynastic empires, one Ottoman and one Habsburg, held sway. In contrast, Malta—though colonized—was already a united micro-state where culturally homogeneous islanders already asserted "that the British never conquered [them], but rather that the Maltese willingly placed themselves under the protection of the British Crown" (Orr 1992: 175).

Even Maltese caution in embracing individualism and secularism of the modern age was in some ways an expression of indigenous nationalism. This was apparent, for example, in the local church's opposition to Napoleon's abrupt ending of censorship. In fact, when the British re-imposed censorship as soon as the French had departed by mandating a governmental license to use a printing press, the church used the full weight of its influence to support re-imposition of censorship.

What brought the church and colonial officials together on this issue was the coincidence that they both had vested interests in perpetuating a long tradition of institutional paternalism in Malta. Also, there existed no freedom of the press in the Italian Peninsula. Among those most vociferously supporting censorship was Canon F. S. Caruana, earlier an anti-French nationalist leader and later elevated in 1831 to Malta's highest ecclesiastical office, that of Bishop.

With neither the Inquisitor nor the Knights present to vie for power with the local church, it was inevitable that the church and colonial government would sometimes find themselves on opposite sides of nationalist concerns. With no tradition of a sharp demarcation between the authorities of church and state, accommodations among the sacred, the profane, and the modern remained to be worked out even as Malta began to experience the challenges of living under British colonialism.

One challenge arose around 1809 when Britain allowed the Protestant Bible societies to establish a presence in Malta and to begin distributing religious literature in Maltese and Italian. In addition to being suspicious of Britain's intentions on religious grounds, the church was fearful that colonial authorities might undermine the preeminence of Italian as the language of the church bureaucracy, the courts, and the élite. When in 1813

Lt. General Thomas Maitland, the British governor and commander-in-chief of Malta, left the Maltese without even symbolic input in the management of their affairs by abolishing the *Università* (Blouet 1967: 173), there was a widespread feeling of betrayal. Maitland further offended nationalist sentiment by suggesting the adoption of English as Malta's official language. Without Maltese input, he suggested that English should replace Italian in the courts and as the language for government contracts (Blouet 1967: 174).

It was the internationally sanctioned Treaty of Paris signed in 1814 that officially recognized that Malta had become a crown colony of Great Britain. The imbalance between a rapidly growing population with decreasing economic opportunities was already prompting numerous Maltese to migrate to other parts of the Mediterranean Basin out of dire necessity. Moreover, Malta officially became a British colony at a time when Maltese cotton was beginning to be undercut by more cheaply produced cotton from Egypt.

These circumstances combined to make early acceptance of British rule rather palatable to the Maltese. And from the English perspective, there still existed a French factor. Napoleon was on record as having stated to a British ambassador: "I would rather see you on Montmartre than in Malta. It is the fulcrum of the Mediterranean" (Ludwig 1942: 484–485). Eventually deciding to keep Malta under her control, Great Britain's concern was less with nation-building and development in a new colony than with neutralizing French influence in the area.

Despite Britain's reimposition of censorship in Malta, it soon became clear to the church that its ancient privileges could not be taken for granted and could best be protected through vigilance. In 1815, the Methodist Missionary Committee in London was asked by British soldiers stationed in Malta to send to them a Wesleyan vicar. With the 1815 arrival of Rev. W. Jowett, Catholic consternation turned into outrage when he and a certain Dr. Cleardo Nandi of Malta set about establishing a Maltese branch of the Bible Society. In 1822, moreover, the first Protestant press was established in Malta under the auspices of the American Board of Commissioners for Foreign Missions (Clair 1969: 21). The colonial government also allowed an Arabic press under the auspices of the English Church Missionary Society to operate between 1825 and 1842 and to be briefly revived thereafter (Roper 1988). Although publications from these Protestant presses were primarily intended to encourage audiences in Greece and Palestine to rebel against their Turkish overlords, the clergy opposed their mere presence on Maltese soil as a threat to the universal acceptance of Catholicism.

Beginning around 1825, the government restricted the missionary activities of groups such as the Bible Society and the Salvation Army and reserved to itself the right to ban public religious ceremonies by non-Catholics if they threatened the peace. In a further effort to placate the church, the

British maintained Catholic precepts regarding education and marriage and exempted the Archbishop of Malta and the Bishop of Gozo from the jurisdiction of criminal courts (Boissevain 1969b: 7). Though colonial authorities leaned overall in the direction of protecting historic privileges of the church, the church reacted with suspicion in adjusting to the new colonial administration. In fact, between 1824 and 1851, five Wesleyan vicars were allowed to enter Malta. The fact that they favored temperance in a society with a long tradition of wine consumption eventually put them all the more at odds with traditional mores as Maltese nationalism matured (Denny 1987: 329–343).

Two paradoxes marked major changes in Malta during the early 1800s. One of Europe's most Catholic countries was colonized by a predominantly Protestant one, and waves of Maltese migrated to the same nearby countries that they had long viewed as their greatest enemies. Even with British protectionism and economic assistance, many poverty-stricken Maltese continued to find it necessary to leave their homeland in search of more promising opportunities in neighboring countries. The fact that European slavery in the regencies of Tunis and Algiers was dying out by the early 1800s acted as a "pull factor," and desperate economic conditions within Malta's rapidly growing population acted as a "push factor" (Smith 1998: 70–71).

Alongside risks and frequent difficulties associated with massive emigration, the church considered any attempt to control population through artificial means totally unacceptable. Between 1815 and 1825, roughly 10 to 15% of Malta's entire population settled outside the country for some significant period of time. While the vast majority settled in Arabic-speaking parts of Northern Africa and the Levant, smaller numbers also went to Sicily, Italy, Marseilles, and Barcelona in Western Europe and to Greece, Constantinople, and Smyrna in the Balkans and Asia Minor.

With the beginning of French colonization in Algeria in 1830, the northeastern Algerian cities of Bône and Philipville became especially popular as destinations for Maltese emigrants. Between 1818 and 1832, between 1,000 and 2,000 Maltese annually moved outside of Malta while between 1833 and 1844, some 2 to 3% of Malta's entire population emigrated. Though these Maltese—disproportionately of the poverty-stricken working class—settled mostly along the African littoral in major cities from Algeria to Egypt, many also chose the Levant, Turkey, and Greece (Price 1954: 59; Smith 1998: 64–65).

At the same time that national pride was being challenged by British colonial rule, it was also being influenced by the back and forth migration of Maltese to neighboring countries. One result of the dispersal of Maltese emigrants in the larger Mediterranean Basin was that the domestic press increased its coverage of various countries in which Maltese were settling in ways that helped to shape an evolving national identity. Newspapers such as *Il Mediterrano, Il Portagogio Maltese, Il Filologo, Malta Times, Malta Observer*, and *Malta Mail* played crucial roles in expanding national consciousness of developments abroad, including particulars associated with colonialism.

Though geographically situated within the margins of Europe, Malta was with regard to its colonial status more similar to the Balkans, the Levant, and parts of Africa than to such European powers as England, France, Germany, Belgium, and the Netherlands that were then involved in empire-building. This oddity was an additional challenge that domestic nationalism had to accommodate. Alongside the coverage of news from abroad, the Maltese press gave considerable nationalist expression to what it deemed shortcomings of the colonial social order at home.

Two of the impediments to modernity in Malta were the narrowness of Britian's imperial objectives and the fact that the church and the state, the two most powerful institutions in society, maintained a feudal hold on almost half of all arable land. An 1823 decree that required the church to sell within a period of one year any real estate bequeathed to it was viewed by the church as more aimed against itself than in the public good. The church perceived an additional threat the following year when colonial authorities allowed Wesleyan Methodists to open their own place of worship in Valletta though it was very modest (Denny 1987: 329). At times, defensive church authorities were reluctant even to support the expansion of education among the unlettered masses for fear that such expansion might introduce Protestantism (Clair 1969: 25).

The local church often challenged the colonial social order in the national interest and the church leadership was hardly in the vanguard of those who wished to introduce liberal ideas and practices into the islands. When colonial authorities abolished the right of sanctuary and restricted the jurisdiction of the ecclesiastical courts to purely spiritual matters in 1828, these actions were viewed by most Maltese as more anticlerical than in the spirit of the modern age. Though by the 1830s Carmillo Sceberras and George Mitrovich began to agitate for freedom of the press, they remained exceptional and were encouraged neither by the local church nor by the Holy See.

Though under Malta's constitution of 1835 the responsibility for governing resided ultimately with the governor, the paternalism of his administration was coupled with the church's paternalism through a highly elitist advisory council that he was allowed to consult. The membership of this council was limited, in fact, to the governor, the lieutenant governor, the commander-in-chief, the chief justice, the Bishop, the chief secretary to the government and one representative each from the nobility, landowners, and the commercial community, all appointed by the governor. Despite such an elite and conservative council, limitations began to be placed on censorship in 1837 and within two years it was completely abolished by Ordinance

No. IV (Clair 1969: 32). In practice, however, it remained unlawful for anyone to insult the Catholic Church, the Church of England, or any other Christian denomination at a time when both church and state were represented in government; that provided considerable protection to both the religious and political status quo.

Though by 1842 Malta's insularity had been penetrated by the presence of 4.5% of its residents who were foreigners, the pace of development was not keeping up with needs. The fact that this was a period when "[o]ver five hundred of the employed were listed as professional beggars and 1,600 lived at government or private charitable institutions" (Smith 1998: 63) indicates economic conditions were dire. Much of the development which took place after 1840—including a development program for the dockyard, the improvement of harbors, and new defense infrastructures—increased the dependence of the Maltese economy on the ebb and flow of British military adventures (Blouet 1967: 175–176, 184–185).

Exceptional as nonmilitary development were some agricultural improvements such as the introduction of the potato, cattle to supply milk, efforts to increase vine cultivation, and even attempts to establish a silk industry. A deterioration in Anglo-French relations between 1846 and 1848 intensified concern about the fact that Malta was one of the most densely populated countries in the world, had a fluctuating economy that was overly dependent on the British military, and depended on imports for three quarters of its food (Price 1954: 105–107).

Typical of an economic boom period was the one that began in 1853 with the outbreak of the Crimean War. In this war where Great Britain along with France, Turkey, and Sardinia confronted Russia over the domination of southeastern Europe, numerous foreign troops used Malta as a supply and refitting station (Blouet 1967: 175; Price 1954: 107–110). Some Maltese even followed the troops to Greece and the Black Sea in an effort to profit from the war activity. Around the same period, other Maltese moved to Egypt where Said Pasha had numerous public works underway, including the building of the Suez Canal.

The canal's 1869 opening increased Malta's importance as a vital link in a British imperial chain that ran the length of the Mediterranean. In much the matter of a board game, Britain agreed with France in 1878 not to interfere with a French move into Tunisia provided that France would not interfere with her move into Cyprus. This paved the way for increased political and economic interference by Great Britain in Egypt, though Britain waited until 1882 before militarily invading the country. This accomplished, Britain had an imperialist lifeline that stretched from the mother country through Gibraltar, Malta, Cyprus, and Egypt via Aden in the Red Sea and on eastward to India, Hong Kong, and Australia.

Against a background of intense Anglo-French colonial rivalry in the mid-nineteenth century, Westminster wished to contain Maltese nationalism. While Malta's 1849 constitution provided for an elected Maltese minority, it provided for a non-elected majority of mostly British officials. Though mere representation theoretically provided Maltese an opportunity to at least participate in policy debates, even this was often denied through parliamentary trickery used by the non-Maltese majority (Blouet 1967: 192–193). The existence of rampant illiteracy, the overarching influence of parish priests as patrons of masses, and the absence of real political parties further reduced the significance of Maltese representation in this weak quasi-elected council. For the masses, domestic nationalism found expression more through association with the church than through symbolic participation in a largely meaningless electoral process.

At the same time that the 1849 constitution was largely frustrating the nationalist aspirations of local politicians, spillover from the *risorgimento*— a movement for Italian unification—was causing a number of Italian partisans of the nationalist struggle in their homeland to settle in Malta. Though the *risorgimento* reached a successful conclusion in Italy in 1870 with the incorporation into a united nation of the papal possessions, its legacy in Malta was still in its early stages. Revolutionary and nationalist ideas, influenced by developments in Italy, would challenge the colonial status quo in Malta, not only with regard to religion but also with regard to language. Most Maltese nationalists viewed English as threatening the preeminence of Italian, and Italian settlers tended to be very supportive of this local opposition to the encroachment of English.

Italian was not a language in which the Maltese-speaking masses were fluent, but it was dominant among the elite and was the language of record in the courts as well as the working language of the local church. Though several decades had passed since the Holy See had broken the centuries-old dependence of the Diocese of Malta on the Metropolitan of Palermo in Sicily, Italian remained associated with high status in Malta. The use of Italian in preference to English by Malta's intelligentsia came to represent historical continuity and religious independence as well as colonial resistance. Hence, though Maltese nationalism was home-grown, it did not evolve in a vacuum. At the same that it was being influenced by nationalist developments in Italy, it was also being influenced by the constant back and forth migration of Maltese to other parts of the Mediterranean.

Nineteenth-century Algeria drew more Maltese settlers overall than any other single destination, though waves of Maltese moved back and forth in greater and lesser numbers to other areas according to the fluidity of opportunities and risks. Perhaps the two most important reasons that numerous Maltese were drawn to the Arabic-speaking world was similarity of language as well as the ease of returning home. Among the types of developments that typically brought Maltese emigrants home were economic failure, epidemics of cholera or small pox, and conflicts of various kinds.

Conflicts drove numerous Maltese from Tripoli in 1827 and 1836, from

Egypt in 1840, from Algeria in 1845, and from Algeria and Tunis in 1864. Fear of cholera drew many home in 1837, 1841, and 1850, and again in 1858. From neighboring countries in the Mediterranean, it was easy for Maltese to return home in times of prosperity as well. Considering that between 1840 and 1890 the re-immigration rate to Malta approximated 85% (Price 1954), the importance that living among predominantly Arab-speaking neighbors had on Maltese nationalism can hardly be overstated. "The issue of Maltese racial identity also played a part—at times an important part—during the period of British rule. . . . the racial issue was never far from the surface, especially in the 19th century when it featured openly in official correspondence and internal colonial office minutes" (Pirotta 1994: 104). At the same time, indigenous nationalism was being influenced by awareness of global prejudices relating to race.

The nineteenth century, for example, was one during which many of the world's peoples were enslaved or colonized and the subjugation of these people was often perceived as resulting from some deficit on their parts. Ethnocentrism and racism existed in many popular and "scientific" varieties, and it was not uncommon to attribute superior or inferior status to whole nationalities based on racial and language classifications no matter how arbitrarily or unreasoned the attributions. Moreover, it was common to consider people as "white" and "non-white" by superficial reference to complexion, place of origin, language, and even on the basis of phrenology, cephalic indices, and head shapes.

At a time when Western scholars mistakenly assumed that discrete groups conceived of as races existed among human beings and could be objectively defined by scientific criteria, many contributed to the confusion by assuming the existence of close biological relationships between peoples speaking related languages. In keeping with "scientific racism," terms such as Semite, Hamite, and Aryan were used in simplistic and confusing ways so as to group people together sometimes on the basis of assumed biological affinities and sometimes on the basis of assumed language, cultural, and personality affinities. *Mediterranean Race*, authored by G. Sergi of Rome in 1900 was among the many works based on such flawed understanding of human variation. Though turning away from the cephalic index, which he correctly recognized as unscientific, Sergi did not turn away from simplistic racial theorizing. In fact, he claimed to use anatomy to identify races based on the shapes of skulls, asserting that long-skulled people and short-skulled people belonged to different races.

In Europe of the early twentieth century, racial concerns often overlapped with nationalist concerns, and in 1912, one of Sergi's disciples, an Englishman named R. N. Bradley, placed Malta at the eye of this distorted thinking with his case study on the Maltese entitled *Malta and the Mediterranean Race*. Bradley (1912: 30–31, 125–126), argued that a dolichocephalic (or long-headed) Eurafrican race descendant from sub-Saharan

Africans had crossed over to Europe at various points such as Gibraltar, Malta, Sicily, the Greek Islands, and Asia Minor and eventually diffused throughout Europe. Bradley (1912: 111, 164–165, 170) argued that the Maltese remained essentially racially pure descendants of the long-headed Eurafrican or Mediterranean race unlike many Europeans nationalities (including the English) which subsequently became culturally and biologically intermixed with a superior brachycephalic (or short-headed) Aryan race from Asia.

Though not all anthropologists of Bradley's day would have been comfortable with his theories, such simplistic theorizing about human variation was not unusual in anthropological circles at that time. As Marvin Harris (1968: 101) has pointed out about the discipline at that time, "anthropology and racial determinism had become almost synonyms." Racist interpretations of human variation—biological, psychological, emotional, and cultural—had a considerable following in the late nineteenth and early twentieth centuries. Though Bradley's theories were not particularly flattering to Malta, he found empathy for them among at least a few Maltese intellectuals (Bradley 1912: 7–8; Luttrell 1975: 16).

While Bradley claimed that his theories proving the existence of two races of Europeans based on anatomical analysis of head shapes was supported by psychology, archaeology, and even kinship and religious practices, they were not made more palatable to most Maltese nationalists by the fact that he included within his long-headed category southern Italians, Irish, Welch, and Algerian Kabyles. There can be little doubt that a legacy of racism in the larger world—both popular and "scientific"—has contributed to defensiveness on the parts of some Maltese about their connections with Africa and with Arabs.

Some Maltese scholars have denied that Arabic-speaking Muslims were ever resident in Malta in large numbers despite overwhelming archaeological, linguistic, and documentary evidence to the contrary. Among Maltese linguists who have argued that the Maltese language was principally derived from Phoenician or Hebrew and could not possibly be derived from Arabic have been some of the most famous, such as De Soldanis and Vassalli—at least in his early writings. Such views about the derivation of Maltese have time and again permeated some strains of indigenous nationalism although the full weight of linguistic scholarship in Malta today opposes them. As long ago as 1912, Bradley (1912: 162) observed: "We can quite understand this pride among an insular people who desire to hold up their heads with the English and Italians and to point to an ancestry as noble and famous as any in the world; we can understand the aversion to being in any way connected with Arabs."

In the words of Orr (1992: 145), "The debate over the origins of the Maltese language has been a protracted and particularly vitriolic one that persists to this day, albeit with far less intensity than in the mid-twentieth century." The Maltese language sometimes has complicated national identity and status for people who speak it as a mother tongue, and it sometimes has touched raw nerves and awakened bitter memories. In colonial Algeria, for example, Maltese settlers not infrequently experienced discrimination from other Europeans, some of whom disparagingly referred to them as "Christian Arabs," "half-Italian, half-Arab," "more African than European," "a type of hard-working Moor," and people "of both continents" (Smith 1998: 117–119).

Part of the difficulty lay in the irony that throughout much of the period of European imperial control of northern Africa, the Maltese were themselves a colonized people with a living standard only marginally higher. The fact that the Maltese were fluent in a language similar to Arabic and were oftentimes willing to live in closer proximity to colonized Africans also contributed to their unfavorable treatment by fellow Europeans. How fluid and complex the situation could be at times is illustrated by an 1889 decision made by Paris concerning colonial Algeria.

France automatically extended French citizenship to children of non-French Europeans resident in Algeria unless they specifically rejected it. This decision had very little to do with what the French thought of Maltese as human beings and a great deal to do with France's willingness to negotiate their status to strengthen her colonial hold on Algeria. Neither at home or abroad was it possible for Maltese to completely escape the impact of irrational discrimination based on language, geography, and colonial status. In colonial Algeria, for example, some economic and social segregation of Maltese from residents from metropolitan France was documented well into the mid-twentieth century (Smith 1998: 31).

In the 1880s—just prior to the introduction of railroad transportation and electric lighting—Westminster sent three commissioners to Malta to conduct inquiries on various matters ranging from taxation to education. Two of these commissioners recommended, among other things, expanding the teaching of English in hopes of increasing the flow of Maltese emigration to Cyprus and Australia. Presented with greatest specificity in the 1880 report of Commissioner P. J. Keenan whose mission was to investigate the system of education, these pro-English proposals were opposed by many nationalists. In fact, the Keenan Report became a focus for strong "anti-reformist" opposition for its recommendations that incited deep nationalist fears about language (Price 1954: 177–178).

Among these recommendations were that English should be taught in the place of Italian as an elective subject, that English should be substituted for Italian in the courts within 15 years, and that English and Italian should be placed on equal footing in the schools. It did not contribute to calm that the Colonial Office raced to execute many of them as soon as possible, though the target date for changing from Italian to English in the courts was eventually extended from 15 to 20 years. In the primary schools, Sigismondo Savona pushed a *"pari-passu"* system of educational reform in line with the Keenan report whereby the language of instruction could remain English or Italian at the option of students' parents. Opposition to these reforms quickly became broad based. With papers such as *Malta, Diritto di Malta, Il Filogio, Malta Mail,* and *Il Mediterraneo* stirring the public, political parties began emerging in Malta by 1883.

On one side was Savona and others in favor of promoting English, arguing that it would facilitate Maltese emigration to English-speaking countries. On the other side, they were strongly opposed by the *Partito Nazionale,* under Dr. Fortunato Mizzi, whose father was Gozitan magistrate Francesco Mizzi and whose mother was Italian. A kind of test case between partisans on these opposing sides took place in 1883 when a contingent of Maltese laborers who shipped out to Australia found that "cheap labor" from Southern Europe was treated in a racist way and considered undeserving of salaries paid laborers from such parts of northern Europe as the British Isles (Price 1954: 181–183; York 1988). When news of their discriminatory treatment reached Malta, the populace was highly indignant and pro-Italian nationalists likened Australian discrimination to trafficking in human flesh.

As a result of the 1884 entrance into Cambridge University of the Most Honorable Count della Catena, or Gerald Strickland, an Anglo-Maltese noble, Maltese nationalism was also set to evolve along a different route. During the three years that Strickland studied at Cambridge's Trinity College, he lobbied continually for enhanced political rights for Malta. In fact, Malta had in him a champion of her rights on English soil as never before (Smith and Koster 1984: 42). Though Mizzi was pro-Italian and Strickland pro-English, by the time Strickland completed his studies, he had entered into a working alliance with Mizzi to present the Colonial Office with a draft constitution that would advance the cause of political evolution in Malta.

Under a new constitution that came into effect in 1887, Mizzi, Strickland, and three collaborators were swept into office (Smith and Koster 1984: 46). This constitution, which provided Malta with its first experience with representative government, allowed Maltese for the first time to elect a majority in a council that was allowed to legislate on domestic matters except in extraordinary circumstances. Ironically, this experiment in representative government did not long endure, as Maltese nationalists with conflicting agendas on the so-called language question would soon destabilize it. In reality, nationalism in Malta was entering a more mature phase where it would increasingly have to cope with diversity of expression.

While some Maltese expressed their nationalism politically through support of political parties, perhaps pro-Italian or pro-English, others drew closer to their religion and deepened their support of Catholicism. In an effort to prove Malta's European credentials impeccable, some Maltese scholars even relied on forged documents (Luttrell 1977: 105–132). As expressions of nationalism multiplied, there hardly existed any segment of society that did not become engaged in the surge.

In 1882, for example, the British Crown responded to complaints of Maltese nobles by instituting a Committee of Privileges of the Maltese Nobility to decide succession to various titles. Struggling for wider recognition of their titles, many nobles argued that their coats of arms proved they were not related to Arabs since Arabs had no tradition of heraldry. Elected president of the Committee of Privileges of the Maltese Nobility in 1887 was none other than the nationalistic Gerald Strickland (Smith and Koster 1984: 85).

Given all the various ways that nationalism could express itself, Strickland found no contradiction three years later when he married into the highest rungs of English society. In a sense, his fashionable late Victorian marriage which drew a "score of Sackvilles, Cochranes, Drummonds and their relatives" as well as "a score of Maltese nobility" (Smith and Koster 1984: 93) was fully compatible with nationalist assertion.

Meanwhile at the other margin of society, more working-class Maltese shipped off to Australia and struggled with nationalist pride to establish themselves as "white" European laborers worthy of the salaries paid to laborers from the north of Europe. And closer to home, other Maltese continued the established pattern of making their way back and forth from Africa and the Levant, searching for a better life, and periodically fleeing various uprisings and plagues. In fact, there was an increase in numbers going to Tunisia and Libya from the mid-1870s because of the lifting of the Ottoman ban on Christian ownership of real estate in those countries. The French takeover of Tunisia in 1881 added to this attraction. Despite the fact that by this time the standard of living in Malta was rising above living standards in predominantly Arabic-speaking parts of the Mediterranean (Price 1954: 133–134, 191), unlike nearby African neighbors, Malta was land-starved.

The convergence of many domestic and international factors put Maltese national consciousness in a state of flux by the last decades of the nineteenth century. The ability to use English had become a requirement for employment in the civil service, and already by 1874, 90% of civil service positions were held by Maltese (Denny 1987: 339). This situation was quite in contrast to that prevailing in most other British colonies in large measure due to Malta's long established university and cosmopolitan elite. Other Maltese were beginning to develop a working facility in English for business purposes. As Maltese society was highly complex at the same time, the unlettered masses leaned heavily on their parish priests and a small literate elite for patronage and for information about their place in the world.

Even in the early twentieth century, nationalist expression through participation in political elections had less meaning for the masses than did

the unswerving support that they gave their church. In 1903 so many disputes involving competing expressions of nationalism were swirling around
language and education that authorities restored the old 1849 constitution—a constitution which allowed for only a minority of elected members.
It was this minority constitution that was still in effect at the outbreak of
World War I when some 20,000 Maltese joined the military to fight for
the Empire. One consequence of this participation was that the war greatly
increased the numbers of Maltese with a working knowledge of English.

In the build-up to World War I when both France and Britain were much
involved in trying to accommodate Italy's expansionist nationalism, the
impact was also apparent to Malta's south. For example, the Franco-Italian
agreement of 1900 that ratified the 1881 French incursion into Tunisia also
gave a green light for Italian incursion into Libya. The Sanusi revolt against
the French—erupting in southern Tunisia in late 1915 before spreading into
Algeria and Niger—foreshadowed many nationalist struggles that would
shortly take root either close to Malta or elsewhere in the far-flung British
Empire of which Malta was a part.

In the course of its evolution, global imperialism became associated with
certain quaint ethnocentric and racist ideas such as "the white man's burden" and "a civilizing mission" that were used as justifying rationales.
When imperialism was at its peak, so was "racist" opposition directed
against Irish immigrating into England. Like Ireland, Malta was a predominantly European and Catholic colony whose nationalists had always taken
strong exception to the contradictions and arrogance inherent in much imperialist rhetoric at the same time that they were aware of each other's
struggle (Frendo 1992: 82). That Malta's traditional ties with her Arabic-
speaking neighbors were undergoing some reassessment seems indicated by
the fact that there was so little interest in studying Arabic at Malta's Lyceum by 1913 that it was discontinued there as a course offering (Camilleri
1977: 171).

Despite a wall of opposition in the British House of Lords, a home rule
bill for colonial Ireland eventually became law in 1914. Although it was
agreed that Irish home rule would be postponed until after World War I,
this legal advance in Irish self-government, no less than the Easter Rebellion
against the British that broke out in 1916, made a big impact on the Maltese. The execution of many of the rebellion's leaders by the British, in fact,
greatly increased support among the Irish Catholic majority for Sinn Fein—
a nationalist party that had been founded in 1905. Though British crushed
the rebellion in a week's time, Sinn Fein defiantly declared itself in favor
of an Irish republic the following year.

With the collapse of Ottoman Turkey at the war's end, U.S. President
Wilson issued his fourteen points stressing that self-determination should
be a right of all people. Though Wilson primary had in mind self-
determination for certain European peoples, Saad Zaghlul and three other

Egyptian nationalists found themselves deported to Malta in 1919 for having dared ask the British high commissioner for independence. As nationalist struggles continued to spread through the Mediterranean and in the larger world, four Maltese lost their lives when troops fired on unarmed demonstrators in Valletta (Blouet 1967: 193). In 1920, Tunisian nationalists founded the Destour (or Constitution) Party to pursue independence, and Abdelkrim began an anticolonialist rebellion in the Rif Mountains of northern Morocco.

When in January of the following year the British granted autonomy to India—the largest colony of the Empire—the tide was beginning to turn. Four months later, nationalist protests against the British erupted in Alexandria. And in December of 1921, a treaty was signed between the British and the Irish that would establish the Irish Free State as a "quasi-independent" British dominion the following year. It was in this context of both regional and global nationalist struggle that Malta achieved autonomy under a new constitution in 1921, the first, in fact, that would grant Malta truly responsible government in the area of domestic affairs (Smith and Koster 1986: 388).

While recognizing Italian and English as official languages, Malta's new constitution prohibited any legislation or administration policies that would diminish or detract from the position of English or reduce its use in education or the civil service. Perhaps as a quid pro quo that the British hoped would calm a Maltese elite, including many who still preferred the use of Italian over English, election to the Senate was limited to the landed, the professional, merchant classes, and the clergy. In providing for such an elitist upper house, the constitution of 1921 was actually rather conservative.

Mussolini, in a virtual civil war with the communists, had been pressing for Italy to declare a protectorate over Albania since 1921. When in 1922 he ascended to power as a fascist leader and intensified the Italian war of colonial conquest against Libya, some Italian settlers in Malta were caught up in fascist exuberance (Frendo 1992: 85), and Libya immediately became less inviting for Maltese settlers. As Italy's colonial war to conquer Libya was unfolding only a year after Malta's constitution of 1921 made Italian one of the country's two official languages, this clouded the status of Maltese in Libya. Moreover, this colonial war involving two of Malta's closest neighbors became a complicating development for Maltese nationalists at home. While some Maltese were so pro-Italian as to dream of becoming part of a greater Italy, others probably identified with the victims of Mussolini's aggression.

Important common threads ran through the various nationalist struggles that were occurring in the southern and eastern sectors of the Mediterranean, including Malta. As growing nationalism in predominantly Arab and Berber areas became increasingly anti-European and anti-Christian, it complicated matters for Malta, a country long accustomed to exporting redundant populations to these areas. Though still colonized at home, the Maltese assertion of a national identity as European Christians forced them into a double bind of being identified with the very European colonialists viewed as oppressors in countries such as Algeria, Tunisia, and Libya.

Despite some parallelism between nationalism in the Arab-speaking countries of Maghreb and in Malta, upsurges in the former reduced economic incentives and increased personal risks for Maltese settlers. When in 1922, Great Britain rather disingenuously declared her protectorate over Egypt ended, this also made Egypt less inviting as a destination for "European" and "Christian" Maltese settlers. For similar reasons, the founding of the nationalist party known as *Etoile Nord-Africaine* in Algeria around 1923, like the Druse uprising in Lebanon and Syria in 1925, was both an inspiration and a threat to Maltese nationalist aspirations.

Against this background, large numbers of Maltese began migrating to new areas in the world that they thought would be more inviting. As the closeness between Maltese and Arabic was an important factor in enticing Maltese settlers to Northern Africa and the Levant in the nineteenth century, the gradual development of Maltese facility in English helped lure settlers to English-speaking societies after World War I. In addition to Australia, which proved especially popular, large numbers of Maltese migrated to Canada, Great Britain, and the United States.

Even as changes occurred in the destinations to which Maltese were emigrating, nationalists with contrasting views of who they really were and how they should relate to the larger world continued to quarrel with each other over the so-called language question. In the course of this dialogue language evolved into a symbol of status, not only for individuals but for the nation. Many Maltese were concerned about how language would impact Malta's perceived affiliation with the larger world, including Great Britain.

Not only had the constitution of 1921 not brought closure to much conflict in the area of linguistic nationalism, it had also left unsolved what, if any, role the Maltese language should have in national identity. It was this unsettled matter of how Maltese would factor into the language question that in 1923 helped, at least indirectly, to ignite a conflict of major proportions between church and state.

A 1923 bill supported by the Nationalist Party and the church providing that both English and Italian should be compulsory subjects was attacked by Gerald Strickland, owner of a major newspaper and prominent leader in the Constitutional Party. Perhaps the exact issues pale in comparison to the fact that strong personalities with solid nationalist commitments became arrayed against each other. As the dueling unfolded, opportunities for compromise disappeared in a war pursued as if between the sacred and profane. The fact that all participants had strong nationalist credentials receded to the background of public consciousness.

Strickland, elected prime minister in 1927, became a lightening rod for insulting accusations of improper conduct by his opponents. In some cases, members of his Constitutional Party and even some church officials circulated unsubstantiated rumors that he was a Freemason, and hence, anti-Catholic (Smith and Koster 1986: 420–421). Further complicating the situation, "anti-reformists" (who were pro-Italian) eventually became aligned with the Nationalist Party and church hierarchy against Strickland while "reformists" (who were pro-English) were more inclined to support him.

Though the British were not interested in a radical restructuring of Maltese society, simply maintaining the peace required them eventually to propose to the Vatican on several occasions between 1920 and 1930 the idea of agreeing to a concordat that would establish greater separation between church and state. The British hoped for a concordat with the Vatican that would forbid clergy from openly taking sides in general elections and holding seats in the legislature. The Vatican made clear to British authorities, however, that as long as Strickland remained in power, no concordat would be possible. A consequence of this position was that representatives of the church continued to participate in government during most of the next two decades, and not without controversy.

A tug of war involving governance in Malta continued, with Strickland and his supporters on one side and Mizzi—an anti-reformist with considerable support from important elements within the church—on the other. This clash between conflicting nationalist visions seemed to reach a head in May 1930 when the Bishops of Malta and Gozo issued a joint pastoral formally forbidding Catholics from voting for Strickland or any of his supporters on pain of committing a mortal sin.

So at odds were the combatants that some of Strickland's supporters were denied the sacrament of penance, and on one occasion, Lady Strickland's routine request for an Easter blessing of the Strickland home was declined (Smith and Koster 1986: 472). The Bishops even reimposed their religious bans of 1930 shortly before the elections of 1932. Meanwhile, the Constitutional and the Labor Parties campaigned for enhancing the position of English while members of the Nationalist Party claimed to support the use of English and Italian on a more or less equal footing.

As various Maltese partisans openly feuded with each other under the guise of working for the national good, they often seemed more opposed to each other than to their imperialist British overlords. In fact, by 1933, the British even suspended the constitution and declared a state of emergency. During the six-year period that the suspension remained in force, Maltese were without any elected participation in government.

This suspension of the constitution, added to the Strickland situation, caused a deterioration in relations between Britain and the Vatican (Smith and Koster 1986: 493–497) that coincided with British concern about Mussolini's growing appetite for empire-building. In addition to Malta's location just south of Sicily, large numbers of Italian colonists were also present just south of Malta in Tunisia and Libya. Italian expansionism, moreover, was threatening stability in the Horn of East Africa adjacent to the sea lanes through the Suez Canal and Red Sea on which Britain was heavily dependent. When in 1935, Mussolini thumbed his nose at the League of Nations and moved beyond Italian holdings in Somalia and Eritrea to launch a full-scale war of conquest against Ethiopia, British concerns increased about the vulnerability of Malta.

These concerns rested both on what was happening internationally and the considerable pro-Italian sentiment in Malta. Viewing the language question in Malta solely from a domestic perspective, some argue that the "British eventually supported and promoted the official use of Maltese as a way of counteracting the political forces of nationalism, which oddly enough, argued for the continued use of Italian as the language of the courts and government" (Orr 1992: 145). Quite apart from the complex factors—domestic and international—that motivated the British to begin supporting the use of Maltese over Italian, Maltese had been emerging in the background as a galvanizing force in indigenous nationalism for some time.

Some grammars and unpublished dictionaries of Maltese had appeared as early as the eighteenth century, including most notably a dictionary written in four manuscript volumes by Agius De Soldanis. Building on the work of De Soldanis, a few decades later Mikiel Anton Vassalli compiled the first dictionary of Maltese to be published. While serving as the first head of the National Library, he encouraged his compatriots to think about the importance of Maltese literary tradition in a nationalistic way.

While a tradition of romanticism in Maltese literature dating from the late 1800s contributed to nationalistic thinking, some discontent around its association with Africa and Asia and problems of rendering it in Roman rather than Arabic letters raised some interesting challenges. After years of using Roman letters to transcribe Maltese, a method proposed by an association of Maltese writers in 1921 began to win wide acceptance (Frendo 1992: 81; Vanhove 1994: 168).

Though even before he became prime minister in 1927, Sir Gerald Strickland was among those who supported the teaching of Maltese along with English, his confrontation with the church did little to advance its acceptance. The national conversation about identity and language took a new turn in 1934 when Maltese was added to Italian and English as an official language; in fact, it was even made the principal language of the courts (Blouet 1967: 196).

With the removal of official status from Italian two years later, Malta's official languages were reduced to two, Maltese and English (Blouet 1967:

196). That the language continued to be a destabilizing issue in Malta even after Italian lost its official status demonstrates that the so-called language question was as much about identity, status, and completing national visions as about language per se. In fact, the official status granted to Maltese was initially viewed by a segment of the Maltese elite as shameful. Some considered it a kind of "*zalza Russa*" or "Russian sauce" (Galley 1994: 46, 51) while others considered it merely "*il volgare*" or "the kitchen language" (Mayo 1994: 32).

"Italian was still the official language of the Curia [i.e., the administrative headquarters of the diocese] in 1936 when in Appendix VI of the *Concilium Regionale Malitense*, Maltese priests were instructed to draw up their annual reports and submit them to their Ordinary in the Italian language" (Aquilina 1970c: 63). Many *Nazionalisti*, or Nationalists, were really elitist Italianites who remained as much unreconciled to the official use of Maltese as of English. Some of them long continued to attend spiritual exercises conducted in Italian, in the words of one Gozitan school teacher, "as though they had a special soul" (Galley 1994: 51).

By 1939, the outbreak of World War II was imminent and Great Britain found extreme pro-Italian sympathies on the parts of some politicians in Malta unsettling. Shortly after Germany's attack on Poland made the war a reality, Britain detained some Italian sympathizers in Malta while deporting about 40 others to Uganda in British East Africa (Farrugia 1995: 49–76). Because of British distrust of indigenous nationalism and the uncertainty of the times, the new constitution that took effect in 1939 failed to provide for an elected Maltese majority. As nationalists considered this an affront to the popular will, Britain promised them a constitution granting autonomy at the war's end.

The chance of Italian ever regaining its status as an official language in Malta was effectively ended on June 11, 1940, the day after Italy declared war on England and Italian bombs began falling in the Islands. In the wake of the war, Guze Cassar-Pullicino—on Gozitan soil—began to urge the preservation of traditional aspects of Maltese culture, including the folklore and language (Galley 1994: 213). Rather in the spirit of Mikiel Anton Vassalli and numerous other scholars, he recognized Maltese as a language of dignity and urged its wider use in government and education. At the same time that Maltese was becoming more esteemed, the use of English also was becoming more widespread.

The almost continuous coming and going of foreign military personnel during the World War II exposed the populace to much English and greatly endeared many people to Great Britain as a mother country. This was reinforced by the existence in Malta of growing numbers of British residents, many living side by side with Maltese families in localities such as Sliema and St. Julian's. By the mid-1950s—in what seemed on the surface an about-face for indigenous nationalism—British influence had spread so profusely that some Maltese entertained thoughts of permanent political integration with the mother country.

Though an anglophile element had existed in Maltese nationalism for decades, its mushrooming after the war was still remarkable for several reasons. First, the Maltese had begun to show unprecedented interest in identifying with their own language and paying homage to their own folk-lore. It was also remarkable given the fact that the early postwar years brought independence to such Mediterranean countries as Syria, Lebanon, Jordan, and Israel, and also to India and Pakistan, the Empire's largest colonies.

So vastly different were competing nationalist visions of what the political future should look like that in 1950 the British had dissolved Malta's Parliament for a short time simply to maintain the peace. On the one side, the Nationalist Party, having failed to bring Malta into a closer association with Italy prior to the war, supported independence. On the other hand, the Labor Party supported integrating Malta with Great Britain, somewhat in the manner of Northern Ireland.

Responding to the interest of many Maltese in integration, British Prime Minister Anthony Eden convened the 1955 Round Table Conference on the political future of Malta. The Round Table reached a quick consensus to offer Malta association with Britain, including representation in the British Parliament if it wished. That the option to integrate with Britain in-augurated a period of considerable conflict in Malta was evidence of the complexity, strength, and viability of Maltese nationalism.

While contrasting positions on integration with Britain separated Malta's major two parties, contrasting nationalist visions of Malta's future also separated Monsignor Michael Gonzi, the Archbishop, and Dom Mintoff, head of the Labor Party. When in 1955 the Labor Party defeated the Na-tionalists, conflict between them rose to the surface rather explosively.

On the one side was Monsignor Gonzi, who had helped to found the Labor Party in the early 1920s, who as Bishop of Gozo in 1942 persuaded Gozitan farmers to send grain to nearly starved and war-ravaged Malta. This hero had been elevated to Bishop of Malta in 1943 and he became the first Archbishop of the Metropolitan of Malta a year later. On the other side was Dom Mintoff, then head of the very Labor Party that Gonzi had helped to found. On becoming prime minister in 1955, Mintoff, believing the realms of the church and state should be separate, refused to pay a call on the Archbishop in keeping with long tradition. Gonzi interpreted his decision as anticlerical.

The more Mintoff attempted to move Malta toward integration with Britain, the more the church hierarchy opposed it. So hostile toward each other did the church and the Labor Party become that on the eve of the 1956 referendum by Mintoff's government to link Malta more closely with Britain, Monsignor Gonzi made a broadcast appealing to voters to disapprove it. While the reason that the Archbishop cited for intervening was that the position of the Roman Catholic religion had not been sufficiently guaranteed, there was little doubt that the personal disdain between him and Mintoff was also a contributing factor. Another reason that this conflict was so sharply drawn was that the British had never attempted any radical restructuring of church and state relations in Malta.

That the referendum result was indecisive and had doomed Labor's plan for integration left bitter feelings between the opposing sides. In fact, shortly before Mintoff resigned from office in 1958, he became embroiled in a major conflict with the local church—this time about whether Malta's most treasured works of art, two paintings by the famous Caravaggio, should be transferred from the Co-Cathedral of St. John and St. Paul to Malta's National Museum. At its root, this conflict was about more than two national art treasures. It pitted a nationalistic elected government against a church that considered itself to have equal claim to protect the national heritage and both of which were concerned with territoriality.

In addition to conflict about the apportionment of church and state responsibility for the safekeeping of two national art treasures, this conflict was related to a dispute that had been simmering between church and state for more than 150 years concerning which of them had legally inherited from the Knights of Malta the custodianship of the Order's Conventual Church (Buhagiar 1991: 359–374). On orders from the Holy See, Mintoff eventually returned the paintings to the Co-Cathedral on the night before his 1958 resignation—a resignation that came about because he was unable to reach terms with Britain that he considered sufficiently protective of Malta's national interest.

The Labor Party—under Mintoff—led the Maltese to the brink of choosing a future that would have emphasized Malta's connections with Great Britain over those with the Mediterranean. However his fervent nationalism, coupled with the unsettled issue within Maltese nationalism of how the church and state should interface in the latter part of the twentieth century, caused Malta to draw back. With respect to Britain, Malta's national interests proved stronger than partisan inclinations. Therefore, as soon as the Labor Party resigned the government, it joined with the Nationalist Party in declaring itself in favor of independence.

Though the NATO and British military "run-down" that followed sharply reduced the number of foreign military personnel stationed in the islands, cultural continuity was apparent in the substantial increase in the number of British tourists and retired settlers drawn to Malta. Cultural continuity was apparent in the fact the church and state retained ownership of much of the arable land. Cultural continuity also was apparent in certain contests between church and state to be preeminent representative of the nation.

When, due to conflict among nationalists that was continuing in 1959, colonial authorities withdrew Malta's constitution leaving all power in the hands of the British governor assisted only by Maltese advisors, government in the Islands become a real anachronism. Libya, Tunisia, and Morocco had become independent and a 1956 international crisis over the Suez Canal had established that Egypt was sovereign over all its territory, including the Canal Zone. Malta's colonial status was all the more anomalous because an upsurge in foreign influences had sharpened national awareness that colonial systems worldwide were being dismantled.

The Maltese were not without continuous exposure to foreign servicemen and tourists, and beginning in the early 1960s, they were able to pick up a number of Italian television stations. There was also regular access to news on BBC, on domestic television, and through rediffusion, a type of cable radio broadcasting system that was generated in-country. This was a period during which Malta was virtually bombarded with news of independence being won by nations large and small around the world. In 1960, for example, it was Cyprus and an astounding seventeen countries in Africa alone. In contrast, Malta's 1960 constitution still provided for power over defense and external affairs to be exercised concurrently with Britain.

In the elections of 1961 which were sharply contested between the Nationalist and Labor Parties, relations between the church and the Labor Party remained so openly hostile that there was considerable church intervention. On April 9, 1961, in fact, the church placed Mintoff and many of the Labor leaders under an interdict for their disrespect to the Bishop, and a few weeks later the Bishops issued a circular condemning Labor Party publications. Just six weeks before the election, the church through the Diocesan Joint Council of Catholic Lay Associations even launched a campaign among the masses to vote against Labor. While approximately two-thirds of the electorate chose to vote against Labor, about one-third did not.

With the Nationalist Party in power in 1961, Prime Minister Dr. Borg Olivier formally requested independence. While Maltese nationalism in some embryonic form is among the most ancient varieties that one encounters in the Mediterranean, due largely to its expression in overlapping secular and religious spheres, Malta was one of the last countries in the region to win independence. During the period of British colonialism, Malta's population increased from about 100,000 to 320,000, and it was able to ascend the world stage with a diversified economic base that depended largely on small industry, tourism, government service, agriculture, and rental of defense facilities. This country finally emerged as an independent royal dominion on September 24, 1964.

This political formula whereby Malta opted for royal dominion status seemed for a while to be a perfect formula that could reconcile Malta's courtly past with independent statehood in the late twentieth century and beyond. Malta gained independence at a time when the world was bitterly divided by the Cold War and there existed considerable optimism about a Third World's pursuit of nonalignment and development.

Following the lead of Great Britain, which changed its pound to a decimal currency in 1971, Malta changed to a decimal lira the following year. Despite being a micro-state with a tiny military organized in a headquarters and three regiments, Malta possessed a spirit of nationalism that led it to take a new bold step in 1974. Under the leadership of the Labor Party, the party that had once argued in favor of a permanent integration of Malta and Great Britain, it gave up its royal dominion status to become simply the Republic of Malta. Looking at Malta from without, this change merely reflected a more daring and assertive manner of being Maltese. Looking at Malta from within, this was an antielitist move intended to appeal to the mildly socialist leanings of the working class from which the Labor Party draws much of its support.

This change meant that Malta began to have its own presidents as head of state rather than governors-general who represented the British Crown. Even more significantly, no rationale any longer existed for officially recognized titles of nobility in Maltese society. In 1975, the Committee of Privileges of the Maltese Nobility, which regulated the Maltese titles, lost its legal status both in Britain and in Malta. Moreover, "Royal" was dropped from the names of many of the most prestigious institutions of Maltese society, for example, the Royal Malta Library and the Royal University of Malta. As this same spirit of postindependence nationalism began diffusing throughout society, Maltese also took over firm control of their broadcasting mass media following a 1975 sit-down strike (Chircop 1994: 361).

In 1979, Malta terminated its military facilities agreements with NATO and, in a further display of nationalism, Parliament—with a Labor majority—declared Malta a "neutral state." In 1984, nationalism took a new turn in what is often referred to as "the schools wars"—really a struggle between church and state over their relative influence in Malta's educational system (Koster 1991). By 1987, however, nationalism was once again directed beyond Malta when by a constitutional amendment, foreign forces were forbidden ever again to be stationed on Maltese territory.

Chapter 6

Ecology and Social Rhythms

How people perceive, value, and allocate time is not coincidental. These behaviors are learned according to norms having to do with adaptation that is imposed on them at many different levels. Malta offers a classical and fascinating illustration of temporal adaptation as dynamic and life sustaining. Though geography, technology, demography, religion, commerce, and government impact social rhythms in every society, the particular configuration that emerges in Malta is fascinating.

According to Halbwachs (1947), contrasting time experiences within our memory correspond to the different social groups to which we belong—hence, our consciousness of and use of "a professional time," "a family time," "a civil time," "a military time," "a visiting time," "a street time," and "a household time" among which we switch back and forth. For Halbwachs (1925, 1947), the memory of the individual depends on the social milieu around him or her just as the collective memory of a people develops out of a larger social framework. Halbwach, like Durkheim who much influenced him, had an intense interest in elementary forms implicit in the reckoning of time. In *The Elementary Forms of the Religious Life*, for example, Durkheim (1938) observed that calendars functioned to express the rhythm of collective activities while at the same time assuring their regularity. In keeping with these perspectives, Halbwachs and Durkheim believed that each people—to some extent constituting "a social species"—also had its own characteristic approach to the collective organization and externalization of time.

Moore (1963: 46) once commented on the importance of synchronization with respect to eating and sexual intercourse in human societies. With respect to the way communities internally synchronize themselves with periodic changes without, Arensberg (1955: 1147) could have been talking about Malta as well as many other places when he noted that they "alternatively show dispersal of their persons (to the fields, to the hills, by the season, by day, etc.) with assemblages of them (in sleeping quarters, in ceremonies, in communal efforts, in war)." Not all of such patterns can be explained at the level of culture alone; some of them undoubtedly have to do with adaptation to environmental cycles or periodicities. In this sense, the feedback between environmental cycles and social rhythms at different levels may be said to be ecological.

The daily fluctuation of temperature (due to the planet's axial rotation) and seasonal fluctuations of the northern and southern hemispheres (due to the planet's tilted axis and its orbit around the sun) are cycles to which every animal must adapt its behavior. It must act in one way when the temperature goes up and in another way when the temperature goes down—during day and night, during summer and winter. (Gibson 1966: 11)

As such cycles influence activity at levels from chemistry to consciousness all over the earth, they do in Malta as well. At the level of chemistry, all people are continuous with their environments to the extent that across the boundaries of their skins, they are engaged in exchanging matter and energy. Apart from the fact that solar radiation is life-maintaining through photosynthesis and the carbon dioxide cycle, diffused radiation from the sky, and especially ambient radiation, reflected from terrestrial surfaces as day alternates with night, have an important controlling effect on physiological and social rhythms through "stimulus ecology" (Gibson 1966: 13). So important are such rhythms to human beings as culture-bearers that there probably exists nowhere a human society that does not in some measure rely on them as time indications. The degree to which societies in different parts of the world have relied on the same cosmic cycles—mediated through culture—to establish both similar and contrasting social rhythms is quite phenomenal (Goodwin 1974: 64).

In much the same way as a heartbeat and pulse are vital signs indicative of life in individuals, social rhythms are indicative of life forces in collectivities of people as they adapt to each other and to numerous influences that shape their environment. Patterned social interaction requires adaptation to such environmental factors as space and time but its recurrence is especially linked to time. Maltese is a Semitic language with a considerable overlay of Italian, French, and English in its lexicon; however, it is a language where it is virtually impossible to talk about time without relying on core vocabulary that is of Semitic derivation.

Words of Semitic derivation frame the time of birth, *tfulija*, and the time of death, *mewt*, time as an occasion, *waqt*, and time as a universe, *ħin*. From Sunday, *il-ħadd* at one end of the week to Saturday, *is-sibt*, at the other, and from spring, *ir-rebbieħa*, to *ix-xitwa*, meaning winter, or at least the rainy season. In Maltese, words of Semitic derivation repeatedly reference the passage and recurrence of time. According to Aquilina (1970b: 52), "These are all Semitic except the names of the months, which we borrowed from Norman Sicily very likely after having dropped the original Arabic months. . . . [However] non-Arabic is Maltese *sena bisestili* 'leap year' from It. (anno) bisestile."

In Malta as elsewhere, there exist systemic indications of time passage which furnish points of reference for the reckoning of time and, also, constrain behavior in accordance with temporal norms. Like language itself, social rhythm functions as a highly complex system of communication. Social rhythm may be thought of as consisting of what linguist Edward T. Hall would have considered "semi-fixed features" of life, both for groups and for individuals.

In numerous Mediterranean societies, autumn is a peak time for marriages to occur, in part for reasons having to do with seasonal plenty. It is not surprising, therefore, that August through October in Malta is especially the high season for marriage. After a secondary January peak, February and March are the months when the frequency of marriage dips to its lowest level, even lower than during the wintry months of November and December. Not surprising, April is extremely unpredictable for marriage, depending on when Lent occurs in a particular year. Nowhere in the Universal Church are Catholics permitted to get married during Lenten season without a special dispensation.

To the extent that death presents the living with circumstances to which they must adapt, it too affects social rhythms. For example, the high season for deaths in Malta is December through April with January the month when they usually peak. Similarly, September is generally the month when the fewest deaths occur. While September has the fewest deaths and the most marriages, the fact that January is a month associated with both a high frequency of marriages and deaths indicates, however, that a number of variables—some of which have yet to be identified—mediate these complex rhythmic patterns.

Among the most elemental indications of time passage and determinants of time-allocation are those imposed ecologically as social life is attuned with a continually changing environment. Climatic conditions in the Mediterranean have affinities both with a temperate zone to the north, where seasons owe their character largely to change in temperature, and with the tropical zone to the south, where they owe their character largely to rain. In contrast to more northerly parts of the Mediterranean Basin where there are essentially four climatic seasons and most rain falls in spring and autumn with a winter break that is less marked than that of summer, Malta's climate is somewhat more tropical. In other words, it is more like that of the southern Mediterranean where there are essentially two seasons.

In Malta as in Sicily, Crete, coastal Syria, and along the coasts of Algeria, Tunisia, and Libya, these two seasons consist of dry, hot summers and mild, wet winters. Though the winters are accented by enough coolness to slow the growing of plants, the seasonal variation in temperature is less important than is variability in precipitation. There average less than 100 days per year when rain exceeds 0.1mm, though there can be significant variation around this average from one year to another. The aridity of the summers, therefore, can be particularly limiting for food production, and only about 1.5% of Malta's annual rainfall comes in June, July, and August. On rare occasions, even a winter has been a period of virtual drought. Not only can rainwater not be taken for granted; Malta is one of the world's few countries without extant rivers.

By a 1582 bull, Pope Gregory XIII altered the Julian calendar to produce the Gregorian calendar where the year begins on the first day of January. This calendar is used in Malta as in most other parts of the world today very frequently to reckon the annual passage of time. Malta's "rainfall year," however, is reckoned differently. It ends in late August and begins in September.

The Maltese dwell in a world where the elements play important roles in framing the conditions of life but where these conditions are widely perceived as mediated by various saints, sometimes in ways that are serious and sometimes in ways that are light-hearted. For example, since Maltese statues of St. Bartholomew usually show him holding keys and his feast day on August 24 occurs about the time when the rainy season begins, Maltese proverbially say "*San Bartilmew għandu l-muftieħ tax-xita*" (meaning, "St. Bartholomew has got the keys to the rainy season").

Over two-thirds of Malta's rain falls from October through March, with about half of the total falling in November, December, and January alone. It follows that the Maltese summer and winter are quite pronounced. It is unfortunate for farming that most rainfall comes in winter when plants grow slowest due to a significant drop in temperature, and some like tomatoes that are sensitive to cold are not likely to survive. The character of "wet" and "dry" years and seasons, however, is determined by a variety of factors in addition to rain. As documented by Bowen-Jones et al. (1961: 52–74), these factors include spring winds, torrential storms accompanied by rapid run-off, the rate of percolation, the rate of subsurface drainage, and soil-moisture conditions, all of which affect transpiration.

Where Malta is located, wintry conditions are not only likely to be rainy but also windy. Since ancient times, these wintry conditions have been hazardous enough to slow shipping considerably (Bradford 1971: 26–27). Winds are extremely important in Malta year-round, and fewer than one day out of ten is likely to be calm. Seasonal winds are given names that also signify the various directions from which they blow. These winds, which both influence and are influenced by the seasons, constitute a kind of space-time grid that is nonrandom and that impacts social life in important ways.

The *majjistral* wind is by far the most common as it blows almost one day out of three from the northwest. It is cold in winter and cool in summer and is commonly associated with clear skies. After this wind, those from the northeast, southeast, southwest, and west are the next most frequent. The northeast wind, which the Maltese know as the *grigal*, or Greek wind, can arrive with gale force and can sometimes be quite bothersome both to shipping and farming. In the rainy months of winter, it can often be especially dangerous. Since ancient times, wintry conditions associated with the *grigal* wind, often seeming to intensify in cycles of approximately three days, have been sufficiently hazardous to slow shipping in much of the Mediterranean.

Soon after the *grigal* begins to subside around March, a wind that many Mediterranean peoples refer to as the *ħamsin* begins to blow up from the Sahara. It typically arrives around the time of Pentecost—which is 50 days before Easter—and extends into *nofs-in-nhar*, the most frequent spring and summer winds blowing through the islands. Blowing sand from the Sahara, the *ħamsin* can partially mask the sun, make the atmosphere parch, and complicate housekeeping considerably.

Though the *xlokk*, or scirocco, is a southeast wind that can arrive in summer, it is associated with autumn. As it arrives with some of Africa's moistness, it can sometimes cause automobiles to be slow in starting and freshly whitewashed walls to be slow in drying. People sometimes complain about the mugginess associated with it. Least common are winds that blow into Malta from due south, due east, and directly from the north. The myriad social and psychological ways that these winds affect people are sometimes referenced in proverbs, adages, and folk sayings, cross-referenced, of course, by the feast days of the saints that occur more or less concurrently, as in the case of St. Bartholomew. The following examples are based on Aquilina (1972: 510–589).

Fital-Vitorja, il-baħar jitla' fl-għolja [meaning that on the day of Our Lady of Victory (September 8), the seas rise high, that is, begin to be rough].

Nhar San Mar ix-xita nar fl-art [meaning that it is so hot on St. Mark's Day (April 25) that rain is like fire].

Il-lvant jimla l-vagant [meaning the east wind brings clouds].

Riħ il-Ibiċ jiehu w ma jġib [meaning the southwest wind easily takes boats out to sea but makes it difficult for them to return to harbor].

February is especially associated with wind and December with rain. Many people find even a little drizzle inconvenient for their going out and tend to curtail optional activities when it rains. As early as late August and the first part of September when it is likely to be only damp, this slowing down of social activity may be observed. On the other hand, the two periods referred to as *mezzu-temp* are, for general purposes, considered to be especially pleasant because the weather is not too hot and not too wet. One may include October and a bit of November and the other perhaps April and May. Considered a favorite month by many people, May is a time when social rhythms begin to quicken considerably.

Faced with the challenges of working with extremely thin soils that are only about eight inches to two feet deep and rainwater which is scarce and most concentrated in winter when conditions are also quite windy, farmers have to be very ingenious and time-conscious in their plant management. With only slight variation, they continue to organize planting to fit one of the three temporal patterns that Bowen-Jones et al. (1961: 52–74) pointed out several decades ago.

According to one of these patterns, rain-fed crops are planted before the onset of the autumn rains and watered artificially until adequate moisture is available, or alternatively, are sown mid-way through the rainy reason when soil moisture is maximal. According to a second pattern, crops dependent on soil moisture are planted late in the rainy season when rainfall alone is not adequate for their support. These crops are likely to be planted on fallow land which has been repeatedly worked during the winter, and most of these crops are likely to need watering after two or three months. According to a third pattern involving irrigated land, three crops a year can often be raised.

Deep plowing is not an annual occurrence, and along with major laying in of manure it is likely to be carried out only about every four years at the height of the summer (Bowen-Jones et al. 1961: 52–74). As soils are so extremely thin in these islands and are a precious resource, plowing is usually shallow so as not to cause damage. It is least risky when the rains have weakened the hard surface of the soils but when they are still not extremely wet. One favorite time for such plowing and for sowing is a summer-like November dry spell that often occurs around the feast day of St. Martin.

In contrast to crops such as carrots, beets, and leaf lettuce which farmers are involved in planting and harvesting throughout the year, other crops are raised in seasonal cycles. The period April through August is important for planting tomatoes, September and October for winter potatoes, September through March is important for planting head lettuce, November through January for wheat, January for strawberries, and so on. Cooks across Malta are conscious of harvest cycles that determine when items appear in the markets and how prices are likely to soar and fall as crops rise and decline in abundance. The harvesting of grapes that later will be pressed for wine is associated with celebration in many parts of the Mediterranean. Grape harvesting in Malta lasts about three weeks, usually beginning in September, in other words, at the time when the last of the peaches and plums are being gathered. Farmers often need extra labor during this period, for in addition to harvesting grapes, autumn tillage is undertaken.

A farmer knows that he should try to harvest his grain by *Imnarja* (the feast day of St. Peter and St. Paul on June 29), that he should harvest his clover by the feast of St. Andrew on November 30, and that the best winter potato harvest is one that is in the sacks by the feast day of St. Nicholas in early December, although they will be available in the fields until mid-February. A tenant farmer always keeps in mind that land rents should be paid by Christmas, or at least by Santa Maria. Likewise, an experienced consumer knows that the price of eggs is likely to increase around *Imnarja* and that milk is likely to be scarce around the day of Our Lady of Victories.

Though the exchange between producer and consumer is sometimes quite direct, farmers also sell their crops in large qualities at huge government regulated produce exchanges that operate largely in the open air. On Malta, there are several such *pikalis*, including at Rabat, Birkirkara, and Marsa. Whereas the one at Rabat has rather restricted hours from around noon to 3:00 P.M., the others operate from around 4:30 A.M. to 8:00 A.M. Getting the produce to a *pikali* at optimal times is as important to a farmer as plant management. The particular *pikali* that a particular farmer goes to, the number he visits, the amount of produce he sells to each, and the hour at which he visits is all part of his sales strategy to maximize profits while economizing time.

As farmers of crops sell in bulk to a *pikali*, dairy farmers—now concentrated largely on Gozo—sell their milk to the government-regulated Milk Marketing Undertaking. Long gone are the days before the World War II when herds of goats were escorted through the streets by shepherds to dispense milk directly to consumers door-to-door, as this practice sometimes spread Malta fever or brucellosis. Moreover, since the war, there has taken place a shift in livestock emphasis from goats to sheep and eventually to dairy cows.

That herding must have in remote times played a crucial role in the founding of villages seems indicated by the fact that the Maltese word for village is derived from *raħal*—referring to a herder rather than a farmer. Malta's small territory with the intensive cultivation of available land was obviously more compatible with sedentary than nomadic pastoralism. A significant amount of the food that feeds her livestock has long come from ħaxix ħarzin—that is, weed grasses pulled from rubble walls and terraces. However, dairy farmers supplement these meager resources by allowing their herds to forage in fields that are fallow as well as by stall-feeding.

In contrast to the life of a farmer, which is greatly impacted by seasonality, that of the herder is ordered by much constancy. Even during festive seasons and on holidays, livestock must be attended. The daily demands on the time of the livestock farmer are fixed primarily by the need to keep animals healthy. This requires regularity in their feeding times, milking times, and the times when he expects his milk to be collected for sale to Milk Marketing Undertaking.

Though in some cases, a livestock farmer begins the day's work as early as 1:00 A.M., a starting time of 2:00 or 3:00 A.M. is more usual. This means that he and his family are often at work two or three hours before a family that raises crops. During some seasons of the year when it is not possible to harvest certain grains in the bright heat of the sun, however, his workday starts earlier, shifting somewhat in the direction of that of the dairy farmer (Goodwin 1974: 94).

The sea around Malta is considerably saltier than the Atlantic Ocean and historically it has been more important for trading than as a source of food. In fact, the Mediterranean countries that tend to be most successful in fishing are those that also border the Atlantic Ocean, from which they capture much of their seafood. The three areas of the Mediterranean with the widest variety of fish are the Bosporus, the Messina Strait, and the Strait of Gibraltar (Bradford 1971: 48). Relatively few large Mediterranean cities rely on fishing as the major work that sustains their residents.

Only Marsaxlokk, Żurrieq, and St. Paul's Bay are sizeable Maltese fishing towns, not one of which was large enough to have parish status in ancient times. Still, fishing contributes in important ways to Malta's rhythm of social and economic life. Local fishermen do not catch enough fish overall to satisfy the Maltese market; ironically this attracts more focus to the periodic nature of their work.

Tiny sardines and anchovies are plentiful in Maltese waters, but of greater seasonal importance is the small red tunny-fish, which spawns in a rather restricted area between Tunisia, Sardinia, Malta, and Sicily in June. After spawning, the larger tunny-fish go into the Atlantic while the others scatter close to the coasts of the Balkans and the western Mediterranean. Fishing for tunny sometimes continues even into winter (Birot and Dresch 1953: 37, 40; Bradford 1971: 43–45).

Catching, cooking, and consuming fish and other delicacies of the sea are activities that bring people together, not only across dinner tables but in boats, in marketplaces, and elsewhere. For fishermen, seasonality is defined not only by the elements and the availability of certain types of seafood, it is also defined by methods of work and the economic rewards of work, which vary from season to season. To some extent, seasonality for fishermen also revolves around various types of ceremony associated with what they catch.

Wilhelmsen (1976: 419–423) has documented at least three different ways that fisherman may identify seasons. One has to do with the name of the most important fish being sought at a particular time, for example, the dorado or *lampuka* season. Another has to do with the availability of a number of species that are sought during a particular period using a particular type of equipment. A third method has to do with the type of gear that is used per se, for example, the *lampara* season. These seasons do not have exact dates and can differ from fisherman to fisherman depending on what his objectives are at a particular time.

Given wintry rains and winds, relatively few fishing boats put out to sea from December to March although it is possible to catch certain bottom species at this time. When post-winter stability in weather conditions is established, attention turns especially to the swordfish season and to the *lampara* or light season. Apart from fishing for *lampuka*, these two types of fishing bring the highest economic rewards (Wilhelmsen 1976: 417).

Each type of fishing requires it own equipment and team of fishermen. The catching of swordfish requires a large boat of the *luzzu* variety, a crew of about three to eight men, and huge nets that drag the bottom of the sea, though lines are sometimes used. While the swordfish season continues from early April to mid-August, June is considered the most important month for catching swordfish. Despite its continued availability, after Santa Marija—on August 15—it is not much sought.

The *lampara* season—extending from early April to early September—is longer than the swordfish season and is usually of greater interest to fishermen. The season gets it name not from the types of fishes that are caught but from the method of deep-water nocturnal fishing with artificial light that is used. This requires fishermen to work in large boats with big nets and with crews of around 14 men.

What brings *lampara* season to an end is the beginning of the much more lucrative dorado or *lampuka* season. Of all fishing seasons in Malta, the *lampuka* season is the most celebrated. The seasonal opportunity to eat *lampuka* is surrounded by a feeling of ceremony and the baking of *lampuka*, encased in short crust in the form of pies, spreads excitement throughout the islands. Beginning around Santa Marija when the *lampuka* are beginning to reach a good size, this season is by far the busiest and most frantic. While a few free spirits fish for *lampuka* anywhere they wish with a line, most of the activity centers about professional fishermen working together in large crews within areas that have been allotted to them by the Ministry of Trade, Industry and Agriculture for a single year.

Fishing crews are larger during *lampuka* season than in any other. In many cases, the extra crewmen are government workers on a shortened workday schedule who, other than in summer, might be sitting behind desks or engaged outdoors at technical or unskilled jobs. Fishermen searching for *lampuka* are equipped with nets and floats.

When the weather is good, these fishermen prefer to carry their boats out in the morning between around 3:00 and 10:00 A.M., but when morning weather is bad they sometimes venture out well into the afternoon. Whereas smaller boats generally return to harbor on the same day at about midnight or shortly thereafter, larger ones often stay at sea for two or three days with crew members resting only a few hours per day.

The unusual cultural importance of this season is underscored by the fact that fishermen often work on Sundays, during festive periods, and even neglect attending Sunday Mass. It is also underscored in the saying "*knonz ta' Settembru jagħmel bil-gziez; konz ta' Dicembru wisq bil-qies*"—meaning that while a September fishing line catches heaps, a December line catches little. While in St. Paul's Bay this season ends with the *biċ* blowing in from the southwest, it only ends in Marsaxlokk when the *majjistral* makes the seas rough. Due in part to the relative lack of tides on this inland body of water, the winds that blow have a more pronounced effect than would be the case on an ocean (Bradford 1971: 37).

Environment, the elements, and culture join forces in numerous ways that impact how farmers, herders, and fishermen organize many of their activities and in this complex process play important roles in temporally integrating Maltese society in general. So numerous are the behavioral loops and feedback mechanisms involved that one can often know the season of the year, the day of the week, and the hour of the day by simply observing patterns of synchronized behavior in a particular location. It is a type of knowledge, moreover, in which temperature, humidity, sounds, and even smells play a part, regardless of whether one is indoors or on a public thoroughfare.

Some patterns in social rhythm can persist over many decades as systematic observations in the towns of Floriana, Senglea, and Siġġiewi stretching over several decades make clear. In all these three towns, for example, pedestrian mobility is bimodal with peak hours of movement occurring between 9:00–10:00 A.M. and 9:00–10:00 P.M. with greater evening than morning mobility both with respect to vehicles and pedestrians. In extraordinarily dense Senglea, where residents do not rely on private vehicles to the same degree as in the other two towns, no build-up of automobile traffic occurs between 7:00 and 8:00 A.M. While in part this difference is related to more limited space for parking in Senglea, it is also related to more limited purchasing power in a town that has become overwhelmingly working class as well as a tendency by residents to work closer to where they live.

While a definite siesta lull is characteristic of social rhythm across the islands, some local variation exists as is evident in these three towns. The siesta lull is most pronounced and occurs most abruptly in Floriana while it is least pronounced in Siġġiewi. One reason the people of Siġġiewi exhibit greater variation in siesta hours is probably because their greater distance from the pivotal employment area around the Grand Harbor prevents a greater number of people from returning home for siesta. Also, Siġġiewi is surrounded by farms, and some farmers in rustic outlying towns like Siġġiewi prefer to take an afternoon rest in the fields—often in simple shelters specifically constructed for this purpose—rather than return home. Still, the fact that some local Siġġiewi residents used to complain about the habits of a local bakery which interrupted their siestas by delivering bread in the early afternoon shows that in this town as in others siesta is seriously observed.

That post-siesta recovery in public mobility occurs here before it does in the Grand Harbor towns of Floriana and Senglea results from factors other than the value placed on taking a siesta. For Siġġiewi residents who do not work locally, there are generally further distances to travel for their afternoon work activities. Furthermore, people in outlying rustic towns like Siġġiewi tend to operate on an earlier schedule overall.

Such people tend to retire earlier and to rise earlier than do people in more cosmopolitan urban areas, especially when those urban areas are centrally located. As Siġġiewi is not only the most rural of the three towns but also the most remote from the high concentration of jobs in *il-Belt* as well as the animated nightlife there and in towns like St. Julian's and Paceville, it is not surprising that many of its residents appear on the streets very early.

While after midnight the streets of Siġġiewi are typically empty of people who are continuing activities of the previous day, there is considerable movement of such people on the streets of Senglea and Floriana as late as 2:00 A.M. In fact, while some people still dressed in evening attire may occasionally be observed moving about in the latter two towns until around 4:00 A.M., a significant amount of Siġġiewi's vehicular and pedestrian traffic associated with the new day is on the move by this time. As Siġġiewi is spread out more than the two, distances to be traveled are also greater and the use of vehicles traffic as compared to foot traffic is greater.

As public bus lines leading to virtually all parts of the island of Malta converge in Floriana, its residents may easily walk to buses going almost anywhere. In reality, buses transport larger segments of people living in Senglea than residents of Floriana and Siġġiewi because Senglea is the poorest and most densely populated of the three localities with the least reliance on private automobiles. Hence, while in Floriana and Siġġiewi morning traffic begins with an upsurge in the movement of private vehicles as well as public buses, in Senglea it commences mostly with an upsurge in pedestrian traffic and the movement of buses. Only in Siġġiewi does it also include a significant number of work carts drawn by horses or donkeys. Though by mid-day, decorated horses may be seen pulling elegant carriages called *karozzini* [sing. *karozzin*] through the streets and squares of Floriana and neighboring Valletta, these are merely used to service tourists.

Both church and state impact social rhythms through temporal regulations they impose on the activities of their numerous employees as well as on the masses of people they represent. The central government is the largest employer in the country, and the church has many employees. In addition to huge numbers of priests, monks, nuns, and laypersons whom the church employs and the many students, patients, and inmates in institutions whose daily activities it controls, it also establishes rhythms for its membership throughout the islands. Like other factors affecting social rhythm in Malta, many regulations of church and state are sensitive to physical cycles and the elements.

Seasonal skewing in the schedules of government workers is especially pronounced in summer. Instead of working from 8:30 A.M. to noon and 2:00 to 5:00 P.M. as is usual, large numbers work from 7:30 A.M. to 1:00 P.M. and then go home. Many pupils in grammar schools study only a half day between Easter and mid-July whereas in primary school, the change to a shortened school day takes place from around the first of June to mid-July. School attendance is often rather poor during July, in part because of the weather and, perhaps, in part because the arrival by this time of multitudes of international tourists creates a vacation atmosphere.

At the parish, island, and national levels, religion influences behaviors in ways that often cause them to be coordinated and synchronized. In the course of a year, for example, every parish hosts a number of religious pageants known as *festi*, or feasts, that unfold partially in churches but invariably involve public processions. These feasts are complex in their organization and can vary considerably from one feast to another in the same locality as well as among various parishes. While many feasts are entirely solemn and religious, others also function in part as showcases to display local pride in competitive and festive ways involving fireworks, street decorations, music, and confetti.

During a one-year period in the village of Marsaxlokk, Wilhelmsen (1976: 134–158) documented the occurrence of one titular feast honoring the patron saint—Our Lady of the Holy Rosary—and seven secondary and tertiary feasts and/or celebrations based on *festa* organization. These included Quaranta ore (or *Kwarantuni*), a procession honoring the Blessed Virgin Mary, St. Gregory's Day, Lapsi (or Ascension), Feast of the Holy Virgin Mary, the Sacred Heart of Jesus, and the original May feast day of the village combined with Ascension. Wilhelmsen (1976: 134–162) documented two other Marsaxlokk feasts that no longer occur, one celebrating St. Mark's Day and a small one three days before Ascension.

Floriana's processions include Corpus Christi, Sacred Heart, Our Lady of the Rosary, and Our Lady of the Catechism, the last of which is held on the day that young children of the parish take their first Holy Communion. In this procession, unlike most others, only young children and catechists take part. A small statue of Our Lady is carried in the parade and a young child marches on each side of the statue. In Siġġiewi, special processions are held for Corpus Christi, Sacred Heart, Our Lady of Sorrows during Lent, our Lady of the Rosary in September, Our Lady of Light, and St. Joseph (Goodwin 1974: 72).

Religious processions in Senglea include the Pilgrimage of Our Lady of the Rosary on the first Sunday of October, a Lenten procession with the statue of the Redeemer, a Good Friday procession with stages of the Way of the Cross, an Easter morning procession with the statue of the Risen Christ, a Feast of the Cross procession on May 3, a Corpus Christi procession, a procession of the Sacred Heart, and a procession of St. Roque on his feast day. Senglea's religious calendar includes another procession with the statue of the Redeemer that takes place on the first Sunday in June. This June procession is in keeping with a historic vow made by the people of Senglea when it was virtually the only locality in Malta spared the ravages of two terrible cholera epidemics (Goodwin 1974: 72).

Throughout any given year in villages, towns, and cities across Malta, many people participate in religious processions. Though such events remain extraordinarily important in the culture of the islands, with the passing of time, they have grown fewer. Though each parish celebrates a number of feasts, it is the one in honor of its patron saints, the titular feast, which is its *festa* par excellence.

In preparation for a titular feast, parishioners must begin work a long time in advance. Money must be collected for the hiring of bands, for decorating the parish church, and for manufacturing or purchasing fireworks in order to compete successfully with the glory and dazzle displayed by other towns. In each locality, residents desire that their parish church will be spectacularly festooned and embellished with rich tapestries and art for this annual event. Members of each parish also hope their local streets will be decorated with the most beautiful banners, statues, and special lights, and their homes will be the cleanest, the most recently whitewashed. They even hope that they themselves will appear the most showy in their "good" clothes—often made or purchased for the occasion—as they receive relatives, friends, and welcome the presence of visitors from far and wide.

The temporal ordering of a *festa* has much in common with medieval ordering imposed on holy days. In principal, the titular feast day of a parish is typically determined in one of four ways: (1) to coincide directly with a movable holy day, (2) indirectly according to a movable holy day by having a fixed relationship with it, (3) to coincide with the Sunday following an actual feast day, or (4) to coincide with a fixed date of the Gregorian calendar. In reality, climatic patterns, history, the status of a church, the seniority of a parish, the patron saint of the locality, other religious events, and a wide variety of other conditions combine to influence the actual time when a titular *festa* will be celebrated. Regardless of a church calendar according to which each day is a saint's day, taking other factors into account, feasts are most often celebrated in summer; in fact, summer is really synonymous with the *festa* season (Goodwin 1974: 75–76).

As Malta has many parishes and hence many titular feasts to celebrate, it would be a disaster for the economy if feast days frequently occurred on workdays; in practice, they only rarely do, when a feast is celebrated on a fixed date. A parish considers it a high honor when church officials allow it the unusual privilege of holding its feast on a fixed date. An additional type of privilege that is highly regarded by parishes is to have a titular feast day that is not only fixed but which falls on a national holiday. An example of a parish honored in this way is Senglea, which has its *festa* on September 8—also a national holiday—known as Our Lady of Victories or *il-Bambina*. In a sense, when Senglea pays homage to its patron saint, so does the entire nation.

The feast day of St. Nicholas, Siġġiewi's patron saint, occurs on the calendar in December, a time when Malta is often quite windy and rainy. This is not a time of year when people are fond of venturing out to celebrate, nor is it a time when the fireworks essential to have a dazzling titular feast would be easy to ignite. Hence, church authorities allow Siġġiewi's titular feast to take place in June.

Only small-scale December celebrations honor St. Nicholas in Siġġiewi, on his special day and also on either the Sunday preceding or following it, when small children of the parish march in procession with a small statue of the patron saint. After the procession, there is a party during which they are given toys. Also on December 5, a Mass with vespers is celebrated and a homily is held in the evening. The following morning, a special mass is celebrated for children as well as a solemn High Mass with a long panegyric. Although weather is uncertain at this time of the year, if it is pleasant, band marches typically take place in the evening.

When a titular feast is scheduled to culminate on a Sunday, formal events usually begin to unfold the previous Sunday—at which time there are special church celebrations and the statute of the patron saint is taken out of its niche in the church. Even at this stage in a *festa* event, there is considerable public celebration both inside the parish church as well as outside on the church square. The following Wednesday, a three-day triduum often commences, during which time vespers are sung in the evening followed by a High Mass at which there are appropriate homilies about the life and virtues associated with the local patron saint.

On Wednesday and Thursday, there typically take place festive outdoor celebrations. By Friday, special lighting effects usually illuminate the streets, and after the evening service, there is likely to be a public band march through major streets of the locality. On the eve of the feast day, the evening church service is usually longer than it was during the triduum due largely to a longer homily and the singing of two different types of vespers. By this time, church attendance is greater and outside manifestations more lively. Also, evidence of fireworks and petards illuminating a darkened sky will be abundant and the band marches more extended. In much earlier times, the Maltese even celebrated an octave prior to a local feast, that is on the eighth day before the day of the *festa* proper.

In parishes where the patron saint is the Virgin Mary, however, the titular feast is still sometimes organized around a novena instead of a triduum, meaning that the initial festivities which usually start a week before a feast day proper may commence at the beginning of the novena, or even on the preceding Sunday. A few localities, including some that celebrate the Assumption of Our Lady as their principal feast day, hold a *kwindicina*, involving 15 days of religious celebrations.

In the morning of the feast day proper, a *Te Deum* or Thanksgiving Mass is celebrated and there takes place a long panegyric focussing on the hagiology of the patron saint. In some localities, this is followed by a band march in the late morning or in the early or late afternoon. At an evening Mass prior to the beginning of marches two kinds of vespers are usually sung.

In terms of sheer drama, nothing rivals the moment after the early evening Mass when a cortege in solemn procession begins to exit slowly through the main door of a crowded church into a square that is filled to overflowing with large and excited crowds. When hoisted high on the shoulders of eight or so men wearing white robes and white gloves, the statue of the patron saint appears on the threshold of the church, frantic jubilation erupts, confetti rains from the balconies of houses, and the sound of applause and fireworks fills the air. With great pomp, and measured steps that alternate with dramatic pauses, a most spectacular procession winds its way through the main thoroughfares of the parish. Though a local band may have provided the musical program on previous days, this is a day when music is invariably provided by paid musicians from elsewhere.

A local *festa* procession, though formally organized, belongs largely to the ordinary people, with almost everyone having the right to exchange their role as spectator and participant-stroller freely and from moment to moment. After the procession, which may last for two or more hours if weather is good, the statue is ceremoniously carried back to the parish church. This is followed by a prayer of thanksgiving and a benediction. Though at this time, the *festa* is officially over, people wander the streets much later than usual. One often can observe many strollers in the streets after eleven o'clock.

Quite apart from feast days, religion orders time, in that parish churches celebrate several daily Masses in the morning and one in the early evening. Before the evening Mass, there takes place in most of these churches a recitation of the rosary and a benediction service, which together last from 20 to 30 minutes. In smaller and less distinguished churches, daily morning Masses are usually celebrated according to the needs of the community and the number of priests or monks available. In Malta overall, the number of priests and monks as a proportion of the population is very large. On the Island of Malta, there are almost two priests for every 1,000 persons while on Gozo, there are almost six. In addition, there are on the island of Malta approximately 1.5 monks for each thousand people in the population. As many priests and monks tend to celebrate at least one Mass each day, demography as well as religiosity is a factor that helps to explain some aspects of social rhythm.

With only minor changes over several decades, Floriana's parish church celebrates at least five daily Masses in summer, four in the morning and one in the evening with the first one around 6:00 A.M. In non-summer months, it celebrates an additional morning Mass, the time of which varies between schooldays and non-schooldays.

In Floriana's Sarria Church—staffed by the Jesuits—it has been traditional to celebrate a daily Mass in summer at 7:30 A.M., except on Sundays, when two morning Masses are celebrated. During the rest of the year, morning Masses increase to two on weekdays and three on Sunday mornings. At Floriana's Capuchin Church, five daily Masses are celebrated with the first one starting near 5:00 A.M. and the last one starting around 8:30 A.M. On Sundays, however, the first and last of these five daily Masses is on a slightly different schedule. Also, on Sundays, the first Mass at this church is celebrated at 4:45 A.M. The rosary is recited daily in the chapel, and after this recitation, only in the month of October—which is dedicated to the Virgin Mary—an evening Mass is celebrated around six o'clock.

In addition to feasts and the celebrations of daily Masses, other religious events contribute to social rhythms. For example, in Siġġiewi, St John's chapel is only opened once a year, on St. John's feast, and festivities are limited to the interior of the church with no out-of-door processions taking place. In Floriana on the days of the apparition of Our Lady of Lourdes, there are special festivities in the Chapel of Our Lady of Lourdes. These days are 18 in number and occur on fixed dates.

Maltese churches—like families and individuals—differ in status and social standing. Parishioners bask with pride in the glory of a local church that is of exalted status, and most especially if it is their parish church. The people of Floriana take pride in the fact that their parish church is dedicated to St. Publius, believed to have been converted to Christianity by St. Paul. Even more important, the parish church in Senglea has the exalted status of a basilica—an honorary title that is bestowed on churches with special historical or religious significance by the Pope. This means that even the priestly hierarchy in Senglea have special titles. At the Senglea basilica, it is traditional to celebrate three morning Masses, with the first one beginning at 5:45 A.M., as well as to celebrate an evening Mass.

At other locations in Senglea, religion imposes a different temporal order on the day, including in the chapel of St. Anne's, now a home for the aged that is staffed by nuns, at St. Julian's Church, and nearby at St. Philip's

Church, which is operated by the Jesuits. Within a distance of a mere few feet, religion helps to impose on synchronized group behavior a patterning such as could hardly be imagined in parts of the world that have become highly secularized. It is ironic in this most Catholic of countries that religion sometimes orders days more as in some parts of the Muslim world—where people are supposed to pray five times a day—than in some secularized parts of twenty-first century Christendom.

Throughout the year a tempo is established with pulsations of the sacred alternating with the profane where religious inputs compromise with those of day-to-day subsistence. In Siġġiewi where farm work must get off to an early start, for example, the first Mass at the parish church is celebrated at 4:00 A.M., followed by five other morning Masses with the last one beginning around 7:00 A.M. As it is not easy to make drastic short-term changes in social rhythms, even on Sundays, the first Mass at Siġġiewi's parish church begins at 4:00 A.M. As a seasonal concession to summer, however, many parishes, celebrate evening Masses an hour later because people have lots of activities to squeeze into their longer days. In some towns, including Siġġiewi, even the first morning Mass in summer is slightly later.

Despite the paucity of wild life in the islands except for migrating birds, during the hunting season, a special Sunday Mass is celebrated in Siġġiewi around 2:45 A.M. for the benefit of the hunters. In Siġġiewi's Chapel of St. Mary and Chapel of St. Mark, Masses are celebrated rather irregularly, while the Chapel of St. John is only opened once a year, on the feast day of the patron saint.

A daily schedule punctuates each day in a particular and striking manner that varies from locality to locality throughout the islands. With bells pealing, people go to and fro from one event to another, in tune with rhythms orchestrated, in large measure, by religion. Church bells punctuate days much as in some countries factory horns, public clocks, and prayer calls from minarets do. In fact the many ways in which bells are rung constitute a quasi-language. In terms of the ringing of church bells, the daily cycle is divided into four parts each consisting of six hours. The system assumes that the listener knows which quarter of the day is occurring at any given time. Hence, church bells—through two contrasting morphemic tones—indicate only the hour within the quarter of the day and the quarter point of the hour that is occurring at a particular moment.

Bells are rung to call people together for liturgical functions, and during these functions they sometimes are rung to emphasize the most salient parts of these services. Bells are rung during funerals, before and during the celebration of Masses, and so on. A *festa* that celebrates the patron saint of a parish is also heralded by the ringing of bells during which periods they are rung more often and more joyously than usual. In most localities bells ring a quarter of an hour before a liturgical function in order to call people to worship, but in rural areas, where people spend much time on scattered farms, bells typically ring half an hour before worship to allow them enough time to arrive on time.

Each week is punctuated with special religious observances that contribute to the feeling that some days are very different from others. Most parish churches on Thursday afternoons, for example, hold an *ora santa* or holy hour. In addition to the recitation of the rosary and benediction, such a ceremony typically involves adoration—where there are readings from the Bible, a short homily about the same, and the singing of hymns. Senglea is a town where this service is not held if the scheduled Mass is to include a wedding. Moreover, the Adoration is not held in Siġġiewi on the Thursday preceding a first Friday of the month, as there are often extra confessions— now called Sacraments of Reconcilation—that need to be heard.

As Friday is associated with the crucifixion of Christ, it tends to be treated in a special way though the Roman Catholic Church no longer demands abstinence from the eating of meat. Generally on Friday evenings, churches schedule a *Via Sagra* or Way of the Cross. At these services, a member of the laity is sometimes in charge of leading the faithful in prayer in front of the fourteen holy pictures or statuettes depicting the traditional stations of the Way of the Cross. During the evening Mass at Siġġiewi parish church, instead of the *Via Sagra*, sung vespers are usually performed. And on Fridays in Senglea, there is likely to be an extra Mass at 10:00 A.M. in the Chapel of the Redeemer, and after the evening Mass, a half-hour Adoration celebration. Though there does occur variation from one parish to another and even from one year to another, such variation tends to reside in minor details.

Most Maltese schools, whether government or religious, begin the day with a communal prayer in the school hall or auditorium. A special Mass is celebrated for students and teachers on the first Friday of each month throughout the academic year. If facilities for this Mass are not available at the school, students are taken to a nearby church. Likewise on the shop floors of many factories, a special Mass is celebrated during the mid-day break on the first Friday of each month for all workers wishing to attend.

Maltese take seriously their religious obligation to attend at least one Mass on certain days designated holy days of obligation, though females on the average are more observant than males and the elderly more observant than the young. Apart from Maltese national holidays (most of which happen also to be religious days of obligation), all Sundays are included. After the Vatican Council II which ended in 1965, church rules now permit a Catholic to fulfill his or her religious duties associated with Sundays and holy days on the previous eve. Saturday has greatly increased in popularity as a religious day. Still, one occasionally encounters elderly and conservative Maltese who, though they attend Mass on Saturday, do not feel comfortable unless they repeat their religious obligation on Sunday.

In much the same way as religion helps to punctuate the day and the week, it also helps to punctuate the year. The 40-day period between Carnival and Easter that is widely known as Lent is an especially important season. Though the Wednesday and Friday fasting which used to characterize it has not been a matter of law for several decades, this is a period when fewer big parties are held. In general, Maltese think of Lent as a period of austerity. Maltese social life slows down considerably, and in almost every sizeable church in the islands, spiritual exercises are organized in preparation for the great feast of Easter.

These exercises scheduled over several weeks usually involve five to eight homilies that start on a Sunday during Lent for sub-groups which differ considerably from town to town. In the parish church of Floriana, for example, there may be separate spiritual exercises for people under 25, for women over 25, and for men over 25. In Floriana, special exercises may be held separately for newly wedded couples under the sponsorship of the church-affiliated Cana Movement. In Floriana's Sarria Church, separate church exercises are sometimes held for the general public, for English-speaking worshippers, and late in the evening for shopkeepers. Other exercises are held in this town at the Catholic Institute and at the Capuchin Church. In Senglea, special spiritual exercises may be addressed to unmarried women at St. Anne's Chapel, for teenagers of both genders in the parish church, for married women in the parish church and in St. Philip's Church, and so on with children even attending spiritual exercises in their schools. This is a time of year when many people are very charitable about giving to others although Catholic Mission Day is in October.

Fasting is still obligatory on *Ras ir-Randan* or Ash Wednesday, the first day of Lent, as well as on Good Friday, the most solemn day of Lent. Fasting in the Maltese context means that no meat is eaten, that breakfast and lunch are light, and that no milk or snacks are permitted between meals. It is not the total abstinence from food and drink as is common among Muslims, but after breakfast, one eats only one large meal and a snack without meat, as opposed to two large meals.

The Friday before Good Friday, some people continue the custom of going to a special place of religious significance to do penitence, while perhaps participating in a procession. In the early 1900s, a procession of this type took place annually in Valletta, with lots of the penitents barefooted. Both Floriana and Siġġiewi hold a religious procession on this Friday be fore Good Friday. On Good Friday, religious processions in Cospicua and Mosta are among those that draw people from throughout Malta, in the case of Mosta, with some worshippers dragging chains down the streets.

On what is called "Easter night," really the evening of Holy Saturday, there takes place a midnight service, in fact, the most solemn of the entire church year. During this service there is the blessing of new fire, baptismal water, and the administration of Christian initiatives. This is the preeminent

time when new adult members are received with the church through the
sacraments of Baptism, Confirmation, and Holy Communion. Whereas
Good Friday is a time of mourning when the churches are draped in black
crepe, the Easter processions that take place in numerous localities are lively
and joyous, though strictly religious in tone.

With the closing of Easter festivities, the Easter season begins and does
not end until Pentecost 50 days later. During this period, more time tends
to be allocated to cleaning and beautifying homes, for in Malta this is the
preeminent time when the parish priest or one of his assistants makes an
annual visit to bless dwellings and to collect tithes. In Marsaxlokk, according to Wilhelmsen (1976: 143), this is usually undertaken during the
octave of Easter by the parish priest who "brings with him Holy Water
and an incense burner which is carried by the sacristan." In some localities,
especially more rural ones, the fields are blessed collectively and the larger
domestic animals individually. Similarly in fishing villages, it is common
for fishing boats to be blessed, although this does not necessarily occur
around the time of Good Friday or Easter (Wilhelmsen 1976: 423).

The last Sunday of a liturgical year, the Sunday before Advent, is dedicated to Christ the King. It is always on the fourth Sunday before Christmas
that Advent begins, and it is Advent which in the Catholic Church ushers
in a new liturgical year. During the nine days preceding Christmas more
time than usual tends to be allocated to religious activity. For example,
regular evening Masses are extended by a short homily about the birth of
Jesus and special hymns are sung. These special celebrations are associated
with the novena of the child Jesus. In Floriana, this Christmas novena is
given a slightly different form every year in order to appeal to young people.

On what is called "Christmas night"—really the eve of Christmas—evening and midnight Masses are celebrated; virtually all churches are filled
to overflowing. Before the Mass proper, special Christmas hymns are sung,
and a short reflection is sometimes delivered by a boy—usually of about
eight or nine years of age. During the three days following Christmas, 40
hours of adoration are held in Siġġiewi and similar events take place in
other towns.

The major transitional periods of a liturgical year—Advent, Christmas,
Lent, Easter and Pentecost—are reflected even in the dress of the clergy.
During Advent and Lent, periods of penitence and renewal, the clergy wears
shades of purple; during Christmas, white or gold, symbolic of joy; between
Easter and Pentecost, red, symbolic of the Holy Spirit; and on ordinary
Sundays, green, symbolic of hope. In contrast to when parish churches are
ornately decorated for titular feasts, during Advent and Lent, bright colors,
banners, and flowers are removed. Until around the 1960s, churches used
to be stripped bare of all unnecessary decoration, including even statuary,
and holy paintings were covered with violet or black cloth.

In reality, the liturgical year of the Catholic Church is made up of two distinct series of feasts which unfold along parallel lines and are the complement of each other. The one that is proper to the season is called the Proper of the Time and the other—which comprises the feasts of the saints—is called the Proper of the Saints. During Advent which is an integral part of the Proper of the Time, a series of feasts is celebrated, such as St. Francis Xavier, St. Andrew, and the Immaculate Conception of our Blessed Lady, which belong to the Proper of the Saints. With regard to the dignity or importance of feasts of the Roman rite in both the Proper of the Time and the Proper of the Saints, ranking occurs. In certain dioceses—for example, Malta or Gozo—certain feasts of saints are considered proper that do not appear in the calendar of the Universal Church. Moreover, as has been pointed out, certain celebrations associated with the Proper of the Saints may be adjusted as a cultural adaptation to regional or local conditions.

Throughout Christendom in ancient times, holidays began as holy days, but as church and state evolved along separate paths, many holidays became secular. Through its local parish organization, the church was traditionally associated with the ordering of time within Maltese localities in ways that the state was not. In Malta—where a clear division between the authorities of church and state has begun evolving quite recently—the movement to create more secular holidays at the expense of holy days is a development that has unfolded largely since 1977.

Of the 15 public holidays that Maltese were celebrating until 1977, the principal raison d'être of 12 resided in their character as holy days. Moreover, the religious hierarchy in Malta tended to associate a special religious significance with the remaining three, namely, New Year's Day (January 1), National Day (September 8), and Independence Day (September 21). For example, it emphasized that New Year's Day was the Octave Day of Christmas dedicated to Mary the Mother of God, a holy day of obligation; and that National Day was also the Nativity of Our Lady. Moreover, the fact that the highest officials of church and state joined together in public celebration to mark Independence Day prevented it from being thought of exclusively in a secular way.

In 1977, the government—with a Labor majority—announced the Vatican had cancelled most religious feast days as days of obligation and that in order to increase national productivity it was abolishing these days as public holidays. While the church reacted by transferring these feasts to the nearest Sunday and advising its membership to participate in Mass on the traditional days of obligation, this state action had two important results. Attendance at Mass on these days of obligation declined, and eight Sundays could no longer be used for local *festi* from which parish priests derive much prestige (Koster 1994: 316). The local councils—first provided for by the government legislation in 1993—further challenged the local authority of parish priests.

Some people now refer to May 1 as May Day or Workers' Day rather than the Feast of St. Joseph the Worker. However four public holidays that remain in the calendar of public holidays are also holy days of obligation—New Year's Day, Feast of St. Paul's Shipwreck, Feast of the Assumption or Santa Marija, and Christmas. With respect to time, moreover, the local councils play no role in its ordering while local religious events continue to mark the passage of each year in accordance with ancient religious traditions.

Still the situation—continuing until very recently—where a theocratic legacy guaranteed the sacred an advantage over the profane in influencing social rhythm within society is changing in profound ways. Apart from Easter, Maltese now celebrate 14 instead of 15 national holidays. Of great significance, the government has dropped four holy days from Malta's public holiday—The Epiphany, Ascension Day, Corpus Christi, and All Saints Day—while it has added three secular holidays. The three new secular holidays are Freedom Day (commemorating the 1979 departure of the last British troops from Malta), Sette Giugno (commemorating the deaths of four Maltese demonstrators killed by the British in 1919), and Republic Day (commemorating the 1974 designation of a Maltese president rather than the British monarch as the head of state). These changes recently made by the state in public holidays contribute to its preeminent authority to use nationalistic symbols and underscore its conquest of church influence in the regulation of time.

While both state and church contribute to the regulation of commercial cycles, the preeminence of former is associated with the government's power to legislate, license, and control working conditions. This power is most apparent in connection with the regulation of its own work force as well as those in large industries and major markets. As Adrian Delia, a lawyer, has explained to journalist Blanche Gatt, social rhythms inhere in police licensing and police enforcement as well as in legislation.

Chapter 155 of the Laws of Malta, the Shop and Hawkers (Business Hours) Act was enacted by Act XXIV of 1957, and it was last amended in 1992. This Act makes provision for the business houses of shops and hawkers and for purposes connected therewith, such as the different kinds of shops, retail outlets, trades or businesses existing, the opening and closing hours of the same, the days on which they are to open, and the exceptions to these rules. (Gatt 2001: 15)

Still, some establishments, hawkers, and consumers elude some of this control by establishing commercial rhythms and cycles emanating from laws of supply and demand enmeshed in the folk life of localities and neighborhoods or on technicalities having to do with services directed toward tourists. An organized segment of Maltese, through judicial action and political pressure, is seeking to persuade the government to liberalize laws and regulations that restrict commerce on Sundays and on certain feast days.

While department stores, shopping centers, and trade shows are available to Maltese shoppers, the importance of hawking in a country as small and densely populated as Malta can hardly be overstated. In fact, hawking acts as a functional adaptation to limited space, and it helps to keep people connected with each other in a more personal way than does participation in large-scale commerce. It also functions as a type of door-to-door or neighborhood delivery system that eliminates the need for people to travel long distances for many things they wish to buy on a regular basis.

Maltese internalize lots of information about the optimal times to purchase fresh foods locally, for example. It is not coincidence that they buy fewer vegetables on Mondays than on other days; this is a conscious strategy to avoid weekend leftovers. Housewives in particular know which days of the week animals are slaughtered at the abattoir and because of their desire to buy meat at its freshest, butcher shops are busiest on the afternoons of those days. When price-controlled food staples are sometimes available in local stores, this brings greater numbers of shoppers to groceries, and additional help sometimes has to be employed to service them.

Though Floriana is only 0.34 square miles in size, it supports two daily open-air morning markets, each on a somewhat different schedule and each on a different side of town. Each market attracts different vendors and different customers though for the most part the merchandise in both is similar, including containers, eggs, herbs, biscuits, non-perishable groceries, lemons, flowers, prickly pears, and other seasonal fruits. This commercial pattern works well for residents of Floriana, who do not like to cross busy St. Anne Street unnecessarily as it is a major throughway leading to Valletta. As fishmongers frequent one of these markets more often than the other, however, consumers wishing to purchase seafood must factor this into shopping strategy.

Knowing how to survive in a place like Floriana means knowing not only about these markets and many shops, it also means knowing such things as that while the man who sells "fancy bread" will come as early as 9:30 on every morning except Sunday, the two sellers of ordinary bread will make their rounds every day except Monday. It means knowing that while one vendor may come regularly beginning around 6:15 A.M., that the other—not being on a fixed schedule—is less reliable in the morning. The residents of Floriana also know that the milk truck can be expected to deliver milk to stores twice a day except Sunday and that if they happen to be present on the street, they can buy milk directly from the driver. Maltese possess phenomenal amounts of information about such things as when a particular salesman of paraffin, cakes, biscuits, ravioli, or soft cheese made from the milk of goats and sheep can be expected in the immediate vicinities of where they live.

There exists sufficient small-scale commerce in the average Maltese locality that it functions as a veritable clock. In fact, so specific are such clocks that they sometimes differ for people living in different neighborhoods in the same town or parish. Though Senglea is much smaller in size than Floriana, commercial rhythms differ according to three major neighborhoods. One is the area close to the two gates through the old fortifications, the only entrance to Senglea by land. Another is the central hub called Civic Center. A third is located at the extremity of the peninsula—called Senglea Point—which looks out at the Grand Harbor and at Valletta beyond.

In general, greengrocers or vegetable and fruit hawkers may be seen from about 6:00 A.M. until noon. However, while they are more likely to be seen near Senglea's parish church in the vicinity of the gates around 8:00, they are more likely to be seen near Senglea's St. Philip's Basilica around 9:00 or 10:00. They are also sometimes seen selling in this latter area in the afternoon—from about 3:00 to 6:00. However, these hawkers do not visit Senglea at all on Sundays, Mondays, or Fridays. The fishmongers—mostly from Żejtun, Marsaxlokk, and Qrendi—make regular rounds, though in *lampuka* season only the supply of fish places limits on their presence.

A hawker of biscuits who used to visit Senglea's Crucifix Street just behind the parish church on Tuesdays, Thursdays, and Saturdays at around 10:00 A.M. did not visit the far end of Victory Street near St. Philip's Church except on Tuesdays and Fridays around 11:00 A.M. A few decades ago at Senglea's only bakery, each Maltese household used to be registered to buy a specified amount of subsidized bread which could either be picked up at the bakery or delivered to their homes. However, vendors in vans sold additional bread there every day except Monday, after a public holiday, or after a local *festa* in the locality where the baking took place.

As some hawkers sell to particular households but not to people who live in adjacent buildings, there exist extremely minute commercial cycles about which residents are expected to be aware. This awareness has to do with such matters as around what time on Friday the woman from Żabbar will arrive to sell capers and when the sellers of mint and basil may be expected from Żejtun.

Much commercial activity in the Maltese Islands takes place in large markets, in grocery stores, along Dingli Street in Victoria throughout the week, and on Sundays when the large open-air market in Valletta known as *il-Monti* is closed. Much of it takes place in restaurants, boutiques and shops that specialize in antiques and books, as well as in the omnipresent squares in front of parish churches, especially at the times when Masses are likely to be well attended. As people come together to buy and sell items ranging from scrap metal, watches, ready-made clothes, and caged chickens and rabbits to fresh produce and left-over military goods, this activity not only circulates money, it circulates culture.

When we see some Maltese taking their casseroles to one of the communal ovens known as *il-forn* between 8:00 and 9:00 A.M. and returning to pick them up around noon, a practice that is most common on Sunday, we also see the circulation of culture. This custom of sometimes baking family dishes in communal ovens is energy-saving and has parallels in many countries of the Mediterranean Basin.

Some sedentary hawkers rest comfortably in the open air with their goods on display while others roam the streets interacting with people in ways that are as much social as economic. When hawkers of paraffin move slowly through the streets of Malta and Gozo, men, women, and children with cans and tins may be seen clustered about their vehicles, conversing and waiting to be served. In towns across Malta, the cries of hawkers in the streets are especially in evidence between June and October.

There exist numerous nonrandom indications of the passage of time that are systemic and which interact with each other to synchronize behavior and facilitate social interaction. They both affect and reflect patterns in the allocation of time. Not all Maltese respond to all of these cycles in exactly the same way. It is assumed that they are internalized somewhat differently based on such factors as age, gender, and social class.

Commerce of all types brings people from various places and from various social classes together in ways that permit them to negotiate, converse, and update themselves on the news. Though much Maltese commerce involves large institutions like banks, corporations, factories, and brokerage firms and unfolds in upscale, formally regulated settings, with regard to the contribution it makes to social rhythms it has no more authenticity than tempos established by commerce that is small-scale. In the final analysis, commercial cycles—both macro and micro—like cycles imposed by church and state, overlap and intersect through processes involving the ecology of adaptation and human give-and-take. While all of these cycles are instrumental to subsistence, they operate within limits imposed by the powerful forces of demography, geography, and climate.

Chapter 7

Status and Social Standing

Institutionalized social inequality, a universal feature of national societies, reveals a great deal about social structure, social interaction, and culture—including worldview. That Maltese have long been status-conscious is beyond question. Exactly what type of stratification system exists in Malta and whether or not it involves classes or more nebulous status groups are matters of considerable debate among social scientists and others. However a Maltese proverb is clear: "One shoes the horse and the other rides."

Social scientists study institutionalized social inequality in terms of many features: occupations, economic status, educational achievement, dwelling types, areas of residence, networks, lifestyles, differential access to policy-making apparatuses, and patterns of mobility both intragenerational and intergenerational. Some look at variables such as "morality," "civic leadership," and "pedigree" whose content are a real challenge to define operationally and which can vary considerably from one sociocultural context to another.

Even once the exact dimensions to be studied are delineated, contrastive techniques may be used to study stratification, including those that are objective, subjective, and reputational. Sahlins (1958: 2) once suggested that criteria for estimating stratification could be divided into those that differentiate and may be called structural, on the one hand, and those that confer privilege and may be called functional, on the other. "To understand the dynamics of stratification," according to Fallers (1973: 162–163), "we must examine the interplay among ideology, social differentiation and the process of allocation of persons to roles." What is clear from all of this is that status and social standing have so many dimensions that all undertakings to study them must necessarily be partial.

In these islands notions of the most prestigious ways to live have evolved over centuries as Maltese have interacted with each other, and with others, through processes of cultural reciprocity. Socioeconomic distinctions in Malta probably appear sharper due to a long history of interacting with foreigners, a complex division of labor, high population density, and nucleated settlement patterns. Though Malta has long been characterized by social specialization, what type and how much has varied a great deal from place to place and from period to period.

In medieval Malta, most people resided in rustic agricultural villages much as their contemporaries did in other parts of the Mediterranean. Clustered in small settlements scattered across the land, some farmed, some herded animals and some occasionally fished. Also, some looked after the medical and spiritual needs of their compatriots. A few families lived lives of ease while enjoying relative high status because they belonged to a wealthy, privileged, and landed nobility (Thake 1996: 25). In the capital city of Città Notabile or Mdina, and to some extent in its suburb of Rabat as well as Birgu, the division of labor tended to be more complex than elsewhere. In addition to a limited number of craftsmen and artisans, some specialists were involved in trade. While trade was especially important in Birgu, religious specialists were also important in Mdina.

Throughout vast stretches of the Mediterranean Basin, status and social standing have long been defined less in individualistic ways than in terms of families. Notions of shame, saving face, and family honor began to take root in the Maltese Islands from an early time and doubtlessly were already in place during Muslim domination. Widely transcending religious and ethnic frontiers in the region, these concepts are associated with gender segregation coupled with a belief in the inherent weakness of females and their innate tendency to bring shame onto men. That it is the duty of society to protect status and reputations by holding females to higher levels of propriety than males has a long history and wide acceptance in the Mediterranean (Mizzi 1981: 168; Wettinger 1980: 65–77).

By late medieval times, a number of full-time and part-time specialists were resident in ancient villages like Żebbuġ and Qormi as well as on the central plateau of Gozo. By the end of the fourteenth century, Mdina had an elaborate commune or town council known as the *Università* that was dominated by an Aragonese and Catalan nobility which had gradually become entrenched (Thake 1996: 11). Despite the fact that spatial strictures in localities such as Mdina and Birgu forced people to live close to each other, a social structure evolved that was highly stratified.

Nobles lived in palatial dwellings, most often in towns, though occasionally in fortified palaces located away from settlements. The size and sophistication of homes were related to the status of their inhabitants. Many large dwellings known as *solerata* usually incorporated in the courtyard an arcaded open staircase that led to an upper level. Smaller townhouses were inhabited by common people who made up the masses in all towns. These houses, at least in Mdina, often clustered around a common courtyard or *cortile domorum*. The masses were likely to reside near their livestock and other domesticated animals. Where populations were dense, this commonly involved having the sleeping quarters on the second story or *ghorfa* and a kitchen on the ground floor adjoining a courtyard or *mandra* which provided shelter for animals (Thake 1996: 16).

Early social class differentiation was not only apparent in contrasting living arrangements, but also in the ownership of land, in material possessions, in obligations to furnish *corvée* labor, and even in the contrasting arrangements made for burial. At one extreme, nobles were buried in marble tombs bearing their coats of honor in chapels whose construction their families had commissioned. Mdina's residents of somewhat lower status were buried in chambered graves under the floor pavement of the Cathedral, while the poorest of her residents were simply laid to rest in common graves.

Differences between nobility and commoners were underscored by the fact that while the former spoke Italian and bore family names that were not of Arabic derivation, the latter were generally illiterate and fluent only in Maltese. Among the masses, differentiation was also made on the basis of such factors as place of residence, economic status, types of work, and in some cases, ethnic backgrounds. The highest church officials were of Sicilian or some other foreign background though the ranks of the priesthood were filled mostly with Maltese.

Whereas the clergy of the Cathedral Chapter came from aristocratic families and served within the aristocratic enclave of Mdina, the clergy elsewhere were usually of humble social origins and lived at the same level as the masses in various local parishes where they served. There existed dimensions of ranking tied to all individuals and groups that made up the corporate body of the church; and throughout the time that the Knights were in control, the church in Malta was linked to the Sicilian diocese with its seat in Palermo.

The arrival of the Order of St. John in Malta added to the complexity of this stratification system as it superimposed on a society with a previously established feudal structure a new nobility resolved to establish the supremacy of its rule. Though society remained rigidly stratified under a foreign elite, this elite was not monolithic. It included the old nobility, certain ranking church officials, and the more recently arrived Knights. The eventual presence in medieval Malta of religious orders from abroad as well as a papal Inquisitor (always a foreigner) introduced additional status complexity into the social hierarchy.

By its very nature, feudalism was a type of stratification that depended on both ownership of land and the right to expropriate the labor of people to work the land. Like the nobility previously established in Malta, the

Knights asserted their rights to be an integral part of the land-owning elite. In this land-starved country virtually devoid of natural resources, the right to monopolize land and the labor of the people who worked it gave the Order extraordinary status in a feudal system.

That the Order operated under a papal charter and was made up of nobles belonging to ruling families throughout Europe contributed to this considerable status. Possessing vast fortunes in an island where people were abominably poor and unschooled, the Knights encountered few obstacles in imposing their views onto the prevailing ideology of status and social standing. Among these were the superiority of Catholicism over alternative religious systems, the divine right of some to rule over others—including the aristocracy over commoners and men over women, European chauvinism, the correctness of chivalry, and absolutism in social control.

Though by virtue of their aristocratic backgrounds the new rulers considered themselves superior to Maltese, the success of their crusading mission depended on their living in symbiosis with the masses who surrounded them. In accommodating themselves to this reality, social relationships of inequality had to become complementary in a decidedly complex way. That the Order refused to allow Maltese to become Knights, probably reflected its view toward commoners and its desire to keep the general populace neutral toward the various *langues* (or ethnic subdivisions) into which it was divided.

Not all foreigners in medieval Malta were members of the elite. For example, numerous retainers of less than exalted status followed the Knights to Malta from Rhodes, and some of these and others compensated for labor shortages connected with the death and destruction that plagued Malta after the Great Siege. Some Europeans also came as manual workers during building booms. Moreover, as the Knights turned Malta into a society heavily dependent on slave labor, the populace was always aware that the most subjugated of society, like the most privileged, were non-Maltese. Though under the Knights, Maltese were numerous as servants, laborers, farmers, fishermen, herders, weavers, and even concubines, they were also present as priests, artisans, traders, navigators, and even architects and physicians.

George Sandys, an English visitor to Malta around 1610, noted marked differences between urbanized Maltese of privilege whom he described as being "altogether frenchified," and poor villagers whom he described as "half clad, and indeed a miserable people" (Sandys 1615: 234). Maltese were clearly not a socioeconomic monolith nor were they uniformly lower in status than the foreigners in their midst. Similarly, Greeks, Turks, Arabs, Italians, Corsicans, Muslims, and Jews in Malta were not of a single status.

For long periods during the Middle Ages, some Jewish Maltese were physicians, some owned land, some were import-export agents, and others operated shops of various kinds. Although a Maltese Jew was once the chief physician and another a diplomatic envoy to the court of Sicily, the Jewish community was periodically subjected to discriminatory restrictions. (Wettinger 1985). As for the masses of Maltese who were Christians, no matter how poverty-stricken and even close to starvation at times, they were not subjected to such restrictions. Hence the precariousness of material conditions for the masses notwithstanding, as Catholics and non-slaves, there was a cushion between them and the bottommost rung of Malta's exceedingly complex stratification system.

"*Liberté, fraternité, égalité*" was the rubric under which the French Revolution unfolded as a defining social construct, and the Knights did not receive the outlook implied by this rubric with enthusiasm. The revolutionary turmoil in France was causing them to lose their lands there—and eventually in other countries. Revolutionary zeal in France also called into question their legitimacy and established an unprecedented separation of church and state. The sentiments of Knights is apparent by the fact that shortly after the execution of France's King Louis XVI on January 21, 1793, the Sacred Council of the Knights in Malta "ordered 'obsequies usual on the death of brother sovereigns' to be celebrated in the Conventual Church in Valletta" (Camilleri 1996: 13). This spirit of the French Revolution—uprooting feudalism and the old order—was like a genie out of a bottle. It would only be a matter of time before Napoleon would unleash it full blown in Maltese society.

The biggest threat facing the islands by the end of the eighteenth century was poverty, not piracy or religious wars. Tired of the Order's arrogance, decadence, and absolute control, the populace was keenly aware of its growing inability to protect them, to provide them economic shelter, or to secure them status in the larger world. Though Malta was generally overjoyed at the 1798 expulsion of the Knights, like Malta's previous rulers, the Knights left behind an indelible stamp on her ideology of status and social standing. Moreover, the Maltese felt pride in the way the Order had transformed their barren country from one of almost total underdevelopment to a home worthy of cosmopolitan nobles drawn from high society throughout Europe.

In the mere six days that Napoleon remained in Malta, he liberally relied on revolutionary decrees to rearrange the stratification system. Through the expulsion of the Knights and elimination of some church privileges, he altered it largely at the top. Through the abolition of slavery, he altered it both at the bottom and at the top. While the freeing of slaves deprived some Maltese of the privilege of free labor, it also deprived the poorest Maltese of any group more unfortunate than themselves they could look down upon.

Maltese—long accustomed to a rigidly stratified society with a foreign aristocracy at the top and a transient slave element at the bottom—were outraged by anticlerical France caught up in the excesses of the Revolution, and by her insulting and rapacious behavior toward them. It was, in fact, this upending of the social system and offense to their national honor that eventually led them to rebel against France and appeal to protectionist noblesse oblige from Britain. Ironically however, in drawing up a "Declaration of Rights" for Malta in 1802 to place their country under British protection, Malta's nationalist vanguard was doubtlessly influenced by the spirit of the French Revolution.

Though during much of the first half century of British colonialism, Malta's standard of living remained rather constant with most Maltese barely able to survive, society remained remarkably stratified. Thanks largely to Price's meticulous study (1954) of reports of various royal commissions and the census of 1842, some characteristics of Maltese social structure during the early and middle nineteenth century are well known to us. The most disadvantaged included people who were chronically unemployed, many of whom lived on alms, begging, thievery, and minimal diets from soup kitchens. With jobs scarce and fertility rates high, the underemployed were sometimes equally desperate. Ragged and homeless, some perished from exposure and disease (Price 1954: 11–12).

Over two-thirds of the gainfully employed were small farmers, fishermen, laborers, and artisans. The typical daily diet of these workers was two pounds of barley bread, three-quarter pounds of vegetables, a little cheese, some oil, a few olives, pasta, and occasionally fish and fruit. In times of plenty, a little was spent for oil, alcohol, tobacco, or church donations. The working masses dressed in cheap, coarse, local cottons and were often without shoes. Their households were large and they seldom had more than two rooms in which to sleep (Price 1954: 9).

With the government owning one third of arable land and the church and other religious institutions owning an equal proportion, the number of private landlords with farmland to rent was rather small. These landlords often found their tenant farmers in debt to them with no means to pay. Saltpan laborers, weavers, spinners, and fishermen were even worse off than most small-scale farmers (Price 1954: 10–11).

As salaries generated on the open labor market varied considerably, one way of hedging against unpredictability was to work for the government. Though Maltese were consistently paid lower salaries than foreign public employees, necessity required them nonetheless to compete fiercely for government positions. Government employees included semi-skilled workers at the bottom, clerks and soldiers in the middle, and teachers, doctors and magistrates at the high end.

In comparison to the masses, physicians, advocates, merchants, and large landowners could afford to consume wheat bread (which they much preferred over bread made of barley), as well as macaroni, meat, and wine in larger quantities. Members of a privileged upper class dressed smartly, conversed in Italian, and indulged in a variety of cultural and leisure activities that set them apart. Their commodious houses were often located on some main square. According to the census of 1842, only around 2,000 families belonged to this professional and landowning class, and even many of these sometimes had difficulty maintaining their standard of living. When the government drastically reduced its land rents in order to assist defaulting farmers in 1842, for example, private landlords—forced to do likewise in order to remain competitive—saw their profits fall sharply (Price 1954: 13).

Though there existed widespread hostility of most middle and upper class Maltese toward the encroachment of English on Italian during the nineteenth century, competition to obtain much sought-after positions in the civil service requiring facility in English began to mollify some. Also, Maltese owners of large merchant houses began to develop fluency in English in order to compete more successfully with the locally based British business.

Though throughout the nineteenth century, Italian remained the language of the Curia, the courts, and the intelligentsia, by the turn of the twentieth century, members of the middle and upper classes had acquired enough English to occupy most civil service positions. In fact, a group of Anglo-Maltese families had begun to gain prominence and carefully imitate English manners. While Malta's elite remained divided in a cultural war over whether English or Italian should have preeminent standing in society, her masses conversed in Maltese. Although this was the only language in which they were fluent, few of them were able to either read or write it. Coupled with intermittent displays of colonial condescension toward Malta, the British response to the unrest over language was to encourage the use of Maltese and English and to make more opportunities available for the Maltese to identify with the Empire.

Sons of some professionals were sent to "public" [prestigious private] schools in England and Maltese officers were sent to the mother country for military training. An aristocrat of Anglo-Maltese heritage, Sir Gerald Strickland, became chief secretary of the Maltese government from 1889 to 1896. Subsequently, he even rose to become a governor in Australia from 1904 to 1909. Considering that in 1901 Malta only had 190 schools in which only 20,000 persons were being educated out of a population of 205,000 (Kendal 1999: 1), it is obvious Maltese of Strickland's status were a rarity.

When in the early 1920's Lord Strickland retired from the colonial service and again plunged into Malta politics, the lines between opposing sides on the language question were more sharply drawn than ever. Even while Strickland's Anglo-Maltese Party (later the Constitutional Party) and Dr. Enrico Mizzi's pro-Italian Particito Nazionalista Democratico (later just the Nationalist Party) battled each other over the language question, society was undergoing major changes. British families and servicemen were drawn to Malta in increasingly large numbers, a trend going on since the World

War I. In the upscale suburb city of Sliema, large numbers of British and Maltese families were beginning to live as neighbors, and somewhat as equals.

For the masses however, the postwar years were difficult ones with high unemployment and a bread subsidy introduced for the first time. Describing Gozo during the late 1920s and early 1930s of her childhood to Galley (1994: 46–53), Maria Callelja recounts that beggars had the lowest status, with an unlettered working class only marginally better off and more often than not bare-footed. It was made up of fishermen, farm laborers, herders, and girl servants who worked in the homes of a tiny elite. Absentee land-lords on Malta, including nobles and religious orders, owned a vast amount of Gozo's farmland. Even many of the farmers who owned small plots of their own were little better off than tenant farmers and were sometimes reduced to supplementing their income by working as farm laborers.

Craftsmen and artisans often found themselves as unable to provide for their families as farmers, and many emigrated to Australia. A small middle class of shop owners and second-level civil servants resided in the island capital of Victoria. It was also in Victoria, on Racecourse Street (now also known as Republic Street), where the few families belonging to the privi-leged business and professional class lived in large symmetrical houses with wrought iron balconies, families that Calleja calls *is-isinjuri*.

Pro-Mizzi by political persuasion, *is-isinjuri* strongly preferred to speak Italian rather than any other language, and when they condescended to speak Maltese, they did so in a highly refined manner rather than in one of the rustic dialects typical of Gozo. Through their large windows dressed in lace one could sometimes get a peak at elegant glasses and silverware displayed in a *ventrina*. Usually well dressed, some of them traveled about in smart horse-drawn carriages (Galley 1994: 46–53). In Gozo of Calleja's childhood, as in the nineteenth century, bread remained one of the indi-cators of status. *Is-isinjuri* and civil servants preferred to eat white bread while the working classes usually consumed bread that was dark.

As low wages, unemployment, and underemployment were chronic prob-lems for numerous men attempting to support households in nineteenth-century Malta, many emigrated while others lived off temporary work or supplemented their regular earnings with part-time jobs. Though Maltese no longer leave the country to settle abroad in large numbers, part-time work continues to be very characteristic of work patterns, and this enables "the Maltese to maintain a relative high standard of living in spite of ap-parently low wage rates" (Boissevain 1969a: 11).

Fully employed men often supplement their household incomes by means ranging from raising rabbits at home, or doing office work at night, to working as clerical or research assistants after teaching or being employed in government offices all day. During certain seasons of the year, some men who ordinarily work on land supplement their incomes by joining fishing crews, and others work as merchants. Even some physicians on public salary practice medicine privately on the side.

Fama (prestige), *pozizzjoni socjali* (social position), a knightship (status of a chevalier), and a prestigious membership in the Union Club, the Casino Maltese, or Casino Notabile contribute to high status in ways that have different degrees of meaning for different segments of society. Hence, it would be as difficult to scale what they mean generally as to scale the many things that Americans or Canadians associate with "status" and "class" (Goodwin 1977: 147–152; Goodwin 2001: 1402).

What gives a person social status varies both within societies and among societies, and Boissevain's assertion (1969a: 55) that there exist local variations in prestige systems appears well founded. Such variations in Malta are probably not immense though Boswell (1994: 133–162) has conclusively shown that they reflect vested interests of people in different areas, different degrees of loyalty to where one resides, and to some extent different areal ideologies. Some research based on reputational data suggests that Maltese may generally rank paying occupations in seven major status levels (Goodwin 1974: 114–118).

At the highest of these levels are university professors, lawyers or notaries, medical doctors, bank managers, architects, elite government officials, and ecclesiastics with important titles such as those associated with the Curias and with Cathedral Chapters. Serving in Parliament is very prestigious though it is considered a part-time job and does not pay much. As members of Parliament are disproportionately of the professional class, however, they have prior careers of working at prestigious jobs and tend not be highly dependent on their political salaries for livelihood. Their work as national power brokers and leaders adds more attention and privilege to the considerable status they already possess.

A legal procurator and a secondary or postsecondary teacher hold positions at the top of a second occupational rung as do a pastor, civil servant in a junior executive position, and a higher clerical officer, though status particulars vary in accordance with requisite qualifications and location. At a third rank in gradually descending order are a primary teacher, registered nurse, enrolled nurse, flight attendant, police sergeant, draftsman, radio technician, chemist compounder, and small-business manager.

Linkages are especially strong between occupational status and educational requirements at this high end of the occupational scale, whereas at the lower levels, the extent to which status is attributed to occupations depends increasingly on economic earnings. Considering that Malta is a country where even highly educated females tend to withdraw from gainful employment on marriage, education for many is an important source of social capital.

The kinds of occupations usually classified within the top three ranks involve some type of postsecondary qualification. A person's attempt to

obtain a high-level occupation without the conventional educational qualifications creates opposition, a social stir, and gossip although, as in many
other societies, occasionally people with good connections manage to slip
in (as some Gozitan villagers say) "through the windows rather than the
door" (Galley 1994: 49).

Further down the scale, a lower ranking clerk, foreman, constable, or a
skilled industrial employee (for example, a fitter or assembly line worker)
is not viewed as meeting as high an educational standard. Also at this
fourth level, though lower, are beauticians, lottery agents or receivers, cash-
iers, hotel receptionists, and plowing contractors. That a plowing contractor is ranked at this level despite being a small businessman who owns
valuable machinery on which others depend reflects a significant social bias
against work associated with food production as well as a bias against
work that takes place in rustic settings.

Though males hardly do any cooking in homes, they dominate cooking
occupations in non-domestic settings. The work of a trained cook who is
not a chef in a highly prestigious establishment is viewed as a fifth-rung
occupation, not much different in status from that of a grocer, a dress-
maker, a sales assistant, a greenhouse worker, or a wholesaler in a produce
auction-house. Except for the plowing contractor and the auctioneer, one
thing that most of the occupations discussed have in common is that they
are neither among the most physically exhausting nor involve work where
people must get dirty while working long hours in the open.

Among occupations directly associated with food production, farming
on one's own land ranks significantly higher than does fishing, herding, or
dairy work. Perhaps this is because working conditions are more predict-
able and some time off is assured during weekends. Also through owning
land an independent farmer possesses a valuable means of production that
is in very short supply in Malta. While more prestige is attached to working
as a barber, a bus driver, a carpenter, or a stone mason than as a herdsman
or fisherman, an independent farmer is usually ranked higher than all these.
Even among fishermen, however, status differences are significant, with
some who are prosperous and own their own expensive boats being re-
spectfully referred to by their fellows as *padruni* or patrons (Wilhelmsen
1976: 397).

Ranking in prestige slightly lower than fishing is the work of a waiter,
ganger, untrained factory worker, and a coffin-maker. Closer to the bottom
of the scale are street vendors, watchmen, and maids, though their work
earns them significantly more prestige than that of street cleaners and refuse
collectors. In sharp contrast to most Mediterranean countries and even to
such highly developed countries as the United States, France, and Great
Britain, beggars long ago disappeared from Malta's streets and true home-
lessness in the sense of people sleeping on the sidewalks is essentially unknown.

Boswell's research (1994: 151–152) suggests that because of social prestige associated with residential areas, urban residents on Malta have regional and local preferences concerning where they prefer most and least to live. Overall, they greatly favor living on the side of the inner harbor next to Marsamxett Harbor rather than on the opposite side next to the Grand Harbor. As between the western region and the eastern region, the western tends to be considered a region of high prestige and the eastern one of extremely low prestige. While this research shows them to be more ambivalent about the status of urban areas in the north, Mosta emerges as the most prestigious northern locality in which to live and remote Mellieħa the least.

Related to such regional generalizations are intra-regional ones that figure in the folk image of what life is considered to be like in various villages, towns, and cities. Much of the way a locality is ranked occupationally depends on the kinds of work that outsiders associate with its menfolk. This is because although single females constitute a significant segment of the workforce at all levels, except for teachers they are heavily represented at the middle and lower levels, and they are often viewed as temporary and tangential participants in the workplace.

Maltese generally prefer work that is nonmanual and attribute higher status to it than manual work. This tends to depress the status of towns such as Marsaxlokk and St. Paul's Bay on Malta as well as Mġarr and Marsalform on Gozo, which are known as places with large populations of fishermen. These values have a similar impact on popular images of towns such as Siġġiewi and Safi on Malta and towns such as Żebbuġ and Sannat on Gozo where large numbers of farmers reside.

Sometimes cities located very near each other may have very different status. For many years, Mdina with its associations with nobility and high-ranking church officials—typically of privileged social backgrounds—towered over its suburb of Rabat in power and status. However nowadays, Rabat is considered a very desirable place to live. Bar women, prostitutes, and their male associates tend to depress the status of some places in Malta, for example, Valletta's Strait Street and some areas in Floriana and the Three Cities. Ironically however, Gzira—whose status is especially blemished by this activity—does not seem to negatively impact the high status of nearby Sliema.

Crosscutting the linkages among various types of occupations and lifestyles distributed across localities is an urban-rural axis associated with economic and political power (Tabone 1998: 4). To the extent that professional and wealthy Maltese provide access to higher levels of society for villagers, they often function well as patrons. The fact that patrons usually reside in towns rather than in rural areas reinforces the prestige long associated with living in certain cities, towns, and suburbs. A disproportionate number of senior civil servants live in these high-prestige localities.

The typical townsman was often described to me by villagers as a white-collar worker who goes to cocktail parties, tries to look like an Englishman—pipe, tweeds and moustache—and speaks English to his children. The villager, on the other hand, is portrayed as an illiterate rustic who spends his money on wine and fireworks, without a thought for the future of his children. Both caricatures, of course, are gross exaggerations, but each, none the less, contains elements of truth. (Boissevain 1969b: 28)

In reality, the status of localities is so multidimensional and complex that it is based on much more than whether they represent town or country. For example, Siġġiewi has a longer town history than Senglea and a more prosperous population, including some university graduates, though it remains largely a town of farmers. There exist non-rustic localities like Senglea, Cospicula, and Vittoriosa which are not highly regarded with respect to occupational status because of the manual work that many of their residents perform at the dockyards, in factories, and elsewhere. Prior to World War II, Senglea had many prominent residents clustered along Victory Street near Our Lady of Victory Church, but it now has hardly any university graduates and is thoroughly working-class although it is located in the populous conurbation known as *il-belt* or the inner harbor area.

Stratification is made more complex by the fact that occupational status does not invariably follow the same pattern as economic status. Though most men who are resident in Senglea work at unskilled, semi-skilled, and technical jobs that pay low wages, they are generally considered to have higher occupational status than fishermen, or even farmers. This means that in a locality such as Siġġiewi where many men farm, they tend to perform lower status work than the men of Senglea while they tend to have higher economic status.

What is considered a status symbol in terms of housing and housing design continually undergoes change. After the Baroque style began to be employed by the Knights in the late 1500s—mostly in Birgu, Valletta, and Floriana—to symbolize prestige and power, it was eventually copied in some domestic architecture (Mahoney 1996: 179). We now live at a time when many well-to-do people are attracted to Gozo for its rustic charm and when Goztian villas and farm houses, that have been renovated in fashionable ways far beyond Victoria's Racecourse Street where *is-isinjuri* have traditionally been located, are sometimes occupied by well-to-do people.

The way people sometimes feel about living in a particular place is determined almost as much by the status of their neighbors or the prevailing lifestyle as by the physical housing per se. As localities and neighborhoods have kinds of ranking, so do kinds of housing in accordance with considerable unevenness in the distribution of income and wealth. While the history of settlement patterns impact housing conditions throughout Malta, that the status of housing is also associated with occupational, educational, and economic status of residents can hardly be overstated.

The good housing stock and high levels of home ownership in Attard, Sliema, and Figura give them a definite status advantage over Senglea and Qormi, where housing stock is often poor and where many residents are renters. A vast status difference is associated with dwelling in a large detached or semidetached villa in Balzan or San Pawl tat-Targà on the one hand, and in a *karrejja* or common tenement (possibly without refrigeration, kitchen, or running water except for an indoor toilet) in towns such as Qormi, Senglea, or Żejtun on the other. The larger proportion of villas in the housing stock of Attard than in solidly middle-class Fgura, as well as the considerable number of villas in Mosta, contribute positively to their status with respect to housing. However, not all localities need to construct villas to be high status as is illustrated by Sliema.

No less important than occupations, economic status, education, and housing, language and language attitudes are important markers of status. Schools teach a standardized Maltese known as *il-Malti bil-pulit* but dialectical variation associated with status persists. Alongside important lexicon variations, a cosmopolitan intonation in Valletta and its suburbs has moved decidedly away from Arabic in the direction of Italian and Sicilian (Aquilina 1970e: 11). Coupled with other cultural differences, dialectical variation sometimes contributes to stereotypes between various classes of Maltese.

One characteristic of dialects of Maltese spoken in higher status towns is that they tend to incorporate more vocabulary and pronunciations of English and Italian as opposed to Arabic derivation. As a word meaning mother, not only is Italian-derived *"mama"* preferred over Arabic-derived *"omm"* in the upper-class areas around Sliema and St. Julians, Italian-derived *"papa"* is also frequently encountered, used both to refer to father and to father-in-law (Boissevain 1969b: 28; Boswell 1994: 134; Sciriha 1994: 126–129).

The relative frequency of such "snooty" usages in this area is quite pronounced when compared, for example, to certain speech patterns in the working-class Three Cities or in rustic Safi, which is located in the Eastern region. In a study of forms of addressing parents-in-law where locality, gender, age, and class were taken into account, Sciriha (1994: 126–129)—in comparing youth-oriented upper class St. Julians with Safi—has found some important correlations associated with all these variables. In addition to such lexical patterns of status significance, Sciriha (1994:122–124) also has documented class and regional significance in a tendency on the part of many working-class residents in the Three Cities area to simplify certain diphthongs in Maltese, especially when they occur at the ends of words. Whether one focuses on irregular linguistic usages associated with the upper class or working class, they are sometimes embraced with pride by their users though they may illicit mockery or disdain from others.

Few factors are more important overall in sorting Maltese into a social hierarchy than education. In recent decades, Malta's educational system has become increasingly complex with numerous alternatives for students and their families, all of which have status implications. One of the first choices that a family has to make is whether to enroll a child in a government institution or one that is private. Private schooling is greatly esteemed and slightly over one quarter of all Maltese children study in private schools that are largely staffed by members of religious orders (Mifsud 1994: 323–341).

A child reaching the age of three or four has been enrolled either in a private nursery school or in a government kindergarten. At age five the child is ready to begin six years of learning in primary school, again the choice will be between either one supported by the government under the direction of the Education Department or one that is private. In either case, the school will almost invariably be limited to children of one sex in keeping with separation as an important part of gender socialization from an early age in Malta. The only exceptions are some private schools and a few government schools—sufficiently few in number that one can count them on one's fingers.

Tracking of students along different paths quickly becomes more pronounced as they begin to study in various secondary schools, for entrance to all secondary grammar schools, whether government or private, is based on examination. Consequently, a segment of students is diverted into government-supported, vocationally oriented "technical" schools. There are many paths along which students may pursue a five-year course of study in a secondary grammar school. There exist private schools staffed mostly by religious personnel, institutes, and other private schools staffed largely by lay teachers. Some of these are international schools and some are government schools, but all contrast in reputation and social standing.

For students enrolled in secondary grammar schools as for their families, the experience is often tense in that everyone is very examination-conscious. What most upwardly mobile students wish to obtain at the end of their course of study is the requisite number of General Certificate of Education (GCE) and Secondary Education Certificate (SEC) "passes" that will enable them to proceed toward university entrance. Entrance into the University of Malta is highly competitive, however, and one can only get there in one of three ways, all involving additional study and difficult examinations. Two means are to receive the required number of passes after Form VI study at a private institution or at state upper lyceums and higher secondary schools. A third means—available only since the opening of the University Junior College in 1995—is achieving there the requisite number of "Advanced (A) level" and "Ordinary (O) level" passes.

As the University Junior College represents a change in the traditional means of reaching the university, and hence a change in the rules about obtaining status through education, its establishment in 1995 brought about considerable protest, including boycotts, demonstrations, and angry letters to newspapers. In Malta, much attention is paid to such educational details as whether one has merely finished secondary school at "O" level or passed comparable GCE, whether one has obtained "A" level qualifications, or perhaps has obtained a teaching certificate or even the ultimate prize, a university degree.

In reality, status through education is complicated by the fact that numerous postsecondary alternatives to a university degree currently exist in Malta, resulting not only in many new opportunities for students and trainees but also in a much more elaborated stratification system. In recent decades, these options—all with their own requirements and associated status—have virtually mushroomed. These include a polytechnic college, specialized trade schools, school of secretarial studies, a nursing school, the institute of hotel catering and tourism studies, an industrial training center in industrial electronics, an arts and design center, an agricultural college, a school of navigation, a school of art, a school of music, and an academy of dramatic arts.

Maltese hold in high esteem the impressive educational achievements of people living in places like Sliema, Attard, and even Figura, though in the case of Fgura many students attend government schools (Boswell 1994: 139). On the other hand, people tend to hold in low regard the habit of discontinuing one's education at the mandatory age of 16, or even younger, as frequently occurs in such localities as Senglea and Marsaxlokk.

Within most societies there exist some cleavages between groups of people that are so pronounced that some real difficulty is encountered in attempting to place them side by side on unidimensional status scales. Boissevain (1969a: 41) has stated that "[t]he most important social differences which cuts through Maltese society is that of sex" and, in fact, the positions of females and males in Malta do in many ways set them apart from each other.

From primary school virtually up to the university, the educational system has reflected this division. For example in the 1940s, two teachers colleges were established, Mater Admirabilis College of Education in Rabat for females and St. Michael's College of Education in St. Julian's for males. Though an amalgamation of these single-sex colleges as part of a reorganization to improve teacher education had taken place by the late 1970s, that this occurred so recently nonetheless reflects the separation that differentiates males and females in Malta.

Mizzi (1981: 86) has delineated aspects of this spatial segregation with great clarity. She has written, for example, that in many ancient cruciform churches women still tend to sit in the middle section, with the girls in front, while males tend to sit on the sides and in the back—though in general men exercise more freedom than females to sit wherever they wish. The greater freedom given to males to use territory more liberally than females is further underscored by traditions whereby females in churches are "forbidden from entering the sacristy, and from being on the altar itself, except during special ceremonies or during feasts" (Mizzi 1981: 97).

Though the washing of automobiles is sometimes considered an extension of domestic work which females are expected to do, males are usually in charge of family automobiles. A much larger proportion of men, moreover, know how to drive than women. Reflective of similar gender difference, boats are usually owned and operated by males though females may travel in them as passengers. Male territories in Senglea include the square in front of the churches, the political clubs, the bars, and the marina during the day while the shops and the homes are more associated with female (Mizzi 1981: 86, 194). Although during *festa* celebrations, the public streets are shared freely by males and females, a common everyday pattern of associating territoriality with gender is well described in a citation about Marsaxlokk by Wilhelmsen (1976: 391). "A woman rarely goes near places where men congregate, and if she enters a bar to purchase something, the men in there will not enter into any conversation with her unless they are close kin or belong to the same household. She may, however, help her husband with fishing gear, but even then she says little to the men."

This physical cleavage between the sexes runs deep and has its behavioral and status parallels in numerous behavioral norms based on double standards and different ways of evaluating the economic contributions of males and females. The contribution of women, even married women, to the economy has long been minimized or underestimated due to its temporary, subsidiary, or part-time nature, coupled with the fact that it did not contribute in positive ways to family prestige. Even in the mid-nineteenth century when two-thirds of all Maltese were laborers, artisans, farmers, and fishermen, shoes were rather uncommon, and the average couple had seven to ten children, women made invaluable contributions to the support of their families though consistently rewarded with inferior remuneration. In addition to tending to their homes and large families, some helped in the fields while others engaged in spinning and weaving (Price 1954: 9–10).

Part-time work, long a means by which gainfully employed males and females supplement their wages, also attracts some married women. Until recently, however, married women have tended to undertake gainful employment somewhat surreptitiously in order that the pretense that they are completely supported by their husbands may be projected for the sake of family status. This way of supplementing family income is seldom openly discussed, in part for fear that information given out might damage one's reputation, the reputation of one's family, or otherwise give ammunition to one's rivals (Wilhelmsen 1976: 401). Also, such matters are not openly discussed because information leakage about one's finances—including especially part-time work—could get back to taxation authorities with the consequence one might have to pay higher taxes. Two proverbs that come to mind in this regard are "il-flus ma jwerżqux" and "senduz magħluq x'hin jinfetah tkun taf x'fih," meaning that "money does not squeal" and "you can never know who is rich or poor without having access to his coffer" (Aquilina 1972: 329, 338).

The vast majority of married women throughout the islands work largely in the essentially rankless job of homemakers in their own homes. For married Maltese women, this traditionally has been the most prestigious occupation of all. The islanders make a sharp distinction between the status of women who work in their own homes and women who work outside their own homes as maids.

Single and married women appear to make equally informed decisions about their futures and both are socialized to be very resourceful in maximizing household resources. Some married women in rural areas help care for small animals and house gardens while also practicing crafts such as lace-making at home. The wives of many fishermen are involved in selling fish, sometimes locally and sometimes farther afield. In numerous villages and cities, women operate ground-floor shops located in or near their homes and others contribute to household resources in ways they find compatible with maintaining a certain social standing and the reputations of their families. Many women who do not work for wages make productive contributions to their households through skillful domestic management that includes sophisticated marketing, conservation, recycling of goods and supplies, domestic artisanship, and thrifty conversion of marginal resources into financial as well as social capital.

Until very recently, Maltese males and females have competed for the same occupations only in a very limited sense. Even at present one frequently encounters job advertisements which specify or imply that only a person of a particular sex will be considered. Given that many men had to leave their homeland for lack of work, a tradition developed—reinforced by church, state, and society—that men should be favored over women in Malta's very limited job market. This tradition was especially intolerant of married women seeking gainful employment as they were expected to be supported by their husbands.

Against this background, a certain occupation for a woman often carries more status than the same occupation does for a man relative to other men, since his options in the job market are quite different. As a consequence, many women have to make hard choices between marriage or a career, age-sensitive choices that were virtually impossible to undo as divorce is not possible.

If as most social scientists agree, sex is the most important cleavage in Maltese society, the second most important is associated with the religion, and Catholicism in particular (Galley 1994: 53). Though in Malta there has always been significant overlap across the social divide between the sacred and profane, this situation makes difficult any effort to place ecclesiastics and lay persons on a common status scale. At times, status scales for the laity and clergy overlap, as is evident, for example, at the well-known Capuchin cemetery in Floriana where burial generally has been restricted to priests and members of well-to-do families (Koster 1983: 308).

Clear status differences separate a pope and a cardinal, an archbishop and a bishop from a canon, and all of these from an ordinary priest. In other words the church carries out its mission through a complex bureaucratic organization, whose upper grades are male, with religious orders and laity at the bottom. Throughout Roman Catholicism, the clergy is divided into two groups of priests: on the one hand, regular or religious priests and, on the other hand, secular or diocesan priests. Bishops are in charge of a geographical territory and diocesan or secular priests take a promise of obedience toward their bishop and typically assist him within his territory. Regular or religious priests—sometimes known as monks and friars—take vows of poverty, chastity, and obedience to the head of their orders rather than to a bishop.

Historically, sons of elite Maltese families were attracted to the diocesan priesthood more frequently than to monastic orders, with the possible exception of the Jesuits (Koster 1983: 308). Unlike seminarians aspiring to become religious priests, seminarians wishing to become diocesan priests typically wished to advance in careers not sequestered from the larger world.

Most of Malta's secular priests begin their priestly education by having the requisite funds from their families or patrons on deposit at a Curia bank. This favorable financial standing permits them the latitude to have considerable choice in where they will serve. As diocesan seminarians without such resources study, thanks to the beneficence of their bishop, they generally have less choice (Boissevain 1969b: 18–19). Even among monastic orders, it often happens that a particular order is viewed as more prestigious or influential than another. Not all are equally well educated or hold equally influential positions within the hierarchies of their orders. Nor do those who perform in the larger world have equally prestigious positions. This notwithstanding, within a particular order, the religious priests obey the same superior, live by vows of poverty, and dwell communally.

Status-related differences sometimes distinguish the secular from the regular clergy. While under the Knights for example, most of the religious orders—except for the Jesuits—tended to remain on rather favorable terms with the Order. The secular priesthood was often viewed as competitive with it. Though exact parallels do not exist between regular or religious priests, "It is commonly held that the regular and secular clergy are always potential competitors as they jointly monopolize the sacraments and try to use these to tie a large number of clients to themselves" (Koster 1983: 312).

In sharp contrast to Gozo where nine out of ten priests are secular or diocesan, over half of all priests on Malta are religious. A somewhat larger proportion of regular priests than secular priests traditionally has been employed at the University of Malta. In fact, the Collegium Melitense, a college begun in 1592 that eventually evolved into the University, was founded by the Jesuits.

The fact that secular priests often work in parishes and live with their families means that they are probably more easily involved with the day-to-day struggles for status that unfold in their families as well as in the parishes where they work. The influence of the Bishop of Gozo is greatly enhanced by the fact that his diocese has significantly more priests, nuns, and religious brothers per capita than the Archbishop of Malta, and the vast majority of Gozitan priests, being secular, are obedient to him. In fact, though only 8% of the national population lives on Gozo, the number of diocesan seminarians there is almost half of the number in the seminary on Malta.

All groups and individuals that are tied to the Church are ranked. Each parish, religious order and parish society has its fixed position in the overall order. The same applies to the clerics who constitute its personnel. Position in the hierarchy is determined by seniority of foundation in the case of parishes and associations—or date of ordination or appointment to present office, in the case of the clergy—in combination with certain marks of honour conferred by the Church authorities. (Boissevain 1969b: 22)

Constituting a single episcopate, the Maltese Islands are divided into two dioceses, Gozo and Comino sharing their Bishop in one and Malta's Archbishop in the other. Despite equivalent authority and jurisdiction in most respects, it is the Archbishop who is the president of the two-person Episcopal Conference and who exercises a few privileges in matters pertaining to both Gozo and Comino. Each Bishop heads a bureaucracy, a major part of which is the Curia, that is, an ecclesiastical court and top administrative officials that assist him in governing his diocese. In keeping with the nature of a bureaucracy, some priests occupy more prestigious and influential positions than do others. In addition to this bureaucracy, each Bishop has his own seminary. It is in the seminary of a particular Bishop where those seminarians who take vows of obedience to him are expected to study. While on Gozo, the Bishop's seminary is located in Victoria; the Archbishop's seminary is located in Floriana.

The major cleavage between the laity and church hierarchy permeates all aspects of Maltese life, including worldview. Some priests have more illustrious family backgrounds than others and are more likely to be found occupying exalted positions within the church, more likely in Mdina or some town with high status. On the other hand, even a diocesan priest of humble background typically finds acceptance in the homes of the elite if he happens to be in charge of the parish where they reside.

Within Catholicism, there exists a hierarchy of order as well as a hierarchy of jurisdiction, consisting of ordained males. Females are not a part of either of these hierarchies. Except for a few females mostly performing typing or other office work in the Curia on the larger island, females are essentially without representation in either the Maltese or Gozitan Curia (Clews 2001: 145–146; Miceli 1994; 90). There do exist bureaucratic structures within various orders for religious sisters, meaning that not all members of an order enjoy equivalent authority. Some orders, moreover, are held in higher esteem than others.

Well beyond the walls of their convents, the influence of religious sisters on social structure is immense. Both in the Maltese and the Gozitan diocese, they are more numerous than the priests and religious brothers combined. In addition to the work sisters undertake in hospitals, prisons, and parishes, the fact that they are so vital in staffing educational institutions means that they are instrumental in recycling and shaping values, including those relevant to social standing. On Gozo, where well over nine out of ten teachers in both public and private schools are females, a large proportion are nuns (Darmanin 1998: 66). That 90% of all nuns reside on the island of Malta in contrast to slightly more than 80% of priests magnifies their relative impact.

In addition to the episcopate, the priesthood, and diaconate, social stratification is reflected in the existence of lower orders and grades, as well as in orders of religious sisters, members of secular institutes, and members of various societies for apostolic life. Catholic laity as represented by lay orders, confraternities, and some other religious organizations often bridge the status cleavage between the sacred and profane. Even political party affiliation has status implications that are to some extent colored by feelings toward the church.

During the 16 years from 1971 to 1987 when the Labor Party had a majority in Parliament as noted by Sultana (1994: 34–35), its "declared intention was the eradication of class difference.... The Labour government also narrowed wage differentials in the public sector from 15 to 5 times [while] arguing for a necessity to construct an 'egalitarian society.' "

Within the membership of the Labor Party, one encounters a segment that is resentful of certain elitist tendencies within the church and is, at times, anticlerical (Boissevain 1969b: 106–107; Wilhelmsen 1976: 233). The working class and lower middle-class masses who are the backbone of this party, though proud of being European and Mediterranean, are often suspect of grand alliances. The Nationalist Party, on the other hand, attracts a larger proportion of people of high socioeconomic status, people less threatened by elitism, with outlooks decidedly more European than Mediterranean.

Though the noble titles in Malta were abolished with the Napoleonic occupation that began in 1798, they were restored under British rule. A Royal commission, in 1877, even made specific recommendations on exactly which titles the British Crown should recognize. In mid-1975, when Labor had a majority, legislation was passed withdrawing official recognition of titles of nobility.

This egalitarian action on the part of Labor came about at a time when there were at least some 30 Maltese holding titles of nobility that had been created by European royalty between the mid-fourteenth and eighteenth centuries. The 1997 legislation that withdrew official recognition of noble titles did not forbid their use for social purposes and did not completely wipe out the fascination of some Maltese with proclaiming noble family linkages—sometimes tracing such linkages back eight or nine centuries to the period of Norman control. In fact, a private Committee of Privileges of the Maltese Nobility still undertakes to decide the succession of titles once recognized officially.

This was barely a year after Parliament—with a Labor majority—amended the Constitution to make Malta "a republic," resulting in a number of symbolic status changes, including—to the chagrin of a segment of society—dropping "Royal" from the names of some of the most important institutions in society.

Additionally, Maltese with the title of "Chevalier" include a rather diverse group of people, including some with monumental achievements, some with just good social connections, and some who just happened to have the 40 or so Maltese liras required for entry into one of the less prestigious orders. As of 2001 (Clews 2001: 405–431), there still existed 14 orders of chivalry in Malta.

Attitudes about status along the dimension of party affiliation are complex. Though the populations of some localities usually identify with one party more than the other, the national population as a whole is approximately evenly divided in its party loyalties. Hence, both parties have broad and overlapping bases of support, and through secret balloting, they turn each other out of office with some regularity. Moreover, at a personal level, associating oneself with the cadre of one political party or the other is voluntary, and one may change affiliation more or less at will, taking status and other factors into account.

As in so many other countries, the very things that some people do to acquire status, others avoid doing—depending, of course, on such factors as age, degree of self-assuredness, value system, political disposition, and family orientation. While some socially conscious Maltese seek membership in ancient religious confraternities and actively vie for prominent roles in public *festi* that celebrate various saints, for example, others consciously limit their participation. In fact, some cosmopolitan citizens look disparagingly on certain compatriots whom they consider overly obsessed with spending money on fireworks for *festi* rather than on education for their children. Similarly, some people speak Maltese in rather conventional ways to gain status while others aspire to status by embellishing it with many foreign words or perhaps even claiming—sometimes falsely—not to be able to read it.

Although it is still true that only about half of the populace regularly read Maltese language books, newspapers, and magazines, more than 98% claim speaking fluency in it (Sciriha and Vassallo 2001). Moreover, the educated elite as well as the masses have embraced their common tongue with unprecedented pride. One note, however; this pride does not extend to Arabic, the principal language from which Maltese is derived. Though large numbers of Maltese are bilingual or even multilingual, being linguistically Eurocentric remains esteemed, with 87% claiming to speak English, 60% Italian, and even 17% French. In contrast, only 3% claim to understand Arabic, and fewer than 2% even consider it an important language (Sciriha and Vassallo 2001).

Another important dimension of status has to do with owning or having access to second homes. In fact, some Maltese families annually undertake ceremonious departures for summer homes or prestigious hotels that may be located a mere three or four miles from where they regularly live. Despite Malta's high population density and the paucity of surplus housing, this custom is not restricted to the well-to-do. In addition to using alternative housing in summer, some residents on Malta with surplus income consider it chic to spend weekends in a second house or flat in more rustic Gozo.

Maltese avoid casually entertaining at home people that they do not consider their equal, and a variety of conservative factors influence highly selective ways in which Maltese interact with tourists. Among symbols of high status in Malta are having a maid, wearing stylish clothing, affiliating with health clubs, owning a yacht, furnishing homes with antique hierlooms—including nice glassware and silver—attending events at the Manoel National Theatre, being socially well connected, getting a good education, marrying well, and maintaining family honor. Moreover, young sophisticates of high status often frequent elite cafes, restaurants, and clubs in areas like Sliema and St. Julian's.

In the same way that the well-heeled men often seek recreation through tennis, golf, sailing, and yachting, their less well-to-do fellows find pleasure in darts, draughts, bocci, or brilli. Similarly, females of different classes often pass their time differently. While the masses of women might spend considerable time shopping, cleaning their homes, and walking with their children in the evening, the more affluent and better educated are likely to devote more time to participating in philanthropic and civic organizations, and, if playing a card game, to prefer bridge rather than *tombla*.

For all women more than for men, however, status is dependent in some considerable degree on correct public comportment, guarded contact with the opposite sex, attention to domestic chores, and regular attendance at church. Though foreign travel is a dimension of status for males and females, it is not an easy one to interpret. While many Maltese are fortunate enough to travel for sheer pleasure, some emigrate because of what they consider to be dire economic opportunities at home or attraction to the broader social diversity and mobility options abroad.

An engaging analysis of institutionalized social inequality by Ronald Sultana involving a comparison of research by M. Vassallo, Edward Zammit, Godfrey Baldacchino, and others demonstrates that contrasting theoretical orientations contribute to diverse views of Malta's stratification system. Among those who tend to minimize inequality, Sultana (1994: 35, 39–40) cites Vassallo who, heavily influenced by Max Weber, believes that the wide diffusion of education has largely rendered Malta a meritocracy that has status groups but not classes. At the other extreme, among those with Marxist perspectives who assume the omnipresence of class exploitation, Sultana (1994: 42) cites R. Miliband who sees society as largely dichotomized between dominant and subordinate classes.

According to Sultana (1994: 43–50), Miliband sees a subordinate mass dominated by a class that Baldacchino has defined in terms of prestigious inter-family connections and disproportionate representation on corporate and government boards as well as differential access to the means of production. Miliband, according to Sultana (1994: 42), is much more impressed by this essential dichotomy than by the existence of a tiny "petty bourgeoisie" that is sandwiched in between. Scholars remain divided about the real nature of Malta's stratification system. However, Sultana (1994: 37) points to findings by Zammit suggesting most ordinary Maltese probably believe in the existence of three or more strata of some kind and the possibility of achieving social mobility across them by means of hard work, investments in education, and good patronage networks.

Chapter 8

Home, Family, and Social Change

Many types of groups fall within the categories of kinship or family, and it is not uncommon for definitions of these groups to change over time and from one situation to another. Some scholars argue that there exists no such thing as "the family" for family meanings are so tied to practice, and can differ based on gender and other factors, that producing a catalog of meanings is impossible. Others offer us meticulous definitions that not infrequently promise more than they deliver. What Maltese recognize as close relatives or *qraba ta' gewwa* is situational—including uncles, aunts, and grandparents for a baptism, but probably also cousins for a wedding or a funeral.

To use the terminology of Tabone (1995: 28), about 16% of families live in flats or apartments, about 14% in some type of maisonette, approximately 11% in a one-story ground-floor dwelling, but almost one-half in adjoining town or terrace dwellings. These terrace dwellings, more than any other type, provide the housing for Maltese, though there has always existed variety. One major exception has been some grand palaces—now more often used as public buildings than as private residences—and another is detached villas of recent vintage. Most terrace houses are of moderate size and consist of two stories though in some areas the stories may number as many as four. Both in cities and rural areas, terrace housing has long functioned well in nucleated settlements that contribute to frequent contacts among family members and neighbors.

Most houses face directly onto streets or sidewalks, without a setback or lawn. Maltese quarry the limestone from which extended rows of housing are constructed. As these quarries yield one of Malta's few natural resources available in abundance, housing is adapted to local conditions in terms of materials, a dense population, and very restricted landmass. Scholars increasingly recognize integral connections among space, place, and family in the determination of home life (Birdwell-Pheasant and Lawrence-Zúñiga 1999). Historically derived in various ways from a combination of African and European styles, Maltese housing provides the physical confines in which home life unfolds and reciprocal shaping takes place in important ways.

Small windows and a minimum number of doorways facilitate privacy and security. In conformity with social requirements for the same, balconies are often enclosed. Shuttering windows, whether on balconies or elsewhere is very common. Malta's terrace houses require good ventilation to be comfortable and are flat-roofed.

"Save water" has long been a common slogan in Malta, and people often count the days that dry spells last. Special prayers sometimes are offered in churches during periods of drought. In a setting where water is in scarce supply, the flat roofs are useful in collecting rainwater and directing it into stone wells. Some families still place perishable items like milk and butter into a pail kept in the well. Some generations ago people might boil some of the well water for consumption. Nowadays, they more often find other uses for it, such as watering their gardens.

Given scarcity of water and thin soils, greenery is sparse and the limestone base is only intermittently covered. Given that limestone predominates as a construction material, a visual unity exists between the buildings and the landscape. Once limestone blocks used for exterior walls of houses are cemented together and covered with plaster, they are sometimes whitewashed or painted a pastel color while at other times they are simply left the ochre color of the natural stone. Both limestone blocks and varied tiles, including marble, are widely used as flooring. From medieval times through the nineteenth century, two major types of town housing were constructed, depending in large measure on local access to affordable land.

One of these types exists in abundance where land is relatively cheap such as Siġġiewi, Qormi, and Żebbuġ. In this type of terrace house most rooms—usually moderately sized, long, and narrow—are found on the ground floor. As this plan often encloses a courtyard where traditionally animals were often kept, it required a big plot of land. Originally, a great many of these houses were single-storied as the shortage of timber inhibited the construction of rooms wider than nine feet or so. In order to roof rooms of this width, one had to slope the walls slightly inwards from bottom to top, decreasing the ceiling span to about seven feet at the roofline. Brackets known as corbels supported thin slabs of limestone used for roofing. For wider rooms, arches had to be built on the ground floor for the roof slabs and, where a second story was to be built, wooden beams supported the stone roofing slabs (Mahoney 1996: 79–89).

A second type of terrace house was common in towns where affordable land was in short supply such as Mdina, Birgu, and Senglea. For this type of smaller two-storied terrace house, the single-storied courtyard plan was, in effect, split into two parts with its front constituting the lower level and its rear constituting an upper level. In many of these houses, an enclosed staircase substituted for an interior courtyard. Being more vertical without an interior courtyard, this smaller two-storied house made more efficient use of land. Some well-to-do Mdina families in medieval times experimented with a variation of roof, influenced more by Europe than Africa, which involved innovative sloping of tiles. As this innovation required timber—a resource in short supply—and failed to conserve water in the manner of traditional houses, it never became widespread (Mahoney 1996: 79–89).

With the towns near the Grand Harbor straining under particularly heavy population densities by the end of the nineteenth century, some big multistoried houses that formerly housed single families began to be divided into substandard tenements or *kerrejja*. Even their basements, in many cases, were let as a multipurpose room to the poor. These conversions contributed to additional overcrowding, poor ventilation, inadequate sanitation, dampness and poor lighting. Such living conditions were uncomfortable and ideal for the spread of disease.

A rather low mezzanine that was sometimes sandwiched between the ground floor and the main upper story of large houses had been gradually disappearing since the end of the eighteenth century, and by the early 1900s, most houses had only two principal stories. What domestic architecture lost with the mezzanine, it often gained by means of a full or partial basement. While the basement was used for garaging an automobile in some cases, in others it supplied extra living space, sometimes for the owners and at other times for tenants (Mahoney 1996: 79–89).

Responding to a dismal housing situation in 1880, the Council of Government approved Chapter 13 of the Code of Police Laws. This legislation provided for important improvement in building control. It stipulated, for example, that all new houses should have rear yards as wide as the width of houses, that internal courtyards should be related to the height of the buildings, and that houses should have adequate lighting, ventilation, sanitation, sewage disposal, and means of controlling dampness. The outside rooms of virtually all houses now have small openings to the outside that are left open year-round to control dampness and protect against mildew. As winters are more humid than frigid, the heat loss that results is more than offset by a fireplace, or more commonly a portable heater operating on paraffin, electricity, or gas. Without doubt, the new standards for domestic architecture brought about by Chapter 13 triggered changes in the way family members interacted with each other as well as neighbors.

Steel beams replacing wooden beams on the upper floors of multi-storied houses between the mid-1800s and World War II meant that the old arches formerly used to support the roofs in some of the wider houses were no longer needed and external walls could be made thinner. Moreover, the introduction of reinforced concrete shortly before the war meant that limestone roofing slabs and steel joists also disappeared. Though houses continued to have high ceilings, by the time of the war, they decreased somewhat though still remaining high (Mahoney 1996: 79–89).

As house plots became narrower and the combination of rear yards and open stairwells extending from the ground floor to the roof began to replace the internal courtyards for cooling and ventilation, housing was improved and land use became more efficient. Many of these terrace houses were so narrow that with their ground floor corridors, there was sufficient space for rooms on only one side.

It is not uncommon for a ground-floor corridor to shift from one side of a house to the other mid-way in its course, meaning that a hallway does not always extend the full length of a house in a straight line. In two-story dwellings, it is often halfway down the ground-floor corridor that one encounters a turn, where a stairway that extends from the ground floor to the roof is located. This architectural feature of a multistory stairwell permits the roof to be used as a functional part of most houses. Rear yards are also an important part of domestic space. They are often used for storing equipment, for small-scale vegetable and flower gardening, or as places to keep pets. Animals such as chickens, pigeons, and rabbits that often supplement the diet are sometimes kept in these yards or on roofs. So common is it to have a small house garden that even in a densely settled and completely built-up city such as Senglea, one encounters vendors of manure with some regularity.

On the ground floor of homes, the rooms nearest the street are normally used for receiving guests and frequently contain the most impressive furniture, trophy cases, and lace curtains. Though it is in these rooms that guests are most likely to be entertained, guests are sometimes received more informally in the kitchen or hallway as well. In homes without a second floor, front rooms sometimes serve a dual function as receiving rooms and as bedrooms. On the ground floor of some houses, one or more of the front rooms has been converted into a shop of some kind with its own door leading to the street. Women as well as men work in these types of shops that, though built into homes, are well separated from the family quarters (Wilhelmsen 1976: 86).

When a family lives on more than one floor, bedrooms are most often on the upper levels. In rural areas, this meant that a family traditionally slept above its animals. As most houses are narrow and deep, it is not uncommon for some bedrooms to lead into one another.

Even in wider Maltese houses where most bedrooms open onto a hallway, it is not uncommon for a family member sometimes to pass through a bedroom to reach a common room used for studying, watching television, or bathing. In such cases, one person may just call out to another that they are coming through if they think that privacy will be a problem.

Family life can be intimate in some Maltese homes with doorways occasionally equipped with curtains as well as doors. At least some families like the fact that with curtains, family members can see from one room to another, and they appreciate the way this facilitates ventilation. This situation differs considerably from social class to social class and from one family to another. Whatever the arrangement in a particular home, a bedroom used by parents typically affords more privacy than one used by children. More privacy is generally available nowadays than when families were much larger in size.

Tabone (1995: 27–28) has pointed out that while almost 50% of all housing units are located in a multistoried, terraced dwellings, another 8% are located in detached or semidetached houses, and 11% in one-story ground floor dwellings. Approximately 16% of housing units consist of flats, many of which are located in apartment blocks. As far as possible in all these types of housing, receiving rooms tend to be the closest to the street or to the front door. Bedrooms, on the other hand, tend to be removed from receiving rooms in order to maximize privacy. That Maltese dwellings are private places with individual identities is underscored by the fact that many houses are individually named—for example, "Free Flat" or "Villa Pace"—rather than known by numbers and street names.

Although much of family life revolves around the preparation and communal consumption of food, approximately 2.5% of families have no kitchen facility of any type (Abela 1998b: 108). The kitchens that exist range from many equipped with a simple hot plate or cooker on a shelf operating on gas, electricity, or kerosene at one extreme to a minority equipped with such "luxury" appliances as refrigerators, freezers, microwave ovens, and gas and electric stoves with ovens at the other. In some households, a modern kitchen is reserved for complex preparations while a tiny cooker known as a *fuklar* is used on a day to day basis (Mizzi 1981: 200), especially as the latter is fuel efficient and tends to keep the house cooler in warm seasons.

Dishes where one could place a pot to stew for a long period are especially common and they readily lend themselves to preparation in the traditional Maltese kitchen equipped with a *fuklar* or the older open clay hearth called a *kenur*, ventilated through a smoke hole. While many of these kitchens are located in garages or back yards, some are tiny indoor cubicles with running water and perhaps some type of refrigeration. Still others are large enough for complete preparations and dining. Since families relying solely on such traditional kitchens lack an oven, dishes requiring baking are delivered to local commercial bakers. Even many families with both types of kitchens reserve their modern kitchens largely as places to be proud of and do most of their cooking in their traditional kitchens (Galley 1994: 34).

Most people prefer to eat at home on Sundays, when the main meals tends to be most elaborate. Even the poor expect more meat in the pot on Sundays. Since Mondays are often laundry days, many housewives cook enough on Sundays to avoid elaborate preparations on Mondays. What many Maltese consider to be a heavy meal starts with pasta. This is likely to be followed by a course of meat with potatoes or other vegetable, and terminate with fruit or dessert. A large meal sometimes involves a small bowl of soup prior to the pasta. Both spaghetti and ravioli are popular and various housewives have their own versions of soups such as *kawlata*, *al-jotta*, and minestrone, known in Malta as *minestra*.

Rabbit stewed in wine has the status of a national dish. It is common for some of the sauce from rabbit stew to be served on pasta as a first course before the meat and vegetables are eaten. A tender roast of lamb is considered a special Easter treat. Another seasonal favorite is lampuki pie (*torta tal-lumpuka* if made from one large fish or *torta tal-lumpuki* if made early in the season from several smaller fish). This is a baked fish casserole containing ingredients such as spinach, cauliflower, chestnuts, and sultanas, that is covered with pastry, which is available from around Santa Marija on August 15th to mid-November.

Stuffed octopus, squid, and cuttlefish served in a spicy tomato sauce are favorites as is *bragoli*, a type of roulade of beef stuffed with chopped eggs, breadcrumbs, parsley, and sometimes olives. Stuffed poultry and baked pasta dishes—for example, *timpana*—are also common. Fresh ingredients are used in abundance, including a variety of cheeses, mushrooms, olives, capers, onions, garlic, and herbs that change according to season.

Fully 99% of homes have a kitchen of some kind, and only 3% lack both a toilet basin and bathroom. Of the 3% of homes without these latter facilities, about one-fourth overlap with those that are also without a kitchen (Abela 1998b: 108). An analysis of substandard housing by gender and age of head of households reveals a disparate impact among women suggesting significant feminization of poverty (Abela 1998a: 101). Further indications of housing problems may be seen in the costliness of housing as well as in the habit of sometimes using any room that is particularly large—including a sitting room or kitchen—also as a bedroom.

On the positive side, 82.3% of dwellings have a separate dining room, 56.4% have more than two bedrooms, and 32.5% contain more than one bathroom. Virtually all homes have a telephone, a television, and a washing machine while slightly over three out of four families possess an automobile (Tabone 1995: 28). Around seven out of ten households own the houses they live in, and almost one out of ten own a secondary or summer residence. These statistics indicate that Maltese are better housed than most other Mediterranean peoples as well as peoples in Europe's industrial north (S. Vella 1998: 80).

Whoever has the ownership of land in Malta is legally deemed to have ownership of the space above it and of everything on or over or under its surface. This means that people who own private properties may construct, plant, or have access to products that the land yields except in the case of certain easements. As most houses are adjoined to others, many laws that relate to land tenure and property rights concern competing rights of neighbors.

Any homeowner may compel a neighbor to fix at joint expense the boundaries of their adjoining tenements. A party wall between two courtyards, gardens, or fields must be 12 feet high if between two gardens in which there are chiefly orange or lemon trees but may be lower if it divides gardens with mostly other types of trees. Among things that neighbors are legally proscribed from placing against common walls are stoves or manure. And a person in whose building there are stairs leading to the roof is supposed to construct a party wall six feet above the level of the roof to maintain privacy between families. There exist certain limitations on planting trees close to a neighbor's property, and where a cistern extends under the tenement of a neighbor, such neighbor may bore a hole and make use of the water (Ansell et al. 1972: 88–94).

In all societies two most important categories of relationships that tie people together in family and kinship groups are those based on marriage-like arrangements and those that are based on cultural interpretations of shared descent. While the first category of relations, sometimes called "affinal" relationships, is perhaps most strongly exemplified in the conjugal ties between spouses, it is by extension also manifest in "in-law" relationships. The second category of relationships, sometimes called "consanguineal" or "blood" relationships ties people together as sons, daughters, fathers, mother's mother, brother, and so forth.

In the larger Mediterranean Basin, one encounters many peoples whose family systems place more emphasis on consanguineal relations as well as others such as the Maltese with family systems that place more emphasis on relationships of affinity or marriage. That throughout the region various types of cousins sometimes marry underscores that while some societies may place more emphasis on consanguineal ties and some on affinal ties, the two categories of relatives are not always different.

Cousin marriages are not socially preferred; in fact, there is a taboo against Maltese marrying cousins closer than the third degree. On appeal, however, the church sometimes grants special dispensations that permit closer cousins to marry (Boissevain 1969a: 27). Cousin marriages underscore that affinal and consanguineal relationships sometimes overlap. This is also evident in the fact that many societies treat marriages as a relationship tying together two groups of consanguines rather than emphasizing the relationship between the spouses as individuals. Mediterranean peoples differ considerably in terms of which cousins one is sometimes permitted to marry, the degree to which marriage integrates a spouse into a new kinship group, and the importance placed on the conjugal tie between spouses.

In areas populated predominantly by Arabs, Berbers, and Turks, the principle of consanguinity or blood relations tends to be held more as a core principle of family formation than the principle of affinity or alliance through marriage. Certain of these peoples even use principles that evolve out of kinship to organize themselves into elaborate lineage systems, more often than not based on the concept of patrilineality or descent through males. In contrast to these peoples, neither large patrilineal descent groups nor extended patrilineal local households, into which women marry as strangers and often remain outsiders, are found in Malta. This is also a distinction between the Maltese and some Mediterranean Christians, for example, the Maronites of Lebanon. Embedded in the Maltese kinship system are no lineages, no patrilineages, no matrilineages, nor ambilineages.

This absence of lineages is not strictly a distinction existing between Mediterranean Europeans and others nor in all cases one simply between Muslims and others. For example while Israeli Jews manifest no tendency toward patrilineal organization, in the Balkan Peninsula of Europe, "the Albanians share with the Serbs and the Montenegrins, the distinction of an extended patrilineal kin-group organization" (Peristiany 1976: 11). It is possible that Malta's lack of lineages helps to explain its absence of blood feuds such as occur in some societies in the region.

The Mediterranean societies that are renowned for blood feuding are, with few exceptions, among those whose kinship systems are organized in terms of fiercely competitive patrilineages that do not overlap. Malta is characterized by bilateral kindreds rather than a lineage system; and in lieu of engaging in kinship feuds, Maltese tend to retaliate against their enemies and competitors in other ways (Wilhelmsen 1976: 375), including gossip. Gossip is an important means of social control that can affect both individual reputations and family honor (Du Boulay 1976: 394, 396, 399; Mizzi 1981: 167, 209, 211; Mizzi 1994: 369–382; Tentori 1976: 279, 282; Wilhelmsen 1976: 369, 373–374). Although it can sometimes be triggered by jealousy and by conflict between kinship groups, it can at other times be triggered by losing face, shame, or a feeling that it is necessary to protect the honor of one's own family.

One encounters a complex of attitudes throughout the Mediterranean which tend to sanction retaliatory behaviors by family members of females who have been defiled or whose reputations denigrated. Though the rules differ situationally and from place to place throughout the Mediterranean, men are expected to get a large measure of their validation as men through retaliation against those who jeopardize the honor of their families.

The means of retaliation sanctioned, as well as the object of retaliation, can vary enormously from one society to another and even among various population segments of the same society (Belmonte 1983: 274, 279; Kenny and Kertzer 1983: 14, 19). In its most extreme forms, retaliation associated with the maintenance of family honor can result in killing. In areas such as Upper Egypt and parts of Lebanon, this may mean that a male relative kills a woman because her virginity, chastity, or good moral conduct is in question. In some conservative areas of Greece or Spain, it may mean that a man thought to have jeopardized the honor of a woman, and hence that of her family, is killed by one of her male relatives with a good measure of social approbation. Milder behaviors associated with this complex sometimes entail forcing unwilling paramours to marry or shaming a family through putrid gossip, such as often occurs in Malta.

Wettinger (1980: 65–77) has unearthed evidence suggesting that perhaps violent retaliation to restore family honor may have had some acceptance in late fifteenth-century Malta although this is hardly known in recent times. Still, from society to society and from one era to another, men of the Mediterranean Basin are generally expected to protect family honor and obtain a good measure of their validation as men through doing so (Mizzi 1981: 82–83).

In the case of Malta, however, females—through their own comportment and the ways in which they undertake their domestic and religious obligations—shoulder much of this responsibility to maintain family honor (Mizzi 1981: 97, 138, 167–168). A double standard of sexual propriety exists for the two sexes and a clear determination of a person's family affiliation and its reputation is extremely important for normal functioning of each member of a family in society. Family honor is particularly important in terms of marriage choices when family groups vie with each other to improve, or at least maintain, their social standing, and reputations count for a great deal (Mizzi 1981: 168).

The fact that Maltese formally reckon kinship without regard to sex does not mean that in day-to-day family interactions they place equal emphasis on the relationships flowing through a mother and a father. In contrast to Greece to the east and Corsica to the west where the stress within a bilateral system of consanguinity is on the father's relatives, in Malta, the stress is matrilateral (e.g., Boissevain 1969a, 1969b; Goodwin 2001; Mizzi 1981). In other words, most Maltese have more frequent interactions and stronger affective bonding with relatives through their mothers than through their fathers.

Newly wed Maltese couples typically prefer to establish households of their own. Considering that distances are short in Malta, there exist degrees of neolocality since a new household is often located only minutes from that of one's family of orientation or rearing. In these cases, it tends more often to be located near the family of the wife than that of the husband, although it is sometimes near the homes in which both were reared (Boswell 1994: 143). By religious tradition and by civil code until 1993, a wife was obliged to obey her husband, change her surname to his upon marriage, and follow him where he wished to reside. A wife who refused to reside where her husband wished was considered as abandoning her marriage and risked losing her right to receive maintenance (Orland 1998: 10–11). In practice, however, husbands have long been more likely to follow their wives. As for Maltese children, they inherit their fathers' surnames. They also often inherit their fathers' nicknames, a practice with parallels in many other parts of the Mediterranean (Chapman 1971: 236–238; Galley 1994: 192–194). These nicknames in some parts of Malta are used as widely as surnames (Wettinger 1999: 333).

Similarly, in those situations where a new couple takes up residence within a parental household instead of establishing a new one, matrilocal residence is considerably more common than patrilocal residence. These postmarital residential patterns, coupled with close relationships between most Maltese wives and their mothers, mean that married men tend to visit their wife's relatives much more often than their own. Also, the relationship between a maternal grandmother and her daughter's children is also likely to be particularly close.

Despite the absence of kinship lineages in the Maltese kinship system, the offspring of the same maternal grandmother are typically quite friendly, especially while she is still living. Moreover, people often recognize that they are related to other people going back at least five generations where marriage decisions are involved (Boissevain 1969a: 26–28; Boissevain 1969b: 38–39). Still, in ordinary conversation, people do not generally refer to family units larger than those descended from a particular grandparent unless they are consciously engaged in tracing genealogy for technical or status reasons. In accordance with typical residential patterns, most households consist of nuclear families or parents left with an "empty nest" after their children have married and moved out.

More often than a few decades ago, an elderly parent or grandparent may reside in a home for the elderly or infirm although he or she has an adult offspring living nearby. Many private residences and some 17 or more church facilities provide housing for elderly citizens in addition to St. Vincent de Paul, a large government hospital that provides care for old people who are infirm.

Due to low mortality rates and relatively low birth rates, Malta's population tends to be older in age than those in many Mediterranean countries, including almost all those in Africa, Asia, and the Balkans. Her population is projected to be older than that of Spain by 2020 and almost as old as that of Italy (Troisi 1998: 36). On the island of Malta, the northern region has the smallest number of older persons, while the highest percentage is found in the Inner Harbor region. The aggregated statistics on Gozo and Comino also reveal particularly large concentrations of the elderly (Troisi 1998: 38). As Malta ages, it also becomes more female since females tend to live longer, in fact, to about age 79. The fact that more young males than females emigrated between 1950 and 1965 also contributes to a lack of sexual balance among the elderly (Spiteri 1998: 125).

It often happens that the elderly are concentrated in older housing in a relatively poor state of repair (S. Vella 1998: 82). It is not uncommon to encounter households made up entirely of elderly people, in some cases of unmarried adult siblings, maybe two sisters or a sister and a brother. A factor that contributes to the existence of this type of household is a strong tradition in this country as in Greece, Spain, Italy, Serbia, and other parts of the former Yugoslavia, that despite age, one should reside with one's parents until marriage (Kenny and Kertzer 1983: 13). In addition to the social pressures that support this tradition in Malta, the fact that housing tends to be scarce and expensive does not encourage individual single people to establish their own households.

For a man to be single at 33 is not considered unusual, and it is even less unusual for a female. However, where a male, who is not in a religious order, is over 35 and still single, people sometimes begin to say things like "we thought he would never marry" or "it is taking him a very long time to get married." Though his situation would be considered very unusual by age 45, it would not likely be attributed to homosexuality.

As homosexuality is a taboo subject in Maltese culture, it receives little public discussion. Despite the existence of a few small organizations or cliques on the margins of society that have recently become identified as "gay," speaking about homosexuality is even more taboo than speaking openly about sex generally (Cole 1994: 595–598; Naudi 1998: 110). Though some changes in attitudes are documented (Abela 1992: 31; Abela 1994: 15), the Maltese are significantly more condemnatory of homosexuality than Europeans generally.

While homosexuality cannot be equated with single or married status, not getting married is typically considered almost a social failure unless one becomes a priest or a nun—which parents generally consider a glorious thing. Even if parents have but a single child, they usually consider it something of a great blessing if a child becomes a priest or a nun. Associated with some status differences, however, it is possible that some segments of the elite may share this outlook less than others.

Abela (2000: 61) has pointed out that by European standards, Malta has a large proportion of single adults most of whom live with their parents, and Tabone (1994: 234) has pointed out that there is a decline in the marriage rate. Not only is singlehood not uncommon in Malta, it is a requirement within the large religious communities made up of priests and nuns in the population. Even as compared to other predominantly Catholic Mediterranean countries, the proportion of Malta's population made up of priests, monks, and nuns is very large. There are on the island of Malta approximately two secular priests to 1,000 persons in the general population while on Gozo, there are almost six. In the case of monks, the proportion approximates 1.5 to 1,000. While on the larger island, there are over nine nuns per 1,000 females in the population, on Gozo there are around twenty. Traditionally, Malta has been heavily dependent on her religious specialists for performing vital services in numerous fields.

Maltese in religious vocations generally maintain close relationships with their families, including many who live communally such as religious priests and cloistered sisters. In contrast to secluded brothers and nuns, who can only inherit small life pensions and after taking their vows nor can dispose of property through a will, most secular priests live with their relatives and are under no such restrictions. Seminary students typically visit their families at home rather infrequently, sometimes only once a month, perhaps on a Sunday afternoon.

Sexual repression—a rather strong element in Maltese society—probably reaches its apex in monasteries, convents, and seminaries. In these places where celibate religious specialists are expected to suppress sexual desire of all kinds, one tries never to mention sex unless it is unavoidable, and, even then, the tendency is to discuss it in very clinical ways. Standard rules in some of these institutions seem designed to avoid situations that could be sexually awkward. For example, some seminaries permit seminarians to swim in numbers of three or more while categorically forbidding them to go swimming in pairs.

Maltese domestic laws, in contrast to those in predominantly Islamic countries, place considerably more emphasis on affinity than on consanguinity. For example, a joint will in the same instrument is a legal option only for a husband and a wife. They also offer strong support to the nuclear family. Where children survive a deceased person, however, limits are placed on the amount that may be received by a surviving spouse as opposed to the children. While spouses as well as children, and even parents, have certain almost irrevocable rights to inherit, domestic laws recognize certain extreme cases—involving murder, attempted murder, or extreme neglect—where a relative who would otherwise have inheritance rights is deemed unworthy or may be disinherited. Whether or not children have been conceived in wedlock and to what extent they have been recognized also affect inheritance rights.

Family organization is everywhere fluid; although many of the contrasting patterns that we see in the Mediterranean can be explained by religious differences, many can not. While polygyny, a system whereby a man may be legally married to more than one woman at the same time, has never had a place among Maltese Christians, for example, it has in recent decades declined throughout the region. Israel outlawed it in 1951, and, though considered permissible by the Koran, the government in Tunisia has out-lawed it.

Traditionally, Maltese society has placed on new wives much pressure to become pregnant as soon after marriage as possible, and there has never been any taboo against women being seen in public simply because they were obviously pregnant. Even very recent research has shown that most people believe it unjustified for a couple to wait until finishing a house before attempting to become parents (Tabone 1995: 48).

As late as the 1920s, having an infant delivered at home with the help of a midwife rather than in a hospital bestowed more prestige on a family. Between the world wars, attitudes about this began to change and now the vast majority of infants are delivered in a hospital with the help of a phy-sician.

While infant mortality rates are currently very low, Maltese culture is rich in religious customs and rituals that women formerly practiced with hopes of having successful deliveries and having their infants survive the perils of early life. With dramatic drops in infant mortality rates, many of these practices have fallen into disuse. Families remain very interested in having children, and they exhibit no negative feelings about multiple births. Many people view life for a child without siblings as a somewhat unfor-tunate one that may entail a dreary existence.

When infant mortality rates were high, there used to be a strong pref-erence that christening take place within the first two or so days after birth, and sooner rather than later if a particular child seemed very weak or delicate. This practice was in accord with the religious belief that if a bap-tized child died, it would go straight into heaven (Galley 1994: 187). Bap-tism and christening are the same thing in Malta, and it takes place in church. As is common in Sicily, Sardinia, Corsica and many other predom-inantly Christian parts of the Mediterranean, prior to baptism, the Maltese sometimes liken a child to a "Moor" or a "Turk"—meaning, a Muslim, Jew, or other non-Christian (Aquilina 1972: 103; Pitt-Rivers 1976: 318–319).

As the mortality rate is no longer high, people do not feel a great need to rush baptism. Baptism most commonly occurs for a group of infants at the same time. With few exceptions, private individual baptisms have been stopped. The whole idea is that this is a sacrament that involves the whole Christian community, and since Baptism involves the admittance of a new member into the community, it is worthy of public celebration.

According to Galley (1994: 40), Gozitans used to choose two godmoth-ers and two godfathers for a baptism in the early 1900s. For baptism now-adays, at least one godparent is obligatory though Maltese parents generally choose two, a man and a woman as godparents, often a married couple. A person who has not reached adulthood or is unbaptisized is not eligible to serve as a godparent. Spiritual kinship that is transmitted through godparents to godchildren, and sometimes to their birth parents, is much less formal and elaborated in Malta and Italy than in some other predominantly Christian countries in the Mediterranean (Peristiany 1976: 2).

In some parts of Greece and Cyprus where Orthodox Christianity is predominant, for example, baptismal sponsors are expected to later serve as marriage sponsors to their godchildren and subsequently as baptismal sponsors to the children of those whose marriages they sponsor (Peristiany 1976: 20). Such a custom is not found in Malta nor is there a custom where sons replace fathers in the role of godfather causing spiritual kinship relations to be inherited across generations as sometimes happens in Greece and Spain. On the Greek island of Nisos, of such importance is the spiritual kinship that ties together the children of a godparent and the godchild that they are considered "siblings of the cross" and an incest taboo forbids their intermarriage to the degree of third cousin, the same as is true of cousins by consanguinity (cf. Pitt-Rivers 1976: 333, 351–361).

By contrast, Maltese godparents are usually close relatives—uncles, aunts, grandparents, or cousins. Where this is not so, they are good friends of the parents or occasionally influential patrons, as is sometimes the case in Spain (Pitt-Rivers 1976: 322). On rare occasions, a priest has objected to the parental choice of a godparent because the individual chosen was not considered by him to be leading a good Christian life.

An uncle, close to the age of a sister with children, is often chosen for a godfather. He is likely to have a close avuncular relationship with her children, and if he is a godfather to them, they may likely expect to receive small gifts of money from him on New Year's day. If godparents are elderly, like grandparents for example, some children may playfully joke among themselves that they hope their godparents will not die before they can give them a few gifts. However, there exist no formal obligations between godchildren and godparents.

Since these relationships usually are superimposed on existing familial relationships, relationships of spiritual kinship tend not to be of great salience. In fact, the Maltese term *parrinu*, referring to a godparent, is used with declining frequency. However, to reduce social distance, a reciprocal term sometimes is used between a godfather and a birth father (Boissevain 1969b: 39). By extension—as is the case in southern Spain—this term (*xbin* in Maltese) is sometimes used more loosely between others to also reduce social distance.

Unlike in southern Spain, Maltese godparents are not expected to select names for godchild. Maltese parents typically select the names for their own children. It often happens that a first boy is named after his father and father's father. For example, a father's father may be named Joseph, a father named Joseph, and a father's son named Joseph. But in the older generations it would more likely be Ġusepe or Ġuse, traditional Maltese equivalents of Joseph. Children are sometimes called by diminutives of their names, for example, Joey for Joe and Frankie for Francis. This can happen for girls as well as boys. As children are traditionally named after saints, they early learn to identify with their saint's day as well as their birthday.

Single-parent households are increasing in Malta as a result of spousal separations, divorces granted abroad, widowhood, and out-of-wedlock births. With regard to out-of-wedlock births, even government statistics tend to be unreliable as most private hospitals will not reveal the numbers of unmarried women they deliver (Bartolo 1998: 119). Though baptisms are usually public celebrations, in the case of children born to unmarried mothers, they are often conducted in private.

As is widespread throughout the Mediterranean Basin, there exists a preference for a first child to be a son. Although various beliefs in potential dangers associated with "the evil eye" are widespread in the Mediterranean, the ways they affect family life differ from one place to another. In many Islamic lands, for example, parents avoid discussion of their children with non-family members for fear that this may attract the evil eye. Egyptian Nubians sometimes go so far as to dress a male infant in female clothes to avoid the evil eye (Fernea and Fernea 1991: 58). Though many Maltese are also wary of the evil eye, this almost paranoid fear of its effect on their children, should they be singled out, is not observed. Some Maltese, for example, consider it fortuitous when a young infant has a lot of hair, even if only a couple of weeks old, and they will sometimes comment on this. While Jews, Muslims, and even many Christians circumcise males during some stage of childhood, the Maltese typically use circumcision only for medical reasons.

It sometimes happens that when a child is 1 year old, he or she is given a little party. Occasionally at such a party, adults may humor themselves by placing a few objects associated with different occupations within a child's reach—maybe six or eight—while encouraging the child to choose one. Although for fun, this is considered symbolic of the type of occupation the child is likely to choose in life.

Breast-feeding is not uncommon in villages though after having its ups and downs in towns and cities for several decades, it is on the decline. When it was more universal, a first-born child sometimes slept in a hamper in the parental bedroom for two or so years as this facilitated nursing and care. In cases where there was an older sister, aunt or grandmother in the household, the time was sometimes shortened. How long an infant sleeps in the parental bedroom continues to be influenced by factors such as household composition, size of the house, arrangement of the rooms, and whether or not a child is being breast-fed.

Whereas mothers are continually involved with rearing of their children, fatherhood gets its validation largely in connection with providing for the material needs of a family, and perhaps from protecting family honor. Leaving many domestic matters to their wives, men spend considerable amounts of time with other men, as is common in the Mediterranean Basin. While this is much less pronounced in present-day Malta than in many neighboring countries, in towns across Malta, one observes men socializing together in piazzas in front of churches on Sundays and at various other locations throughout the week (Borg and Mayo 1994: 220).

Fathers are not much involved in rearing children before they are 4 or so, and even then, they are more likely to be involved with sons than with daughters. Some fathers really do not pay much attention even to their sons until they are about to finish grammar school when fathers are more likely to become concerned about their taking off in a good direction in preparation for the future.

Childhood is not expected to be a time of strict regimentation but children are socialized not to "make dirt" as a matter of pride (Mizzi 1981: 199; Pons 1961: 23–24). In a typical village setting, everyone knows everyone, and it is not unusual for a young girl or boy to visit with another child of the same sex even at a very young age. In this regard, boys and girls are treated roughly the same except that girls are encouraged to take more interest in domestic work. General social awareness is probably stressed less than family awareness in the socialization of young children— except where they are involved in an organization such as Scouts.

A development that begins to change this somewhat when a child reaches 5 or 6 is when he or she begins to study Catholic catechism or Christian doctrine. Catechism is taught in sessions organized by the church on weekday evenings in classes where children are separated by sex. In virtually all cases, it is when children are about 6 or 7 years of age that they have their First Communion. It is generally the parish priest who determines the exact time when a group's First Communion will take place. In some parishes it is determined on a rather fixed schedule in accordance with a holy day, for example on Our Lady of the Catechism in Floriana. First Communion Mass is typically followed by a procession. On returning to their homes, the children involved are given small parties attended by relatives and perhaps friends. Following their First Communion, a greater expectation exists that children will be taken to church with their parents on a regular basis, and at least on Sundays.

As was true when children study for their previous classes in Christian doctrine, when they take classes in preparation for confirmation, the classes are separate for each sex. In the 1950s and 1960s, a year or a year and a half only separated first Holy Communion and Confirmation usually, with Confirmation coming after. So the same outfits could sometimes be worn for both occasions, with a little alteration—white suits for boys and white dresses for girls. This has changed now because although Holy Communion comes for most children when they are about 6 or 7, Confirmation comes later, maybe at age 10. This means that a different outfit is usually required these days.

Confirmation is grouped, not on an individual basis. In large parishes, 40, 50, or 100 children are sometimes confirmed at the same time. The children who are confirmed together do not have any life-long bonds with each other like members of a club or "age-grade" simply because they were confirmed at the same time. If only because of the numbers of families impacted, a rite of confirmation is an important event for a significant group of people in a parish. Moreover, close relatives who may not live in the parish where the confirmation is taking place often attend.

Confirmation is usually considered a little more important to children than the first Holy Communion in the sense that the Bishop is likely to be present. Also for Confirmation, a child typically gets an additional godparent, and the new godparent is usually of the same sex as the child. After Confirmation takes place, a party is usually held. Once children have been confirmed, parents typically become much more concerned with their religious practices, for example that they attend confession weekly. It is very common for Maltese, including children, to go to confession on Saturdays and to receive Communion on Sundays.

As children age, their sleeping arrangements sometimes change. If siblings are of different sexes, they are likely to be moved to different bedrooms by the time they are 9 or 10 on the initiative of the parents. But sometimes this may not happen until later, perhaps until they have virtually reached puberty—especially if the family is large, the house is small, or if they do not prefer to sleep alone.

If a child passes exams at the end of grammar school and manages to win admittance into a secondary school of high standing, it is considered a tribute to the whole family. If, however, this does not happen, the family is likely to pass it off by saying that the child would have passed if they had studied more, or perhaps that the child does not seem to be one of those good "kids" who are very interested in their future.

Between the age of 13 and 15, children begin to experience a significant transition in their maturing and relations beyond the family assume a bit more importance. A child may be allowed to go off on a picnic or to a club for youth of their own sex, and he or she may ask for small sums of money to spend. There is high expectation that a teacher or some other responsible adult will supervise any such outing. Even at this age, a young person would need a good reason to request permission to travel from an outlying village to Valletta. An acceptable reason might be for him or her to get an application to take an examination or to buy something very special. In the case of a girl this age, she would usually be expected to travel with her sister, her mother, or at least, a girl friend.

When a boy is about 15, parents try to keep him from staying out too late and try to make sure that he picks the right boys as school friends. Parents are usually more interested that their 15-year old children concentrate on their studies than on social relations with the opposite sex. In fact, most Maltese parents do not favor mixed education for teenagers because it is considered a distraction.

Traditionally, sex has been a taboo subject in Maltese families with parents generally telling children little about it, though in some rural areas, parents are compelled to make reference to sex in regard to farm animals. Where puberty must be discussed, its reproductive significance tends to be emphasized less than the moral importance of abstinence. Despite these traditions, pubescent children are increasingly exposed to television programming from overseas and to some newspaper articles that entail discussion of topics that are sex related.

Still if a family were at the dinner table and a young adult child wished to mention a newspaper article about a subject such as contraception or abortion while a teenage child was also present, older adults would probably change the subject immediately. It the adult child persisted, they would likely become angry. Even with their adult children, parents tend to discuss sex reluctantly and with language that is very camouflaged. For example, instead of using a word specifically meaning sexual intercourse, they would probably use a euphemism meaning "to sleep with."

Saturday nights tend to be especially important for teenagers as a time when they wish to go out. The kinds of things that 15-year-old children request money for include going to the cinema and buying drinks when they go swimming. In some families, older teenagers and young adults, even while students, are expected to make a financial contribution and in others they are not. While there exists significant variation among families in the amounts of spending money they provide teenagers, parents with meager resources as well as those who wish to control their children closely tend to provide very small amounts. Though this may depend in part on economic circumstances, it is just as likely to be a question of the particular values held in specific families. Unmarried youth between 16 and 24 spend an average of about five Maltese *liri* when they go out during the weekend (Abela 1992: 25) and younger children considerably less.

Fathers no longer place a pot of basil on a window ledge as they were still sometimes doing in the early twentieth century to announce the eligibility of a daughter. In fact, families are not usually overanxious that their children should start dating early. Nowadays, parents do not expect their children to begin dating before around age 18 and even this age would seem early to many. Dating in the sense of many trial romances is not considered normative by Maltese standards even today. Rather, dating from the very beginning is thought of as a relationship that can possibly lead to marriage.

In the working classes and lower middle classes, there has been a tradition whereby many females discontinue their formal education at age 16 and become gainfully employed. Still, an 18-year-old girl on a date is usually expected to take someone with her, and both sets of parents typically want to know exactly with whom the date is to take place and something about the family background of the date. Obviously parents can not monitor such matters as closely in larger cities like Hamrun or Sliema as they can in small villages. By the time a man dates a third girl or woman in a village setting, he will likely begin to get a bad reputation as someone who is not serious; as a result, it may become difficult for him to ever marry inside that particular village. Similarly, a girl who has had her second or third boyfriend would likely be viewed as pretty difficult, especially in a village setting.

When young people break the news to their parents that they are going out with a particular person, this is considered a very serious development. And when, eventually, the girl is invited to a boy's house to meet his family, the relationship is considered a very serious one. So the first time that they expect a boy to go out with a girl is when he is a university student or perhaps has started working. Marriage at younger than 18 years of age is very unusual, and even if a girl 18 marries, people might wonder if there were a special problem that prompted such an early marriage. If she were only 17, there likely would be gossip.

Marriage is viewed as an opportunity for two groups of related people to establish ties between each other, and there are many status considerations that come into play with each side interested in obtaining prestige. An unmarried Maltese woman has a right to a dowry from her family and if necessary even the right to obtain one by suing. A family, however, has the right to refuse a dowry if a woman marries someone of whose public conduct it disapproves. The fact that females have traditionally been married with dowry in Malta means that a family's status can rise and fall with the amount of such dowry. Where large dowries are involved, families are not shy about displaying them (Mizzi 1981: 142).

The dowry may be provided from the property of the mother or the father or both and may consist of clothes, jewelry, cash, furniture, kitchen appliances, a house, or land. In the case of the well to do, its exact nature is sometimes even specified in a marriage contract. In Malta, daughters and sons have a right to inherit equally from their parents. However, as is typical in Greece and Cyprus, a Maltese wife's dowry is considered an advance of her portion of her inheritance from her parents.

When the parents or guardians of a potential bride are dead, the legal responsibility for providing her with a dowry falls upon the grandparents, and then upon the father's and mother's brothers and sisters. However, if these relatives are dead or incapacitated, it falls upon a girl's brothers. "Thus, brothers and sisters have true rights of maintenance against each other if the lineal ascendants to the second degree are dead" (Boissevain 1969a: 29). Family heirlooms are among the valuables often passed down in a dowry.

The Maltese tradition of marrying daughters with a dowry that the son-in-law traditionally managed meant that an important relationship of trust had to be established between a son-in-law and his parents-in-law. The importance of in-law bonds—and hence the centrality of conjugality—is underscored by their extension into legal maintenance responsibilities for one's parents-in-law, and even one's grandparents-in-law, where they are indigent (Ansell et al. 1972: 12). Given that in-law relationships are so important, intra-village marriages are common, although Maltese in small villages often find their spouses from outside of their localities. Similarly, although residents of Gozo and Malta have long intermarried, it is more common for people to find marriage partners on the island where they live.

Many young people meet and flirt during *festi*, at wedding feasts, at discotheques and cafes, at various outings, or simply while walking and chatting—accompanied by friends of the same sex. In a 1990 study of youth culture conducted under the auspices of the Diocesan Youth Commission which involved interviewing a sample of 734 unmarried residents on the island of Malta between the ages of 16 and 24, it was found that approximately half of all postsecondary youth go to discos often or very often. While the respondents believed that 67% frequented discos to meet their friends, 56% did so to find a partner and 55% "because there exist no alternative places for youth entertainment" (Abela 1992: 24–25). In reality, alternative ways of spending leisure do exist for young people (Abela 1992: 21–23).

The days of old are gone when a gesture as innocent as a boy's buying a piece of nougat for a girl during a *festa* might signify a romantic interest. Still, the beginning of courtship still evolves through stages. As documented by Mizzi (1981) an initial courtship stage may involve a few meetings of which the families may not be aware. Later stages may involve gradual meetings between fiancés with their prospective in-laws and meetings between members of the two families with each other. Often mothers are more directly involved than fathers in the early stages of this process. More recent research points to the persistence of traditional mating "stages of casual dating, going steady, engagement and marriage" (Abela 1992: 22).

Quite apart from the tremendous exposure of the Maltese to foreigners through the tourists that come to Malta, telecommunications, and mass media programming originating abroad, large numbers of Maltese youth travel abroad, especially for holidays, shopping, cultural tourism, and to visit their overseas relatives (Abela 1992: 63–65). One consequence of such regular exposure to foreigners at home and abroad is cross-cultural marriage. However it is more common for Maltese who marry foreigners to emigrate than for foreigners who marry Maltese to reside in Malta. Marriages between Maltese and foreigners that seem the most favored are those involving Americans, Northern Europeans, Canadians, and perhaps Australians. Marriage with Arabs is viewed by segments of the Maltese population as problematic for religious and other reasons.

The "oppressor consciousness" inside us leads us to collude in oppressive structures. In order to be counted, we Maltese totally identify ourselves with the concept of being European, rather than with being Southern European or Mediterranean. This "Europeanness" reveals its most unsavoury aspects in our racism and the concomitant tendency to construct anybody who does not fit the 'European image' as being "other". This is one reason why, for example, the Libyan community in Malta has never been accepted by the rest of the population despite the existence of historical and economic ties between Maltese and Arabs. (Borg and Mayo 1994: 219)

People sometimes suspect that some of the growing number of marriages involving Arab men and Maltese women may be marriages of convenience so that the husbands can obtain Maltese citizenship. Recent changes in the law are intended to curtail marriages of convenience my mandating that any foreigner must be married and living continuously with his wife in Malta for five years before being eligible to apply for citizenship. Though Maltese are often somewhat dark by European standards, fairness of complexion, though not essential, is often considered a plus in a potential spouse, especially in a female (Boissevain 1969a: 28).

Common belief has it that the skin of the Maltese is more or less white. In fact, however, black children have existed in our care systems for many years. They were often the product of relationships occurring outside marriage, and as such were doubly stigmatised. The fact remains that these children grew up in our society, often made invisible by virtue of living in the residential homes for children, eventually becoming adults. They are Maltese as any other citizen. But they were never made to feel accepted. Several leave Malta at the first chance, never to return to the country they were born to, but which never accepted them.

Nowadays this is even more of an issue. We now have more and more foreign people settling in Malta. Whereas until a few years ago, this category consisted mainly of retired English people or ex-British servicemen married to Maltese, now we have more and more people of North African origin often married to Maltese, and an increasing number of refugees. As the number of foreign people increase, these groups are gaining in visibility. In the process, prejudices into which we are socialised since childhood, such as "Arabs are dirty" . . . "dogs," "dangerous" or so on . . . unavoidably come out into the open and have to be challenged. We need to ask whether our attitudes reflect social prejudices and reinforce the discrimination faced by "non-white" people in Malta. (Naudi 1998: 109–110)

During recent decades, Malta and Libya have undertaken a number of joint capital undertakings at the governmental and private enterprise levels. Though a joint intergovernmental ministerial committee to promote Maltese-Libyan trade meets regularly, alternating meetings between Libya and Malta, Maltese privately continue to be cautious toward their Arab neighbors, especially in terms of making joint commitments to intimacy. According to research published by Abela (1992: 65), "Youths retain the traditional Maltese attachment to Europeans. In their majority our respondents like best the British (55%), the Italians (22%), followed by Germans (14%), Scandinavians from Sweden (5%), Denmark (4%) and Norway (3%), the Swiss (4%) or other foreigners (7%) and least of all Arabs (1%)."

As marriage has traditionally been life-long—since Malta remains one of the few countries anywhere with no legal provision for divorce—it has been common to enter into it only after considerable investigation and circumspection, including paying close attention to the views of one's family. As well as affecting one's personal status, a marriage can affect the status and marriage prospects of one's close relatives (Tabone 1995: 42). Reputation in terms of stability and morality is considered a very important consideration, though even more so in the case of a potential bride than in the case of a potential groom.

Of the respondents in the 1990 study of youth culture conducted under the auspices of the Diocesan Youth Commission, 23% had experienced going out with a tourist by themselves. The dating of tourists, however, was more common for youth who had completed a secondary level of education and who lived in the Outer Harbor, South Eastern, or Northern Regions of Malta (Abela 1992: 69). For obvious reasons, marriages with foreigners permit less investigation than marriage where both potential spouses and their families live in Malta and a disproportionately large number of children born out of wedlock involve relationships between Maltese and foreigners. While 16% of the respondents in the youth culture study felt that their parents would not oppose their marriage to a foreigner, and 50% believed that their parents would eventually consent, 10% thought that it would not be possible to change family opposition to their marriage to a foreigner (Abela 1992: 69).

In recent surveys where Maltese are asked whether or not they think there should be a legal provision for divorce where a marriage breaks down, at least two-thirds usually answer no (Abela 1992: 31; Abela 1994: 15, 18–19; Tabone 1995: 41). Whereas a majority remains overwhelmingly opposed to divorce, this is more pronounced among males than females. This general opposition, moreover, is much greater than that recorded for such other predominantly Catholic Mediterranean countries as Italy, France, and Spain. Since the 1980s, however, a growing minority of Maltese has begun to concede some circumstances in which separation and divorce may be justified. "Generally, respondents identify in descending order of importance, violence, unfaithfulness, a partner's homosexual tendencies, lack of love, a partner's dependence on alcohol, unsatisfactory sexual relations, incompatible personalities, long illness, conflicts with each other's relatives, inability to have children, and financial problems as sufficient reasons for divorce" (Abela 2000: 65).

Baptism and confirmation are as important rites of passage for young children as obtaining an education and starting a career are for them later. For young adults, engagement and marriage—but most especially marriage—are extremely important rites of passage. Civil marriage has recently become available as an option in Malta and slightly more than 10% of couples marry in this way (Tabone 1994: 234). The vast majority of Maltese still prefer a religious wedding where the parish priest of the bride usually celebrates the Mass. In fact, couples sometimes find it necessary to book the church and reception hall some two or three years in advance (Tabone 1995: 40). Even a significant proportion of couples who are wed in a civil ceremony eventually choose to have a religious wedding.

Research shows that larger percentages of Maltese than Europeans generally find it important "to hold a religious service to mark important events in life such as a birth, marriage or death in the family" (Abela 2000: 175). Among the rites of passage that are extremely important for adults are becoming parents, and eventually grandparents. The matrilateral grandmother—that is the one on the mother's side—plays an especially pivotal role in families. Many parents and grandparents measure their success in life in terms of their offspring. Eventually reaching advanced age also involves certain lifestyle changes and rites. Older people exhibit higher levels of religiosity and are more concerned than the young with visiting notaries to write wills. As in most societies, elderly Maltese focus more on death than younger people. At whatever point death occurs, however, it presents the family system with challenges and responsibilities.

Many Maltese consider it almost taboo to discuss death with a person on the verge of dying. Some people are even reluctant to bring in a priest under these circumstances because they fear the effect that it may have on a person close to death. Eventually, however, the priest is likely to be summoned because virtually all Maltese believe that if people die without final confession, this may deprive them of a chance to rid themselves of sin and eventually get to heaven.

Individuals and societies experience passage and change in ways that are interconnected though they experience them somewhat differently. For individuals, death is inevitably the final part of the life process. Society, especially as mediated through families, must ultimately search for culturally acceptable ways to mourn, to readjust, and to reproduce if they are to survive. Though the rules as to what is culturally acceptable are continually changing, they invariably unfold within the constraints of beliefs, values, symbolism, status, technology, and resources.

Despite the existence today of cellular telephones and mass media, churches often support grieving families by using bells. Bells are rung in special ways to announce death, often two similar rings followed by a different one—but this does not occur in exactly the same way in all parishes. Though mortuary customs change tremendously over time, in the final rite of passage the family remains central.

When a person dies in the hospital—or is badly maimed in a fire or accident and thereafter delivered to a hospital—it is a nursing aid or religious who washes and prepares the body for burial. Family members merely deliver the clothing needed for burial there. Otherwise, it is at home that a deceased person is typically washed and dressed in preparation for his or her final rite, emphasizing the centrality of the family—a widespread custom in the Mediterranean, including in Sicily. If during this process, the eyelids are open, they are likely to be closed and the mouth bound with a bandage as is also done in some parts of northern Africa, including especially Algeria.

Apart from a priest, one of the first persons a family member contacts when a death occurs is a *tat-twiebet* or *id-deffin*. While technically a *tat-twiebet* is a coffin-maker and *id-deffin* is a funeral undertaker, or the one who buries, what they do can overlap according to various regions in Malta. Though some families opt to use wooden coffins imported from Sicily, around 30 coffin-makers and undertakers do business in Malta. When a family approaches them, they proceed to get a health certificate from a doctor certifying that everything is in order. Since in the case of natural deaths the doctor approached is usually the one who has been treating the deceased, the doctor does not usually have to examine the body to issue such a certificate. In some cases, it is the commissioner of funerals who attends to this.

As wood is extremely scarce in Malta, it is traditional for coffins to be chosen for size according to the dimensions of the deceased. There are four major classes of coffins with the most expensive costing about six times what the cheapest costs. Although around 1950 the most expensive coffin would have cost only about £50, by 1970 the price of an equivalent coffin was about £70; by 1990, it had risen an equivalent amount in Maltese liras.

While the price range for coffins manufactured in Malta and Sicily is equivalent, what can elevate the cost in both cases are decorative attachments, for example, carved or molded angels. It is not Maltese custom to place coffins into larger outer boxes or vaults before they are placed in the ground. However, when a coffin is not going to be placed in a family crypt and instead will be covered with earth, a costly zinc lining must be placed on the inside. This zinc, however, is covered with coffin cloth. Bodies lie flat in coffins and, apart from a pillow for the head, it is not traditional to surround them with fancy cushions. Some families like the symbolism of burying loved ones with a cross.

With a black hearse at its head, the funeral procession is not difficult to recognize. It usually starts from a hospital or from the home of the deceased, depending on where the body was prepared. Though many people receive their final rites at a chapel located in a cemetery, some families prefer to return a loved one to a parish church before burial.

Although some aspects of status probably affect attendance at funerals, a deceased adult's gender, age, or marital status does not seem to much

matter. During church funerals, except for the likelihood of additional can-
dles; including a Paschal Candle in front of the Passion of Christ, a church
is as usual, without special draping. A funeral Mass can be more or less
elaborate, depending, in part, on what kind of costs a family wishes to
bear, and these differ in different parishes. The Mass of Christian Burial is
referred to by some Maltese as the Mass of Angels. Funerals tend to be
shorter than previously. Considering that Maltese families of several centuries ago hired professional weepers and often used bagpipes or other
instruments to accompany their loved ones to their graves, funeral processions are also quieter and more solemn.

For burials in country, the rules of the Health Department specify that
there must be a wait of at least 24 hours, including 24 hours after an
autopsy if one has been performed. If a coffin arrives at the cemetery before
the 24 hours has elapsed, it is put under shelter until these hours have
passed. In Addolorata Cemetery, the largest and most beautiful in Malta,
there is a special room that is used for this purpose.

Throughout the Mediterranean, burial shortly after death without embalming has long been the norm among Muslims, Jews, and Christians,
and Malta presents no exception. About the only time that there may be
an in-country delay in burying a deceased person beyond a day or so is
when the results of an autopsy are awaited or when a close relative from
outside of the country is awaited. Though a body may rarely be refrigerated
for a few days, embalming takes place only when a body must be sent
abroad, and this is undertaken only in a hospital.

Throughout the ages Maltese families have buried their loved ones in
places ranging from dolmens, catacombs, and chapels to vaults and a wide
variety of burial grounds. The diverse range of burial grounds presently
available for families to use include some for military personnel, some
owned by the national government, some by religious orders, and others
owned by parishes—for example, in Mallieħa. Santa Maria in Xewkija is
the most prestigious burial ground on Gozo while on Malta it is Addolorata.

Designed by Emanuele Luigi Galizia (the most prolific of major Maltese
architects of the late nineteenth century) after he toured Italy, France, and
England, statuary-filled Addolorata was modeled after Cemetière du Nord
in Paris. As some burial grounds are more prestigious than others, so are
some locations within a burial ground. At Addolorata, for example, there
are fancy, private graves as well as common graves, with the latter being
located behind the small Gothic church crowning Tal-Ħorr hill.

Members of Maltese families have a strong preference to be buried near
one another. Family members openly discuss with each other what kinds
of family graves they are considering purchasing, almost in the way that
family members talk together about what kind of houses they require. Maltese make a sharp distinction between burying a relative in a common

grave—which is considered shameful—and burying a relative in a family grave—a practice considered highly desirable.

The average family grave has compartments for perhaps four or five coffins as well as a space below for bones. It is taboo to open such a grave in less than a year even if another death occurs in the same family. In this unfortunate circumstance, a family must use a different grave. Every few years, people who own family graves may request those who work at cemeteries to "clean" them. This means that deteriorated coffin material will be removed and the bones of those who died some time ago are placed in the lowest level so space is available for other coffins when it is needed.

For the cleaning of a family grave, relatives gather at the site in the spirit of solidarity and emotional sharing. This is an experience denied families with relatives in common graves where bones can be relocated to some unknown place after a year and mixed with the bones of strangers—a discomforting occurrence that Maltese associate with misfortune and low status. While final rites in Malta are consistent with values and beliefs about family solidarity and status, the cleaning and reuse of family crypts is also ecologically functional in a country with an extremely dense population where the soils are very thin.

People are socially categorized in life, and they are also categorized in death. Families bury a baby, unlike an adult, in a small oblong coffin covered with white linen coffin cloth. Also, it is likely to be carried to a burial ground in a private car, though a hearse is sometimes used. If an infant has not yet been baptized, it is buried in a special part of the cemetery—though this is subject to change from period to period and from place to place.

Letting go of loved ones in all societies involves a period of difficult readjustment to day to day life in which ritualistic interactions take place between those most affected and the larger community. Mourning in Malta once required close relatives to abstain from cooking food for three days during which time they would be sent food by neighbors and more distant relatives—mirroring a virtually identical custom in Tunisia (Abu-Zahra 1976: 170). During still another era, they had to refrain from cooking any of their food in a public oven for three months and, if extremely wealthy, distribute an oven-full of bread to the poor.

While cultural details change, the difficulty that families encounter in readjusting to day-to-day life and in becoming just another segment within society after a death has occurred is a constant. Though fewer women in mourning wear black for extended periods of time and fewer men wear a black armband or a black patch sewed to a coat than just a few decades ago, newspapers continue to carry memorial notices that reflect family solidarity and the strong bonds that still connect the living and the dead in Maltese culture.

All Souls Day remains an important time for remembering and praying for the dead, and flower sellers are much in evidence at this time of the year as the graves of Christians in all parts of Malta are decorated. Maltese are not reluctant to pray for the souls of the dead, whatever the apparent circumstances of death. The living allow for the possibility that the deceased may have been forgiven at the last moment of life and that prayer may assist their souls in eventually getting to heaven.

The family is such a pivotal institution that it impacts and is impacted by cultural adjustments that sweep all aspects of social life. A very different area of life where the family is leading the way with social change has to do with gender relations. Since gender evolves both in domestic and public domains, it is not an aspect of culture over which the family has exclusive control. Still, gender differentiation is typically manifested in a very profound way in families and families often feel obliged, for the safety of their members and concern with aggregate family honor, to insist on conformity with traditional gender roles.

Family systems in all societies tend to be more patriarchal than matriarchal, but it is not unusual to find traces of matriarchy within them (Ember and Ember 2001). In this respect, the traditional Maltese family system is no exception; though manifesting some matriarchal features, it is strongly patriarchal. Well into the late twentieth century, many of Malta's legal codes disadvantaged women and prevented them from achieving legal maturity with men. Hardly anywhere was this more apparent than in the domestic sphere.

The gaining of the right to vote by Maltese women in 1947 did not eliminate numerous legal disadvantages for them, neither in the family nor in the larger society. Until quite recently, for example, those employed by the government or even a quasi-governmental agency had to resign from their jobs should they marry. At the same time, there was great social pressure on females to marry. This so-called "marriage bar"—discriminating exclusively against females on the basis of their marital status—was finally eliminated through a 1981 amendment enacted by Malta's Parliament. With this one step the legislature began to dismantle the legal basis for traditional patriarchy, beginning with the economic system as it intersected with marriage.

The government, the largest employer nationally, was in this way forging ahead to portray itself as a model of unprecedented egalitarianism in the pubic sector. This does not mean, however, that women no longer encounter discrimination and barriers in retaining their positions when they marry and have children; it means that this occurs less frequently and less in the public sector of the labor market than in others (Camilleri 1998: 79; Cristina 1998: 133; Delia 1998: 48). Reinforcing this change was the elimination of the legal requirement that a vacancy in a job previous held by a male had to be filled with another male.

By 1990, new legislation made it possible for married women to become employed without their families suffering from very heavy tax penalties. It also became possible for married women to have an option to file their taxes separately from their husbands (Baldacchino: 1998: 72; Camilleri 1998: 78). The following year, a white paper entitled "Equal Partners in Marriage" emphasized that marriage should "be built on love, solidarity, equality and cooperation" (Orland 1998: 9). Of great significance society-wide, this was the year that the national constitution was amended to include a provision against all forms of sexual discrimination. By this 1991 amendment, the Constitution now provides "The State shall promote the equal right of men and women to enjoy all economic, social, cultural, civil, and political rights and for this purpose shall take appropriate measures to eliminate all forms of discrimination between the sexes by any person, organization or enterprise; the state shall in particular aim at ensuring that women workers enjoy equal rights and the same wages for the same work as men."

Hence, as in most other parts of the Western world, the law has been declared to be on the side of women who wish to be gainfully employed despite marital status. Moreover, within the Ministry for Social Development there has been established an Equal Status for Women Department. Given such structural changes buttressed by law, undoubtedly there will come to be more married couples where both husband and wife will work for wages. Still, mere legal changes will not change the Maltese culture drastically overnight, and at present most men and women feel that men should be preferred in paying jobs.

In 1993, Act XXI of the Constitution amended important parts of the Civil Code dealing directly with family matters to bring them into line with the spirit of the previous changes, in fact, to make them among the most visionary in the Western world. For the first time in Malta's history, the possibility for symmetry between spouses began to replace traditional relationships that emphasized complementary differences.

Under these changes, widely dubbed "the family law," wives enter marriage with the legal option of retaining their maiden surnames. The concept that the spouses enjoy equal rights and have equal responsibilities in their marriage and toward their offspring replaced the prior concept that the husband must maintain the wife in marriage. Household work is recognized as a contribution to family maintenance on a par with gainful employment. The old concept of *patria potestas*, holding that the husband was the sole head of the family, has been jettisoned for the concept of equally shared spousal and parental authority. Passports may be issued for children only with the signatures of both parents.

Except for stock market transactions or where small sums of money are involved, the family law vests in spouses the authority to jointly administer community property. It also requires the signatures of both spouses for lending, selling of property, making of donations, installment purchasing, and borrowing. As far as it goes, this legislation puts spouses on an equal footing vis-à-vis each other in terms of borrowing. There still exist certain prejudices against considering females good credit risks, however, due, for example, to their lower average salaries and the assumption that they more casually leave the job market to attend to family (Delia 1998: 48; Orland 1998: 15). Clearly the law has not immediately eliminated all difficulties that women encounter in acquiring capital.

Even within the family, an additional hurdle exists. Though any married person now has the right to trade or engage in gainful employment without the need to obtain spousal approval (as long as that work involves no borrowing), a spouse may withhold approval needed for his or her partner to borrow capital. In practice, more husbands than wives are likely to feel their gender status threatened by having their spouses operate a business and, hence, are more likely to object to the requisite acquisition of capital (D. Vella 1998: 86).

The family law provides for safeguarding community property (including the matrimonial home) from the unilateral alienation by either spouse, and it also permits spouses to choose a system whereby some property may be owned and administered by them separately (Tabone 1995: 102). Significantly, it gives wives the right to administer the belongings they bring into their marriages—namely, their dowries—without the need for spousal approval (Orland 1998: 14).

Reflecting on the many legislative changes that have recently impacted the family system, Tabone (1995: 100) is probably focussing on the future more than the present when he states: "*In practice* [emphasis mine], the distinctive father and mother roles are becoming parental or family roles" and "The contemporary Maltese family tends to be characterised by symmetry rather than complimenatrity" (p. 102). While the family system is definitely changing in Malta, much that has long been traditional about the system, including roles, has thus far changed only gradually. Moreover, values appear to be changing faster than behavior, and differences exist among various segments of society based on factors such as age, sex, level of education, economic status, marital status, parental status, and probably, religiosity and area of residence (Tabone 1995: 116–135).

Although Maltese women have finally reached legal maturity, Delia (1998: 50) has expressed the view: "The change in laws needs to be accompanied by a change in the culture of families and work." Many social practices continue to disadvantage females, if only because of prejudices, attitudes, discrimination, their greater illiteracy, the greater emphasis on passivity in their socialization, the fact that they alone can become pregnant, are afforded less "free time," and have imposed on them a double standard of comportment in society. Although the overall impact of recent changes in legislation regarding gender status and family structure bring Malta into closer alignment with Europe and pull her further from the family systems of her predominantly Muslim neighbors, her family system remains rather conservative in several respects.

One ironic consequence of broad adherence to Catholic teachings with regard to family organization has been a traditional emphasis on having large families and minimal participation of married Maltese women as full-time workers in the labor force (Darmanin 1998: 60). In fact, although gainful employment by females is increasing, Malta's pattern is more Mediterranean than European per se. The Food and Agricultural Association of the United Nations (2000) reveals that based on statistics gathered during 1990–92, the percentages of females in the labor force for Cyprus, Egypt, Lebanon, Morocco, Syria, Tunisia, and Turkey were 38%, 29%, 27%, 26%, 18%, 21%, and 31%, respectively.

Given that in 1994 only 29.8% of Maltese women were employed, as measured by official statistics, this level of female participation in gainful employment is very low by European standards. It compares to percentages of 42.9% in Italy, 44.1% in Spain, and 47.2% in Ireland, all predominantly Catholic countries, the first two of which are also located in the Mediterranean. In non-Mediterranean and predominantly Protestant Denmark, Norway, and the United Kingdom, the comparable percentages reach as high as 73.8%, 71.1%, 66.2%, respectively (Camilleri 1998: 75).

Progressive family law in Malta promises to make it easier for mothers to work, and under improved conditions. But the scarcity of affordable childcare institutions and the reluctance of mothers to use them leads to a greater dependence of the nuclear family on grandmothers as babysitters (Baldacchino 1998: 54; Camilleri 1998: 80; Cristina 1998: 135; Delia 1998: 48; Spiteri 1998: 123; D. Vella 1998: 88). While imposing on grandmothers, this dependence deprives them of retirement, and it increases the likelihood of their interference in the affairs of nuclear families. This is a dependence, moreover, that potentially can prevent many middle-aged and elderly women from exercising their own options to become gainfully employed or have unencumbered free time.

From the point of view of the child, a possible advantage of being reared by a stay-at-home mother is a long period of maternal bonding close to hearth and home. Social pressures associated with religion and status, the paucity of employment slots, and a genuine interest in providing the best childcare encourage many married couples to play out traditional spousal roles. Still, feminist awareness and more egalitarian expectations in marriage and in the workplace are beginning to weaken this pattern.

While the new family law has made it easier for women to be employed away from their homes, it has only minimally changed general expectations that, in addition, they should perform most domestic work. In terms of values, Tabone (1995: 105–107) has documented that 73.3% of males agree that housework should be shared between married couples while only 1.3% think that a husband doing housework enables a wife to virtually turn him into a woman. He has also documented that the behavioral input of men in domestic work did not much change during a recent 10-year period. Many people traditionally feared that requiring boys to help with domestic work would turn them into homosexuals. Now 72.3% of parents agree that sons should help with such work, though only about 56.5% do so (Tabone 1995: 112–113). Although even the gender values of children are beginning to change, the laws intended to eliminate gender discrimination are ahead of actual practice both in the labor market and in the family (Laiviera 1998: 26).

While over half of women agree that married women should be free to undertake gainful employment, slightly fewer than a quarter of those under 60 years of age actually work outside their homes and almost a third of these work only part-time. While some married women find that part-time work enables them better to balance employment with family responsibilities (Cristina 1998: 134; Delia 1998: 49) many others find other work opportunities closed to them. As in most capitalist economies, the labor market in Malta is segmented with many disadvantaged employees, including women, more likely to be working part-time without benefits (Darmanin 1998: 61–62, 65). Even legislation passed in 1996 that requires annual and sick leave for people who work part-time as their primary employment has not fully rectified this problem (Camilleri 1998: 82).

With respect to family planning, the fact that couples married in 1901 had an average of between eight and nine children (Central Office of Statistics 1963: xliii) and couples in recent decades are having an average of between two and three suggests that some effective means of birth control is apparently being used. This notwithstanding, the overwhelming majority of people are opposed to the use of artificial contraception (Tabone 1995: 55, 92, 97) and these means of birth control as well as abortion remain illegal.

An area in which the family law of 1993 has most challenged traditional Maltese family customs has to do with the socialization and custody of children. People have long assumed that the rearing of children was more a responsibility for mothers than for the fathers, a fact that partially explains why fathers have not traditionally attended school events for children. Such an assumption no longer resides in the law. In fact, for men and women who work for the government or quasi-governmental entities, a right is provided in law to take one year of parental leave without pay for caring for children under 5 years old (Camilleri 1998: 80; Cristina 1998: 133). Though such benefits are not legislated for private companies or industries, they contribute to a new way of thinking about parental roles in society.

Apart from the Vatican, Malta remains the only state in the Mediterranean and the only state in Europe that does not permit divorce. This situation has not prevented a recent upsurge in the number of single-parent families (Cristina 1998: 131). When a separation occurs, either parent—at least in theory—may receive custody of any children. The family law places on both people in a separated marriage responsibility for child support and maintenance of their spouse as required and within the limits of their means. In practice the strong traditional Maltese assumption that in most cases children should be in the custody of their mothers is stronger than the new family law. Hence, though both parents are assured visitation rights with the children after a separation occurs (Orland 1998: 11), it is more often than not the mother who is the custodial parent and the recipient of child support payments.

While there are taking place in Malta radical changes in values concerning how the family system should function in the twenty-first century, traditions associated with such a pivotal social institution change slowly. Fathers much more than mothers continue to be thought of as the material providers for families. Leisure time is more an expectation of married males than of married females as the latter, much more frequently attached to the house, may continue doing things relating to its upkeep far into the evening.

However, husbands take their wives out more than they used to and this is beginning to change former time-allocation patterns for males and females. There is more acceptance by Maltese males that women are full persons not obliged to work continually for a family and a man. Though many fathers are not much involved in rearing children before they are 4, and even then, they tend to be much more involved with sons than with daughters, one sometimes sees a man pushing a pram along the street or carrying an infant onto a bus.

Cooking a meal at home continues to be considered a task for females, unless it is an unusual circumstance or a husband is considered an exceptional cook. Female passivity and domesticity and male dominance are traditional values that are still reflected in children's textbooks (Laiviera 1998: 19–20). After a family meal, wives and girls are expected to wash the dishes much more often than boys. In younger families, however, it is not unusual for a husband to help with drying the dishes. Boys are expected to help with such domestic chores as taking out the rugs twice a year for special cleaning or beating, and families are continuing to expand the range of domestic work that boys do.

As cultural changes afford women options to achieve in ways not available in the traditional family, women will not have to forgo marriage in order to achieve outside the domestic domain, and even in public life, as previously. It is not coincidental that three of the most notable Maltese women to achieve high status in public life had to forgo marriage. One was Miss Helen Buhagiar, a leader in the Democratic Action Party from its founding in 1947, the same year that her struggle—along with others—to gain the right to vote for women was finally successful. Another was

Miss Mabel Strickland. Miss Strickland was recognized as a stateswoman in Maltese politics long before 1947. She eventually followed in her father's footsteps as a major newspaper publisher, served in Parliament, and was head of the Progressive Constitutional Party. Miss Agatha Barbara, a leader in the Labor Party, was the first woman elected to parliament when female eligibility was initially established in 1947 and most women thought of politics as a preoccupation for men. In addition to being elected each time she ran, Miss Barbara became the first female to serve as a government minister. Moreover, after Malta became a republic, she eventually became its president.

The extraordinary influence of unmarried women such as these in public life during their long careers can hardly be overstated. When Miss Strickland died in 1988 she was almost 90 years old and she was laid to rest in the Cathedral in Mdina next to her father. When the Honorable Miss Barbara died at 78 in early 2002, a state funeral was held to mark her passing at St. John's Co-Cathedral in Valletta.

There no longer exists an assumption that daughters in large numbers will discontinue their formal education at age 16. Already females constitute the majority in the University of Malta faculties of art, education, health care, social welfare, pharmacy, law, and medicine. They are also between 30 and 50% of the student body in theology, science, economics, accounting, management, and dentistry (Delia 1998: 49). Many of these changes affecting the structure and operation of the family began first among more educated and cosmopolitan segments of the population. Now they are also changing life for the masses, in part because of television and cinema, the presence of so many foreign tourists, fundamental changes in the Maltese family law, and a national pride in being "up to date" and European as well as Mediterranean. Against this background of continuing change, Tabone (1995: 247–250) suggests that there now exist at least five types of Maltese families: the traditional, the conventional, the modern, the deprived, and the progressive.

Chapter 9

Dawn in a New Millennium

Several Maltese proverbs express concern that the Maltese Islands may one day sink beneath the sea. Though there exists no reason to assume that this is a threat short-term, an island micro-state, only lightly defended, still searching for its identity and place in a turbulent world, Malta faces many challenges associated with survival in an age of globalization. Far from sinking, Malta is still discovering what it means to be a bridge.

Under the most favorable of circumstances it is difficult for a country that is virtually devoid of natural resources and that is highly dependent on a constant influx of tourists to sustain its economy to maintain a viable independence. Thus far, Malta has been meeting the challenge well. Malta's greatest resources are its industrious, well-educated population and its rich cultural heritage. As compared to most countries in the world, Malta is prosperous, at peace, and relatively crime-free.

At the national prison in Paola, there are seldom more than 85 prisoners in custody at any one time. Typical crimes relate to growing cannabis, circulating counterfeit money, theft, homicide, and entering the country illegally. Also a juvenile court sits at the conference hall of the Center for Social Welfare which also houses the Commission against Drug and Alcohol Abuse. Among voluntary organizations which also make use of the center's facilities is the Action Team on Violence against Women.

A range of progressive social security legislation that is administered through the Ministry for Social Development provides a broad social network for the needy at a time when families turn increasingly to the government for assistance in an environment of social change. Benefits become available in the event of injury or disability, for a surviving spouse, for dependent children, and for retirement pensions. Qualifying individuals and families with grave financial difficulties may receive means-tested support through the Social and Family Affairs Department which in 1993 emerged from the amalgamation of the Department of Social and Family Welfare with the Department of Care of the Elderly. In addition to offering financial assistance, the Social and Family Affairs Department provides for a variety of crisis intervention and counseling services in areas ranging from probation and rehabilitation to adoption and fostering. It also assists Maltese who are physically and mentally challenged.

Malta is home to many professional organizations, historical and heritage societies, and international clubs. Its rich range of organizations includes many which are concerned with social development, personal development, environmental issues, sports, other leisure pursuits, and cultural development—including in the arts. The Manoel Theatre built in 1731 by Grand Master Manoel de Vilhena is maintained by the government as a national theater for the arts and a number of performance artists work in hotels, dance halls, restaurants, bars, and outdoor venues.

A long artistic tradition continues that includes the making of furniture, jewelry in gold and silver including filigree, glass, sculpture, lace, tableware, dolls, ceramics, brassware, copperware, and miniature cribs and figurines, as well as painting. Many artists who can not support themselves full-time as artists also work at second jobs. For example, some housewives undertake lace-making as cottage industries at home. The government assists the arts by means of its public relations outreach and by means of its involvement with the Malta Government Crafts Center in Valletta, the Ta Ciali Crafts Village outside of Rabat on Malta, and the Ta Dbiegi Crafts Village in Gozo.

Fewer Maltese are emigrating than in the past though Malta remains one of the world's most densely populated countries with a density of 1,184.4 persons per kilometer. This means that apart from tiny Monaco, Malta has by far the most dense and most urban population in the Mediterranean. The next highest densities, which are 417.5 persons per kilometer in Lebanon, followed by 296.1 in Israel, pale by comparison.

Clearly, Malta must carefully balance the inevitability of change with cultural protectionism if it is not to be overwhelmed, not by the sea but by the larger world. Given Malta's small size, even tiny demographic changes can reverberate with great effect. Malta's current rate of annual population growth of .05% is one of the lowest in the region. Some Maltese view their annual population growth as threatening; however, nearby Libya's annual population growth rate is an astonishing 2.2%, a rate that is exceeded in the Mediterranean only by those of Israel and Bosnia-Herzegovina. Malta is already one of the most densely populated countries in the world, and its long-stagnant population is once again growing and not projected to peak before 2025 (Clews 2001: 214). Though Malta is still largely culturally and ethnically homogeneous, that it is growing larger and more culturally diverse at the same time poses some novel challenges. That this is occurring, moreover, at the same time that females are remaining in the job market longer than they did traditionally might eventually contribute to ethnic tension and create a perceived need for more aggressive population control, even of Malta's very low levels of immigration.

This is not to imply, however, that Malta did not adapt to considerable diversity in the past. The first known Jewish burial grounds in Malta were probably where we find ancient Jewish tombs near Rabat dating to Roman times. Even in the seventh century, as many as a third of women in some parishes were married to European foreigners. Moreover, ancient burial grounds for Muslims date back to the Middle Ages. The first Protestant church built in Malta was consecrated in 1844 (Bonnici 1973: 191). And the same Emanuele Luigi Galizia who designed Malta's national Addolorata Cemetery designed the chief Protestant cemetery at Ta'Braxia, and in 1874 was commissioned to design the Turkish cemetery. Though Malta until this point in its cultural development has managed to assimilate most of its newcomers in terms of religion, language, and ethnicity, it is attracting new settlers from throughout the Mediterranean Basin, the British Isles, and elsewhere that could pose new challenges.

Malta's Jewish community numbers about 120 persons of different religious beliefs ranging from Orthodox to Reform and atheists. There is a community of about 60 settlers from India, many of whom are merchants in Valletta and Sliema. Highly significant, perhaps 600 Maltese are married to Arabic-speaking Muslims with the largest number being from Libya and a significant number being from the Palestinian diaspora. Additionally, there are a few Chinese who live in Malta as well as a considerable number of illegal immigrants, mostly from such Eastern European countries as Bulgaria, Albania, and Russia. Though these segments of the populations are rather small and are not sharply cut off from the rest of society through any deep ethnic cleavage, they do cause Malta to be more of a mosaic than in recent times.

Diversity has not always settled easily on Malta. For example, Pirotta (1994: 105) has pointed out: "There is evidence that strongly suggests that the issue of racial identity has left a lasting impression on the Maltese and that, even after independence, Maltese political thinking has remained conditioned by the experiences of past centuries." All countries encounter challenges in molding people of different heritages, religions, and value systems into national solidarities that work harmoniously. In addition to miniscule communities of Buddhists, Hindu, Bahá'ís, and Jehovah's Witnesses, Malta has larger minority communities made up of Orthodox Christians, Anglicans, Jews, and Muslims.

Against this background, a 1973 decision by Malta to permit the construction of a mosque and a school to teach Arabic was an extraordinary development. The government even donated the land for this purpose—in

Paola, close to where the Turkish Cemetery is located. Al-Dawwa al-Islamia, the Islamic Call and Missionary Society, under the sponsorship of Libya, undertook the construction. Malta made a further concession to diversity in the late 1980's when the mosque and Islamic Center were given diplomatic immunity. Since this time, the center has expanded its curriculum beyond the teaching of Arabic and it is now functioning as a normal school.

Although Libya did not reciprocate by allowing the construction of a Catholic church and school on its territory, the need for Malta to obtain Libyan oil at a moderate price helped to persuade the government that this arrangement was in its best interest. On the other hand, Malta has not given in to a standing request for expanded burial facilities for Muslims. Giving in to this request would commit Muslims to permanently use one grave per person. Such a nonintensive use of land would be very much at variance with traditional Maltese burial practices that accommodate several coffins together and recycle graves through periodic cleaning. As this situation makes clear, Malta's lack of natural resources both led it to become more open toward Libyans and to resist innovations in burial practices that would strain its small repository of land. Mollifying Libya in this way seemed at the time to be in Maltese national interest, as well as progressive.

However, Maltese definitions of what seems progressive continue to change and to create some controversy. In recent decades, the government tightened its control over the University of Malta where many professors are priests. A "Corrupt Practices Act" was introduced forbidding church interference with elections, *Privilegium fori* which made bishops immune from criminal prosecution was repealed, and the privileged position of the church was abolished (Koster 1994: 314–315). Though an overwhelming majority of Maltese now approve of changes that provide for greater separation of church and state in major areas of public life (Abela 2000: 187; Council of Europe Publishing 1997: 33), increasing pluralism in society has the potential to complicate this emerging modus vivendi.

Being Maltese remains virtually synonymous with being Catholic, but increasing recognition is being given religious minorities. Already as a result of amendment of the burials ordinance, church officials can no longer prohibit any Maltese citizen from being buried in the Addolorata Cemetery, regardless of his or her standing with the church (Koster 1994: 315). Although divorce is still not permitted, recent changes in the law provide for the possibility of civil marriage as well as ecclesiastical marriage. One effect of this change is that in cases where Catholics and non-Catholics marry, they are not compelled to be married according to canon law nor rear their children as Catholics.

Malta's centralized location in the Mediterranean, which formerly gave it special economic importance as an entrepôt, as a base of operations for holy wars, and as a military base within the British Empire, is something of a mixed blessing. Quite apart from being strategic, Malta's location involves a liability of exposure. On several occasions, external conflicts involving Israelis and Arabs in contests of violence have spilled over onto her soil. Also, foreign personalities associated with overseas crime syndicates—for example from Sicily—have occasionally made an appearance in the islands, and many believe that a disproportionate amount of crime committed by foreigners is associated with Libyans. Now that the Constitution forbids any further stationing of foreign troops in Malta, the country's income and employment are generated largely through the peaceful use of its good ports, beaches, and moderate climate. However, it is impossible to open one's arms to the world without being transformed.

That Malta annually attracts tourists equal to roughly three times its national population is both a great economic achievement and a threat to its culture and quality of life. Television sets can receive programming from Italy, and sometimes from nearby northern Africa, especially with the benefit of satellite dishes. In additional to global networks like CNN, the islanders are exposed to such a plethora of mass media that the issue of media colonialism has been raised (Chircop 1994: 361–364). These outside cultural influences exist in addition to the constant influx of tourism. In fact, they are to some extent a requisite of twenty-first century living when everyone—including tourists—expects to be constantly "in touch." Of all the countries in the Mediterranean, only in France, Israel, and Slovenia does one find significantly more personal computers per 1,000 inhabitants than in Malta.

Though most Maltese live a cultural religiosity that is closely associated with Catholicism, one result of Malta's greater diversity and increased exposure to the outside world has been an upsurge in the questioning of some traditional norms and an increase in secularism (Abela 1992: 48–72; Abela 2000: 179). Married and widowed people are generally more religiously active than those who are single or separated. Although Malta is continually exposed to foreign influences, it continues to be characterized by a very low level of secularization (Abela 2000: 181, 185).

That over two-thirds of Maltese are employed in services, and slightly less than one-third in industry, is indicative of a postindustrial level of development, although Malta-based industry is small-scale. In fact, only 20 or so of Maltese industries employ more than 250 people. Many of her approximately 2,500 enterprises are involved with parts assembly and other aspects of small-scale manufacture. That a single electronics firm produces two-fifths of all exports indicates a lack of industrial diversity, a situation which naturally entails some economic risk. The key industrial sector, which involves shipbuilding and repair, with most contracts coming from abroad, is subsidized and its long-term prospects of being self-supporting are in question.

Malta has an economy in whose service sector tourism is of primary importance and in whose industrial sector shipbuilding and dry-dock repair are of primary importance. The economic importance of industry is more or less equivalent to that of tourism. Whereas tourism accounts for between one-fourth and one-third of gross national product (GNP), it furnishes employment for a somewhat larger proportion of the population. Unfortunately, however, this employment is highly seasonal—reaching its peak between July and September.

Tourism is heavily concentrated on the island of Malta and is skewed toward a low-spending British clientele though present marketing focuses on achieving greater diversity in vacationers. In addition to large-scale accommodations for tourists, there exist numerous pensions and flats. In Malta's highly centralized, capitalistic economy, the government is the largest employer, and its monopolistic control extends to all utilities, fuel, the airline, shipping line, shipyards, and even to many factories and hotels. The Mediterranean countries of Slovenia and Croatia have recently begun to compete for a similar tourist market. However, as Malta has the advantage of a more southern climate and tends to offer better quality, though at a slightly higher price, its tourist industry continues to thrive. Although Malta obtains benefits from tourism, it also incurs costs that are social and environmental, as well as economic (Baldacchino 1997; Findlay and Wellisz 1993; Odermatt 1996; Pearce 1997).

Important among Malta's imports are machinery, energy resources from Libya, and other products vital to the viability of its tourist industry, such as transport equipment, live animals, food, beverages, tobacco, and chemicals. Malta's exports are in large measure tied to parts assembly but include chemicals as well as food. The country runs a permanent merchandise trade deficit. The European community accounts for slightly more than three-quarters of Malta's trade and most of her incoming direct foreign investment. In contrast, trade with northern Africa is barely more than 3%, most of which is with the single country of Libya.

Although agriculture accounts for only about 3% of employment, it accounts for about 4% of GNP. This is remarkable considering the small size of the islands, the high population density, the thin soils, their poor quality, and the limited water supplies. According to World Bank data on all countries of the Basin, only Libya and Israel are more disadvantaged than Malta with respect to freshwater resources per capita. Against this background, the ingenuity of the Maltese farmers and herders in sqeezing productivity from scant resources can scarcely be overstated. However, Malta's long growing season and the bounty of edible resources in the surrounding sea count as economic blessings.

Malta's GNP per capita of $9,210 (also designated by the World Bank as its gross national income) is well above the average among its Mediterranean neighbors. It is higher, for example, than that of all its African neighbors except Libya, higher than that of all its Asian neighbors except

Israel, and higher than that of Slovenia, Bosnia-Herzegovina, Croatia, Yugoslavia, and Albania in Europe. Recent legislative initiatives relating to family organization and gender relations are beginning to address Malta's low rate of female participation in the labor market. Women—both married and single—are entering the job market in larger numbers than at any time previous and remaining gainfully employed in unprecedented numbers after marriage. Despite the inevitability of economic cycles, the economy tends more often than not to be characterized by moderate levels of unemployment and rather low inflation.

Malta's written constitution provides for a highly centralized parliamentary democracy at the national level despite the recent additional of local councils. Her two major parties—the Nationalist Party, with a conservative belief in free enterprise and Christian democrat values, and the Malta Labor Party with a moderately socialist outlook—rather frequently alternate as the majority party in Parliament, also known as the House of Representatives.

Along with nonalignment, Malta's Labor Party stresses the leveling out of incomes and a mixed economy. By contrast, the National Party leans a bit more to "the right," in the direction of Europe, and has a greater commitment to gaining full membership in the European Union (EU). However, even the prospect of full EU membership will not solve all of Malta's problems. For instance, in Sweden, a member of the EU, the most frequently used racist epithets is *svartskalle*—meaning "blackhead" (Pred 2000: 73, 80)—and most Maltese not only have dark hair but somewhat swarthy complexions as well. Although the twenty-first century is an age of globalization, it is also an age in which we struggle to liberate ourselves from racism and from cultural provincialism that can be oppressive. Whether a full EU member or not, in the long run it may prove just as challenging for Malta to be *just* European as *just* Mediterranean.

Significant cost sometimes is associated with following EU regulations and such cost might be heavy for an economy as small as Malta's. On the other hand, Malta's tourism industry expects some concessions from full EU membership and undoubtedly some technical assistance will flow in Malta's direction. Even while Maltese continue to debate what the long-range merits of such full membership will mean, other dialogue continues to take place about how best to profit from the country's roots as a cultural bridge spanning the Mediterranean.

This is apparent in discussions about how Maltese telecommunications infrastructure may make the country function as a hub for the greater Mediterranean (Chircop 1994: 366). Resulting from the Hospitaller tradition of the Knights, Malta has inherited an excellent medical education system, one presently relying on the University of Malta, along with St. Luke's Hospital located in Guardamangia, as the principal teaching hospital. This expertise can clearly be useful to many of Malta's neighbors. At the University—where some 7,000 students matriculate in faculties as wide-ranging as architecture, civil engineering, the arts, theology, and dental surgery—already 6% are foreigners. Nothing better demonstrates that Maltese nationalism is still evolving in the dawn of this new millennium than the ways the Maltese alternate between wanting to go it alone, wanting to be European, and wanting also to be a part of something larger.

Bibliography

Abela, Anthony M. 1992. *Changing Youth Culture in Malta*. Valletta, Malta: Jesuit Publications, Diocesan Youth Commission.

———. 1994. *Shifting Family Values in Malta: A Western European Perspective*. Floriana, Malta: Institute for Research for the Signs of the Times.

———. 1998a. "Feminization of Poverty." In *Gender Issues and Statistics*, edited by Anthony M. Abela. Malta: Department of Women's Rights, Ministry for Social Policy.

———. 1998b. *Women and Men in the Maltese Islands: Statistics from the Census of Population and Housing*. Malta: Department for Women's Rights, Ministry for Social Policy.

———. 2000. *Values of Women and Men in the Maltese Islands: A Comparative European Perspective*. Malta: Commission for the Advancement of Women, Ministry for Social Policy.

Abu-Zahra, N. 1976. "Family and Kinship in a Tunisian Peasant Community." In *Mediterranean Family Structures*, edited by J. G. Peristiany. Cambridge: Cambridge University Press.

Ackerman, James S. and Myra Nan Rosenfeld. 1989. "Social Stratification in Renaissance Urban Planning." In *Urban Life in the Renaissance*, edited by Susan Zimmerman and Ronald F. E. Weissman. Newark: University of Delaware.

Ahmad, Aziz. 1975. *A History of Islamic Sicily*. Edinburgh: Edinburgh University Press.

Amari, M. 1937–1939. *Storia dei Musulmani di Sicilia*. 2nd ed., rev. Cantania: C. A. Nallino.

Ansell, Meredith O., Ibrahim Massaud al-Arif, and Carmelo Mifsud Bonnici, comps. 1972. *Laws of Malta*. Harrow, UK: Oleander Press.

Aquilina, Joseph. 1958. *The Structure of Maltese*. Valletta: Royal University of Malta.

———. 1970a. "A Brief Survey of Maltese Place-Names" [orig. 1970]. In *Papers in Maltese Linguistics*, a collection by Joseph Aquilina. Malta: The Royal University of Malta [corrected reprint of 1961 printing by Progress Press Co. Ltd., Valletta].

————. 1970b. "Maltese as a Mixed Language" [orig. 1958]. In *Papers in Maltese Linguistics*, a collection by Joseph Aquilina. Malta: The Royal University of Malta [corrected reprint of 1961 printing by Progress Press Co. Ltd., Valletta].

————. 1970c. "Maltese Lexicography" [orig. 1953]. In *Papers in Maltese Linguistics*, a collection by Joseph Aquilina. Malta: The Royal University of Malta [corrected reprint of 1961 printing by Progress Press Co. Ltd., Valletta].

————. 1970d. "Race and Language in Malta" [orig. 1945]. In *Papers in Maltese Linguistics*, a collection by Joseph Aquilina. Malta: The Royal University of Malta [corrected reprint of 1961 printing by Progress Press Co. Ltd., Valletta].

————. 1970e. "A Survey of the Constituent Elements of Maltese" [orig. 1958]. In *Papers in Maltese Linguistics*, a collection by Joseph Aquilina. Malta: The Royal University of Malta [corrected reprint of 1961 printing by Progress Press Co. Ltd., Valletta].

————. 1972. *A Comparative Dictionary of Maltese Proverbs*. Malta: Royal University of Malta.

Arensberg, Conrad. 1955. "American Communities." *American Anthropologist* 57: 1143–1162.

Backman, Clifford R. 1995. *The Decline and Fall of Medieval Sicily*. Cambridge: Cambridge University Press.

Baldacchino, Godfrey. 1997. *Global Tourism and Informal Labour Relations: The Small Scale Syndrome at Work*. London and Washington, DC: Mansell.

————. 1998. "Nistghu Nkejlu l-Bidla fir-Rwol tal-Mara fl-Ekonomija Maltija?" [Can We Measure the Change in Women's Role in the Maltese Economy?]. In *Il-Mara Maltija wara s-Sena 2000* [The Maltese Woman beyond the Year 2000], edited by Angela Callus. Birkirkara: Pubblikazzjonijiet Indipendenza.

Bartolo, Gillian. 1998. "Women in the Press." In *Gender Issues and Statistics*, edited by Anthony M. Abela. Malta: Department of Women's Rights, Ministry for Social Policy.

Belmonte, Thomas. 1983. "The Contradictions." In *Urban Life in Mediterranean Europe: Anthropological Perspectives*, edited by Michael Kenny and David I. Kertzer. Urbana: University of Illinois Press.

Bernal, Martin. 1987. *Black Athena: The Afroasiatic Roots of Classical Civilization*. Vol. 1. New Brunswick, NJ: Rutgers University Press.

Birdwell-Pheasant, Donna and Denise Lawrence-Zúñiga eds. 1999. *House Life: Space, Place and Family in Europe*. New York: Berg.

Birot, Pierre and Jean Dresch. 1953. *La Méditerranée et le Moyen Orient*. 2 vols. Paris: Presses Universitaires de France.

Black, Annabel. 1996. "Negotiating the Tourist Gaze." In *Coping with Tourists: European Reactions to Mass Tourism*, edited by Jeremy Boissevain. Providence, RI: Berghahn Books.

Blouet, Brian. 1967. *The Story of Malta*. London: Faber and Faber.

Boissevain, Jeremy F. 1969a. *Hal-Farrug: A Village in Malta.* New York: Holt, Rinehart and Winston.

———. 1969b. *Saints and Fireworks: Religion and Politics in Rural Malta.* London: The Athlone Press of the University of London.

———. 1994. "Festa Partiti: Parish Competition and Conflict." In *Maltese Society: A Sociological Inquiry*, edited by Ronald G. Sultana and Godfrey Baldacchino. Msida, Malta: Mireva Publications.

Bonanno, Anthony. 1990. "Malta's Role in the Phoenician, Greek and Etruscan Trade in the Western Mediterranean." *Melita Historica* 10: 209–224.

Bonnici, Arthur. 1973. "Thirty Years to Build a Protestant Church." *Melita Historica* 6: 183–191.

Borg, Carmel and Peter Mayo. 1994. "The Maltese Community in Metro Toronto." In *Maltese Society: A Sociological Inquiry*, edited by Ronald G. Sultana and Godfrey Baldacchino. Msida, Malta: Mireva Publications.

Boswell, David M. 1994. "The Social Prestige of Residential Areas." In *Maltese Society: A Sociological Inquiry*, edited by Ronald G. Sultana and Godfrey Baldacchino. Msida, Malta: Mireva Publications.

Bovill, E. W. 1958. *The Golden Trade of the Moors.* London: Oxford University Press.

Bowen, E. G. 1972. *Britain and the Western Seaways: A History of Cultural Interchange through Atlantic Coastal Waters.* New York: Praeger Publishers.

Bowen-Jones, H., J. C. Dewdney, and W. B. Fisher. 1961. *Malta: Background for Development.* Durham: University of Durham.

Bradford, Ernle. 1961. *The Great Siege.* London: Holder and Stoughton.

———. 1971. *Mediterranean, Portrait of a Sea.* London: Hodder and Stoughton.

Bradley, R. N. 1912. *Malta and the Mediterranean Race.* London: T. Fisher Unwin.

Braudel, Fernand. 1972. *The Mediterranean and the Mediterranean World in the Age of Philip II.* 2 vols. London: Collins.

Brett, Michael. 1969. "Ifriqiya as a Market for Saharan Trade from the Tenth to the Twelfth Century A.D." *Journal of African History* 10: 347–364.

Brown, T. S. 1975. "Byzantine Malta: a Discussion of the Sources." In *Medieval Malta: Studies on Malta before the Knights*, edited by Anthony T. Luttrell, 71–87. London: The British School at Rome.

Brydone, Patrick. 1774. *A Tour through Sicily and Malta, In a Series of Letters to William Beckford, Esq.* Vol. 1. London.

Buhagiar, Mario. 1975. "Medieval Churches in Malta." In *Medieval Malta: Studies on Malta before the Knights*, edited by Anthony T. Luttrell, 163–180. London: The British School at Rome.

———. 1991. "The St. John's Co-Cathedral Affair—A Study of a Dispute between Church and State in Malta over Property Rights." *Melita Historica* 10: 359–374.

———. 1997. "Gozo in Late Roman, Byzantine and Muslim Times." *Melita Historica* 12: 113–130.

Busuttil, Joseph. 1968. "Diodorus Melitensis." *Melita Historica* 10: 32–35.

———. 1971a. "Maltese Harbours in Antiquity." *Melita Historica* 5: 305–307.

———. 1971b. "Pirates in Malta." *Melita Historica* 5: 308–310.

Camilleri, Agnes M. 1996. "The French in Malta (1798–1800)." Master's thesis, California State University Dominguez Hills.

Camilleri, Frances. 1998. "Il-Mara fil-Post tax-Xoghol u fit-Trade Unions" [Women at Work and in Trade Unions]. In *Il-Mara Maltija wara s-Sena 2000* [The Maltese Woman beyond the Year 2000], edited by Angela Callus. Birkirkara: Pubblikazzjonijiet Indipendenza.

Camilleri, Joseph J. 1977. "The Abolition of the Class of Arabic at the Lyceum." *Melita Historica* 7: 171–174.

Cassar, Carmel. 1988. "The Reformation and Malta." *Melita Historica* 10: 51–68.

Central Office of Statistics. 1963. *An Enquiry into Family Size in Malta and Gozo.* Valletta, Malta: Central Office of Statistics.

Chalandon, F. 1907. *Histoire de la domination normande en Italie et en Sicilie.* Paris: Librairie A. Picard et fils.

Chapman, Charlotte Gower. 1971. *Milocca: A Sicilian Village.* London: Schenkman Publishing Co.

Chircop, Saviour. 1994. "As We Sit Together, Should We Use the Phone? A Research Agenda for the Study of Media in Malta." In *Maltese Society: A Sociological Inquiry*, edited by Ronald G. Sultana and Godfrey Baldacchino. Msida, Malta: Mireva Publications.

Ciappara, F. 1976. "The Landed Property of the Inquisition in Malta in the Late XVII Century." *Melita Historica* 7: 43–60.

Clair, Colin. 1969. *Malta: The Spread of Printing Series.* Amsterdam: Vangendt and Co.

Clews, Stanley J. A., ed. 1996. *The Malta Yearbook 1996.* Sliema, Malta: De La Salle Brothers Publications.

———. 2001. *The Malta Yearbook 2001.* Sliema, Malta: De La Salle Brothers Publications.

Clissold, Stephen. 1977. *The Barbary Slaves.* Totowa, NJ: Rowman and Littlefield.

Cole, Maureen. 1994. "Outsiders." In *Maltese Society: A Sociological Inquiry*, edited by Ronald G. Sultana and Godfrey Baldacchino. Msida, Malta: Mireva Publications.

Council of Europe Publishing. 1955. *Administrative, Civil and Penal Aspects, including the Role of the Judiciary, of the Fight against Corruption: Proceedings, 19th Conference of European Ministers of Justice—Valletta, Malta, 14–15 June 1994.* Strasbourg: Council of Europe Publishing.

———. 1997. *Structure and Operation of Local and Regional Democracy: Malta Situation in 1997.* Strasbourg: Council of Europe Publishing.

Crawford, Francis Marion. 1900a. *The Rulers of the South: Sicily, Calabria, Malta.* Vol. 1. New York: The Macmillan Co.

———. 1900b. *The Rulers of the South: Sicily, Calabria, Malta.* Vol. 2. New York: The Macmillan Co.

Cristina, Dolores. 1998. "Bilanc bejn il-Familja u l-Karriera" [Balance between Family and Career]. In *Il-Mara Maltija wara s-Sena 2000* [The Maltese Woman beyond the Year 2000], edited by Angela Callus. Birkirkara: Pubblikazzjonijiet Indipendenza.

Darmanin, Mary. 1998. "Gender Sensitive Statistics and the Labour Market." In *Gender Issues and Statistics*, edited by Anthony M. Abela. Malta: Department for Women's Rights, Ministry for Social Policy.

Delia, Lino. 1998. "Ligijiet, Mentalità u Ekonomija: In-Nisa u x-Xoghol f'Malta" [Laws, Mentality and Economics: Women and Work in Malta]. In *Il-Mara*

Maltija wara s-Sena 2000 [The Maltese Woman beyond the Year 2000], edited by Angela Callus. Birkirkara: Pubblikazzjonijiet Indipendenza.

Denny, N. D. 1987. "British Temperance Reformers and the Island of Malta 1815–1914." *Melita Historica* 9: 329–345.

Du Boulay, Juliet. 1976. "Lies, Mockery and Family Integrity." In *Mediterranean Family Structures*, edited by J. G. Peristiany. Cambridge: Cambridge University Press.

Dunbabin, Jean. 1998. *Charles I of Anjou: Power, Kingship and State-Making in Thirteenth Century Europe*. London: Longman.

Durkheim, Emile. 1938. *The Elementary Forms of the Religious Life*. New York: The Free Press of Glencoe.

Earle, Peter. 1970. *Corsairs of Malta and Barbary*. London: Sidgwick and Jackson.

Ember, Melvin and Carol R. Ember, eds. 2001. *Countries and their Cultures*. 4 vols. New York: Macmillan Reference USA.

Evans, J. D. 1968. "Malta in Antiquity." In *Blue Guide: Malta* by Stuart Rossiter. London: Ernest Benn, Ltd.

———. 1971. *The Prehistoric Antiquities of the Maltese Islands: A Survey*. London: The Athlone Press.

Fallers, Lloyd A. 1973. *Inequality: Social Stratification Reconsidered*. Chicago: University of Chicago Press.

Farrugia, Karmel. 1995. *Polluted Politics: Background to the Deportation of Maltese Nationals in 1942*. Malta: Midsea Books Ltd.

Fernea, Elizabeth Warnock and Robert A. Fernea. 1991. *Nubian Ethnographies*. Prospect Heights, IL: Waveland Press.

Findlay, Ronald and Stanislaw Wellisz. 1993. "Malta." In *Five Small Open Economies*, edited by Ronald Findlay and Stanislaw Wellisz. New York: Oxford University Press.

Fiorini, Stanley. 1986. "The Resettlement of Gozo after 1551." *Melita Historica* 9: 203–244.

Food and Agriculture Organization of the United Nations. 2000. *Women, Agriculture and Rural Development: A Synthesis Report of the Near East Region*. RPAWANE 2000 [database online: http://www.fao.org/docrep/x0176e/x0176e00.htm].

Freeman-Grenville, G.S.P. 1973. *Chronology of African History*. London: Oxford University Press.

Frendo, Henry. 1992. "Intra-European Colonial Nationalism: The Case of Malta: 1922–1927." *Melita Historica* 11: 79–93.

Gaillard, Jean. 1997. "La Marine Française à Malte (1798–1800)." *Melita Historica* 12: 195–207.

Galley, Micheline, ed. 1994. *Maria Calleja's Gozo*. Logan: Utah State University Press.

Gatt, Blanche. 2001. "Open Sesame." *The Malta Independent on Sunday*, February 25: 15.

Gibson, James. 1966. *The Senses Considered as Perceptual Systems*. Boston: Houghton Mifflin.

Goodwin, Stefan C. 1974. "Time-Allocation and Urban Adjustment: A Maltese Case Study." Ph.D. diss., Northwestern University.

———. 1977. "Dimensions of Social Stratification in the Maltese Islands." *Pro-*

ceedings of the Alpha Kappa Delta Sociological Research Symposium. Richmond, VA.

———. 2001. "Malta." In *Countries and Their Cultures*, edited by Melvin Ember and Carol R. Ember. Vol. 3. New York: Macmillan Reference USA.

Guillaumier, Alfie. 1972. *Bliet u Rhula Maltin* [Maltese Towns and Villages]. 2nd ed. Malta: Lux Press.

Halbwachs, Maurcie. 1925. *Les cadres sociaux de la mémoire*. Paris: Alcan.

———. 1947. "La mémoire collective et le temps." *Cahiers Internationaux de Sociologie* 2: 3–31.

Harris, Marvin. 1968. *The Rise of Anthropological Theory*. New York: Harper Collins.

Hawkes, C.F.C. 1940. *The Prehistoric Foundations of Europe to the Mycenean Age*. London: Methuen and Co., Ltd.

Hawley, Amos H. 1971. *Urban Society: An Ecological Approach*. New York: The Ronald Press.

Idris, H. R. 1962. *La Berberie Orientale sous les Zirides, Xe–XIIe siècles*. Paris: Librairie d'Amérique et d'Orient, Adrien-Maisonneuve.

Iliffe, John. 1995. *Africans: The History of a Continent*. Cambridge: Cambridge University Press.

Johns, Jeremy. 1998. "Malik Ifriqiya: The Norman Kingdom of Africa and the Fatimids." *Libyan Studies* 29: 89–96.

Julien, Ch.-Andre. 1966. *Histoire de l'Afrique du Nord*. Paris: Payot.

Kendal, James. 1999. "Malta." In *Catholic Encyclopedia* [electronic version]. http://www.knight.org/advent/cathen/0957a.htm.

Kenny, Michael and David I. Kertzer. 1983. "Introduction." In *Urban Life in Mediterranean Europe: Anthropological Perspectives*, edited by Michael Kenny and David I. Kertzer. Urbana: University of Illinois Press.

Koster, Adrianus. 1983. "The Knights' State (1530–1798): A Regular Regime." *Melita Historica* 7: 299–314.

———. 1991. "Clericals Versus Socialists: Toward the 1984 Malta School War." In *Religious Regimes and State-Formation: Perspectives from European Ethnology*, edited by Eric R. Wolf. Albany: State University of New York Press.

———. 1994. "Malta's Relations with the Holy See in Postcolonial Times (Since 1964)." *Melita Historica* 11: 311–323.

Laiviera, Reneé. 1998. "Trawwim-ghall-Ugwaljanza" [Equality]. In *Il-Mara Maltija wara s-Sena 2000* [The Maltese Woman beyond the Year 2000], edited by Angela Callus. Birkirkara: Pubblikazzjonijiet Indipendenza.

Lane-Poole, Stanley. 1968. *A History of Egypt in the Middle Ages*. London: Frank Cass and Co.

———. 1970. *The Barbary Corsairs*. Westport, CT: Negro Universities Press.

Laspina, S. 1971. *Outlines of Maltese History*. 12th rev. ed. Malta: A. C. Aquilina & Co.

Law, R.C.C. 1978. "North Africa in the Age of Phoenician and Greek Colonisation." In *Cambridge History of Africa*, edited by J. D. Fage. Vol. 2. Cambridge: Cambridge University Press.

Lévi-Provençal, E. 1950. *Histoire de l'Espagne Musulmane*. Vol. 3. Paris: G.-P. Maisonneuve et Larose.

Lewis, Bernard. 1969. "What Is an Arab?" In *Peoples and Cultures of the Middle East*, edited by Ailon Shiloh. New York: Random House.

———. 1982. *The Muslim Discovery of Europe*. New York: W. W. Norton & Company.

Lloyd, Christopher. 1973. *The Nile Campaign*. New York: Barnes & Noble Books.

Ludwig, Emil. 1942. *The Mediterranean: Saga of a Sea*. New York: Whittlesey House.

Luttrell, Anthony T. 1975. "Approaches to Medieval Malta." In *Medieval Malta: Studies on Malta before the Knights*, edited by Anthony T. Luttrell, 1–70. London: The British School at Rome.

———. 1977. "Girolamo Manduca and Gian Francesco Abela: Tradition and Invention in Maltese Historiography." *Melita Historica* 7: 105–132.

MacMichael, Harold Alfred. 1967. *A History of the Arabs in the Sudan and Some of the People Who Preceded Them and of the Tribes Inhabiting Dàrtur*. New York: Barnes and Noble.

Mahoney, Leonard. 1996. *5000 Years of Architecture in Malta*. Valletta: Valletta Publishing.

Masonen, Pekka. 1995. "Conquest and Authority: Ancient Ghana and the Almoravids in West African Historiography." *Saharan Studies Association Newsletter* 3: 4–9.

Mayo, Peter. 1994. "State Sponsored Adult Literacy Programmes in Malta: A Critical Review." In *Sustaining Local Literacies*, edited by David Burton. Clevedon: Multilingual Matters Ltd.

Miceli, Pauline. 1994. "The Visibility and Invisibility of Women." In *Maltese Society: A Sociological Inquiry*, edited by Ronald G. Sultana and Godfrey Baldacchino. Msida, Malta: Mireva Publications.

Mifsud, Emmanuel. 1994. "Schooling and Socialization: Rituals, Symbols and Hidden Messages in a Private School." In *Maltese Society: A Sociological Inquiry*, edited by Ronald G. Sultana and Godfrey Baldacchino. Msida, Malta: Mireva Publications.

Mizzi, Sibyl O'Reilly. 1981. "Women in Senglea: The Changing Role of Urban, Working-Class Women in Malta." Ph.D. diss., State University of New York at Stony Brook.

———. 1994. "Gossip: A Means of Social Control." In *Maltese Society: A Sociological Inquiry*, edited by Ronald G. Sultana and Godfrey Baldacchino. Msida, Malta: Mireva Publications.

Moore, Wilbert E. 1963. *Man, Time, and Society*. New York: John Wiley and Sons.

Morris, A.E.J. 1994. *History of Urban Form: Before the Industrial Revolutions*. 3rd ed. Essex: Longman Scientific & Technical.

Naudi, Marceline. 1998. "Issues of Gender and Disability." In *Gender Issues and Statistics*, edited by Anthony M. Abela. Malta: Department of Women's Rights, Ministry for Social Policy.

Negbi, Ora. 1992. "Early Phoenician Presence in the Mediterranean Islands: A Reappraisal." *American Journal of Archaeology* 96: 599–616.

Norwich, John Julius. 1967. *The Normans in the South: 1016–1130*. London: Longmans.

O'Connor, David B. 1997. *Ancient Nubia: Egypt's Rival in Africa*. Philadelphia: University of Pennsylvania.

Odermatt, Peter. 1996. "Negotiating the Tourist Gaze: The Example of Malta." In *Coping with Tourists: European Reactions to Mass Tourism*, edited by Jeremy Boissevain. Providence, RI: Berghahn Books.

Oliver, Roland and Brian R. Fagen. 1975. *Africa in the Iron Age, c. 500 B.C. to A.D. 1400*. Cambridge: Cambridge University Press.

Orland, Lorraine Schembri. 1998. "Il-Ligi tal-Familja: Shubija bejn il-Mizzewgin" [The Marriage Law: Friendship between Married Couples]. In *Il-Mara Maltija wara s-Sena 2000* [The Maltese Woman beyond the Year 2000], edited by Angela Callus. Birkirkara: Pubblikazzjonijiet Indipendenza.

Orr, Donald John. 1992. "Development Issues in a Small Island Economy: A Case Study of the Maltese Experience." Ph.D. diss., University of Pittsburgh.

Pearce, D. 1997. "Tourism Planning Approach of Malta." In *The Earthscan Reader in Sustainable Tourism*. London: Earthscan Publications Ltd.

Peristiany, J. G. 1976. "Introduction." In *Mediterranean Family Structures*, edited by J. G. Peristiany. Cambridge: Cambridge University Press.

Pirotta, Godfrey A. 1994. "Maltese Political Parties and Political Modernization." In *Maltese Society: A Sociological Inquiry*, edited by Ronald G. Sultana and Godfrey Baldacchino. Msida, Malta: Mireva Publications.

Pitt-Rivers, Julian. 1976. "Ritual Kinship in the Mediterranean: Spain and the Balkans." In *Mediterranean Family Structures*, edited by J. G. Peristiany. Cambridge: Cambridge University Press.

Pons, Connie Attard. 1961. *Manjieri Tajba Fis-Socjetà* [Good Manners in Society]. Malta: A. C. Aquilina and Co.

Pred, Allan. 2000. *Even in Sweden: Racisms, Racialized Spaces, and the Popular Geographical Imagination*. Berkeley: University of California Press.

Price, Charles A. 1954. *Malta and the Maltese: A Study in Nineteenth Century Migration*. Melbourne: Georgian House.

Redmond, John. 1993. *The Next Mediterranean Enlargement of the European Community: Turkey, Cyprus and Malta?* Brookfield, VT: Dartmouth.

Roper, Geoffrey. 1988. "Arabic Printing in Malta, 1825–1845: Its History and Its Place in the Development of Print Culture in the Arab Middle East." Ph.D. diss., University of Durham (UK).

Rout, Leslie B. 1976. *The African Experience in Spanish America*. Cambridge: Cambridge University Press.

Runciman, Steven. 1958. *The Sicilian Vespers: A History of the Mediterranean World in the Later Thirteenth Century*. Cambridge: Cambridge University Press.

Sahlins, Marshall. 1958. *Social Stratification in Polynesia*. Seattle: The American Ethnological Society.

Sandys, George. 1615. *A Relation of a Journey Begun A.D. 1610*. London: W. Barnett.

Sciriha, Lydia. 1994. "Language and Class in Malta." In *Maltese Society: A Sociological Inquiry*, edited by Ronald G. Sultana and Godfrey Baldacchino. Msida, Malta: Mireva Publications.

Sciriha, Lydia and Mario Vassallo. 2001. *Malta—A Linguistic Landscape*. Malta: University of Malta Press.

Sire, H.J.A. 1994. *The Knights of Malta*. New Haven, CT: Yale University Press.

Smith, Andrea Llynn. 1998. "The Colonial in Postcolonial Europe: The Social Memory of Maltese-Origin Pieds-Noirs." Ph.D. diss., University of Arizona.

Smith, Denis Mack. 1968. *A History of Sicily, Medieval Sicily: 800–1713*. London: Chatto and Windus.

Smith, Harrison and Adrianus Koster. 1984. *Lord Strickland: Servant of the Crown.* Vol. 1. Valletta: Progress Press Co. Ltd.

———. 1986. *Lord Strickland: Servant of the Crown.* Vol. 2. Valletta: Progress Press Co. Ltd.

Spiteri, Jane. 1998. "In-Nisa Anzjani" [Women in Old Age]. In *Il-Mara Maltija wara s-Sena 2000* [The Maltese Woman beyond the Year 2000], edited by Angela Callus. Birkirkara: Pubblikazzjonijiet Indipendenza.

Sultana, Ronald G. 1994. "Perspectives on Class in Malta." In *Maltese Society; A Sociological Inquiry*, edited by Ronald G. Sultana and Godfrey Baldacchino. Msida, Malta: Mireva Publications.

Tabone, Carmel. 1994. "The Maltese Family in the Context of Social Change." In *Maltese Society: A Sociological Inquiry*, edited by Ronald G. Sultana and Godfrey Baldacchino. Msida, Malta: Mireva Publications.

———. 1995. *Maltese Families in Transition: A Sociological Investigation*. Santa Venera: The Ministry for Social Development.

———. 1998. "Ir-Rwol tal-Mara fis-Socjetà Maltia: l-Aspett Socjologiku" [The Roles of Women in Maltese Society]. In *Il-Mara Maltija wara s-Sena 2000* [The Maltese Woman beyond the Year 2000], edited by Angela Callus. Birkirkara: Pubblikazzjonijiet Indipendenza.

Tentori, Tullio. 1976. "Social Class and Family in a Southern Italian Town." In *Mediterranean Family Structures*, edited by J. G. Peristiany. Cambridge: Cambridge University Press.

Thake, Conrad Gerald. 1996. "Mdina: Architectural and Urban Transformations of a Citadel in Malta." Ph.D. diss., University of California, Berkeley.

Trimingham, J. Spencer. 1979. *Christianity Among the Arabs in Pre-Islamic Times*. New York: Longman Group Limited and Libriarie du Liban.

Troisi, Joseph. 1998. "Elderly Women, Choices and Challenge." In *Gender Issues and Statistics*, edited by Anthony M. Abela. Malta: Department of Women's Rights, Ministry for Social Policy.

Trump, D. H. 1972. *Malta: An Archaeological Guide*. London: Faber and Faber Ltd.

Vanhove, Martine. 1994. "La langue maltaise: un carrefour linguistique." *Revue du Monde Musulman et de la Mediterranée* 71: 167–183.

Vella, Andrew P. 1975. "The Order of Malta and the Defence of Tripoli 1530–1551." *Melita Historica* 6: 362–381.

Vella, Denise. 1998. "In-Nisa fin-Negozju u l-Kummerc" [Women in Commerce and Business]. In *Il-Mara Maltija wara s-Sena 2000* [The Maltese Woman beyond the Year 2000], edited by Angela Callus. Birkirkara: Pubblikazzjonijiet Indipendenza.

Vella, Sue. 1998. "Access to Housing, A Gender Issue?" In *Gender Issues and Statistics*, edited by Anthony M. Abela. Malta: Department of Women's Rights, Ministry for Social Policy.

Wellard, James Howard. 1970. *Desert Pilgrimage: Journeys to the Egytian and Sinai*

Deserts, Completing the Third of the Trilogy of Saharan Explorations. London: Hutchinson.

Wettinger, Godfrey. 1974. "Early Maltese Popular Attitudes to the Government of the Order of St. John." *Melita Historica* 6: 255–278.

———. 1975. "The Lost Villages and Hamlets of Malta." In *Medieval Malta: Studies on Malta before the Knights*, edited by Anthony T. Luttrell, 181–216. London: The British School at Rome.

———. 1980. "Honour and Shame in Late Fifteenth Century Malta." *Melita Historica* 8: 65–77.

———. 1984. "The Arabs in Malta." In *Mid-Bank Limited: Report and Accounts, 1984*, 22–37. Malta.

———. 1985. *The Jews of Malta in the Late Middle Ages.* Malta: Midsea Books Ltd.

———. 1999. "The Origin of the 'Maltese' Surnames." *Melita Historica* 12: 333–344.

Wilhelmsen, Finn. 1976. "Marsaxlokk: An Ethnography of a Maltese Fishing Village." Ph.D. diss., Wayne State University.

Wright, John. 1969. *Libya.* London: Ernest Benn, Ltd.

York, Barry. 1988. "With Brave Hearts and Strong Arms: Maltese Immigration into Australia, 1883–1949." Ph.D. diss., University of New South Wales (Australia).

Zimmerman, Susan and Ronald F. E. Weissman. 1989. *Urban Life in the Renaissance.* Newark: University of Delaware Press.

Index

About the Author

STEFAN GOODWIN is Associate Professor, Department of Sociology and
Anthropology, Morgan State University, Maryland.